WINNING THE BID

A Manager's Guide to Competitive Bidding

Neil Tweedley

FINANCIAL TIMES
Prentice Hall

An imprint of **Pearson Education**

London · New York · San Francisco · Toronto · Sydney
Tokyo · Singapore · Hong Kong · Cape Town · Madrid
Paris · Milan · Munich · Amsterdam

Pearson Education Limited
Head Office:
Edinburgh Gate
Harlow
Essex CM20 2JE
England

London Office:
128 Long Acre
London WC2E 9AN
Tel: +44 (0)20 7447 2000
Fax: +44 (0)20 7836 4286

Web www.business-minds.com

First published in Great Britain 1995

British Library Cataloguing in Publication Data
A CIP catalogue record for this book can be obtained
from the British Library.

ISBN 0 273 60971 8

3 5 7 9 10 8 6 4 2

Typeset by PanTek Arts, Maidstone, Kent.
Printed and bound in Great Britain by
Biddles Ltd, Guildford and King's Lynn

*The Publishers' policy is to use paper manufactured
from sustainable forests.*

CONTENTS

To Georgina and Jack

PREFACE

The notion of competitively bidding for business has been around since the earliest days of the market economy. When two or more suppliers begin to produce and sell similar things the consumer has a choice and the suppliers face competition. The buyer has to make some value judgement on which supplier to purchase from. Meanwhile, each supplier tries to convince the buyer to purchase from them. Competitive tendering has evolved to allow the buyer to take control of the purchasing process and bidding is the suppliers' response. Although sometimes used by the domestic consumer, it is the business client who has developed and refined this process to the point it has reached today.

Most purchases begin with the identification of a need; this could be for an airport catering service, supply of office stationery, a new computer or any other business requirement. The clients have several options open to them to get what they want. They can shop around, look at products or services from different suppliers, or scan catalogues. If they find what they want at a price they can afford they can buy it. Suppliers have an equal number of ways of persuading the client to buy their products and advertising, marketing and other promotion methods have evolved to exert influence on the client's buying decision.

This simplistic approach does not always work for more complex purchases. For example, when the client needs large volumes of certain items, when what they want does not conform with normal standards, when there is a wide range of prices or when the price is unknown. In these circumstances the buyer needs to find out prices from several suppliers. They can either specify what they need, or ask suppliers what they have that might meet their requirement. In some business areas such as building works or car repairs the client asks for estimates of the task required and the price. Alternatively, they may ask suppliers to compete by submitting their best prices and solutions. The supplier's response is called their bid.

A typical bid works like this. The client will specify as precisely as possible what it is they think they want, or alternatively, they will summarise their business needs or problem areas. They then invite suppliers to submit proposals on how these problems could be addressed or these needs fulfilled. This can be either through an open, published invitation, or by inviting a few selected suppliers whom they feel can comply with their requirements. More responsive and proactive suppliers will find out about the opportunity and begin preparing for it before the invitation is issued. By doing this they will hope to steal a march on the other bidders and gain a competitive advantage. When the invitation to bid is received, the bidder will have to decide whether they want to prepare a response or not. First they will analyse the opportunity to see whether it fits with their business objectives. They will then look at the issues of competition and price to assess their chances of winning and justify the cost of bidding. The client will normally allow a reasonable amount of time for the suppliers to prepare their responses, which will depend on how difficult they judge the solution to be.

When the bid submission date arrives, bidders will submit their proposals for the client to evaluate. The client selects the supplier that best meets their needs in price, suitability of the solution and other commercial factors. They then place an order or contract with the winning bidder.

The role of the bid manager in the bidding process is to ensure that their bid is the one the client selects. Bidding is a selling process but it differs from straightforward sales whereby a product or service is tendered to the general market because suppliers must prepare a more detailed proposal that meets the needs of the client precisely. It also needs more effort by the bidding companies and the cost of this can be high. As there is usually only one winner the losers cannot easily recover these costs.

As buyers become more sophisticated, they expect more from their suppliers and this also makes it harder to win. And the competition in bidding can drive down price and increase performance demands.

A supplier who wants to succeed at bidding starts early and performs a thorough analysis of the advantages and disadvantages of the opportunity. They balance the risks against the benefits that will accrue when they are successful. They improve their chances of success by knowing their client, positioning themselves with them and understanding the competition they are likely to face. A good bidder will withdraw if the opportunity does not match their business objectives or if the chances of success are poor. Good bid techniques ensure that nothing is overlooked during the assessment process which could turn profit into loss, or could cause material deficiencies in the offer they make. Good bid techniques apply sound business principles, quality, and process control to achieve consistent and regular success.

A supplier not so well versed in the good bid guide will often tie up people and resources on bids that are difficult or impossible for them to win. Bad bidders do not know the risk involved or the cost implications to their business. They do not know when to withdraw and cut their losses, but often continue just for the sake of it and because it is easier than getting out. Bad bids are prepared in haste and without a thorough analysis. They result in bids that do not win, or even worse, in bids that win but lose the supplier money.

Many companies do not bid for new business, relying instead on their traditional selling channels, managed client relationships, marketing and promotion. These are worthy techniques and may suit certain types of businesses. Other companies find that the risk and uncertainty inherent in bidding make bidding an unattractive proposition. Some companies may not want to extend their markets beyond the scope of their current sales activities whilst others do not enter major bids because of the high costs involved. Many are deterred because of previous failures or because they do not have the skills and resources necessary to mount a successful challenge.

This book is for those people who want to bid more successfully and win more business. It is aimed at those businesses that face problems in their bids caused by ineffective processes, lack of success, poor profitability, or high costs. The process of bidding is dealt with at two levels. It tackles the conceptional level where strategy, ideas, policies, plans and tactics are necessary to lay a foundation for success. At the practical level it deals with the organisational, management and control issues that are needed to translate ideas into actions. The purpose of this book is to help *you* win profitable business and to reduce the chances of your having to carry out unprofitable contracts. After all, winning profitable business is what bidding is all about.

INTRODUCTION

Businesses today are operating in increasingly competitive markets. In this complex trading environment they have to find commercial stratagems and policies that will win. This is often complicated by the effects that powerful consumer groups and governments have on how they can secure new orders. Buying policies in the private and public sectors are constantly being reviewed. Pressures are being exerted on current and potential suppliers to become more responsive, more proactive and more innovative in their approaches. To survive and win needs vision and insight.

The search for greater choice and value for money leads to more purchases being made by competitive methods. The perceived benefit of these methods has resulted in a phenomenal rise in the number of bids and tenders. Even quite simple purchases, which previously may have been stock replacement, are put out to competitive tender. Doubtless, a compulsive view of competition sometimes has the reverse effect and instead of creating benefits it works to the detriment of the buyer and seller. No-one therefore who has worked extensively in a competitive purchasing environment takes it lightly. All recognise that it can be costly and involve more effort, both to the buyer and the supplier. Nevertheless, competition can bring real benefits and knowing when and how to buy using competitive methods is down to the skill of the purchasing manager. The supplier is in the same position; knowing when and how to participate in competition depends on the skill of the bid manager. Often however, suppliers have more to lose if they get it wrong.

This book aims to help those suppliers who sell by competitive bidding and who need to be more successful. Many successful bids come about seemingly as the result of a haphazard arrangement of factors, often more by luck than judgement, demonstrating the triumph of arrogance over understanding. Usually too much time is spent on inward-looking analyses, and in trying to identify likely project costs on the assumption that winning is automatic. Competitive tendering is a game, played by certain rules. The trick and skill in winning, is to make sure that as far as possible, the rules are of your choosing, not your competitors. In today's competitive marketplace businesses can no longer rely upon good fortune and hard work. The cost of competitive bidding is becoming higher. The competition is becoming fiercer and buyers are more sophisticated, while the choices available to them are more varied. To be consistently successful in bidding there must be a purposeful framework supporting the business objectives.

Bid management brings together a wide range of business management sciences and disciplines that provide such a framework: sales and marketing, risk management, competitive analysis, pricing, taxation, line management, team management, time management, change management, negotiating, business planning, project planning, quality planning, strategic planning, contract law and so on, all can combine within the scope of a single bid. Not only are all these management skills required, but they have to be applied and completed within a very short time span. Is it any wonder that the commercial skills needed to be a successful bid manager are scarce? Achieving success in this arena requires clarity of focus on real opportunities which in turn gives rise to a need for teams of skilled and resourceful people who can handle the complex interplay that exists in the bid cycle. Particularly important is the emphasis on building and maintaining a good relationship with the client. This is usually critical to the success of the bid and necessitates staying aware of the strategic situation surrounding every prospect.

This book addresses the tough bidding oppportunities now facing businesses so that they can continue to improve their success rate in competitive bidding situations against aggressive and competent opposition and in short timescales. Success requires that bid managers and bid teams be able to work under pressure, maintain high level of commercial awareness and perform the leading role in managing resources. To win consistently through competitive tendering requires more than just a good pitch. When competing on a global scale, every business has to be very certain of the risks and benefits inherent in the opportunity. The costs are high, as are the stakes. Development of successful business often requires you to bid for highly complex, multi-disciplined projects or investments. Sound commercial management of income generating projects is critical. In the global market businesses will find themselves frequently bidding for projects designed to enhance their position within a region or with a specific client. The value of the longer-term opportunity may be much greater than the individual value of the bid.

Bidding, winning, successfully managing the project and achieving profit will enhance your position. Bidding, winning and failing with the project could cause significant damage to your long-term aspirations. So selecting the opportunities that meet your strategic objectives, which you can deliver *and* which provides profit, is critical.

This book specifically targets the key personnel involved in winning valuable and complex new business. It aims to provide these people with a coherent and comprehensive analysis of the bid cycle from both the supplier's and buyer's view. As managers they have to make decisions calling upon support from many sources. Getting that support, gathering together all the information, and assessing the value of any specific judgement requires planning and processing. The working practices of the businesses have to both meet the requirements of the individuals performing them and provide information to the strategists and managers who need it. In some areas this will mean amending or consolidating work flows to achieve consistency and cohesion. This book will be a useful tool but it cannot entirely replace the experience and expertise of the individual. It can, however, serve as a checklist and source of advice and information. Producing a proposal of any kind requires a series of careful analyses and difficult management decisions and so accurate information and appropriate management skills are essential. Bidding will involve many people in much effort over a short time. Winning the bid requires innovation and creativity. These are all abilities that your competitors will be seeking and so should you and this book gives you the information you need to help you develop those unique capabilities and to help you in winning your bid.

1

BIDDING TO WIN

There are few companies today that are not bidding competitively for new business. For some, it has long been the traditional way of gaining significant contracts, while for others this is a very new method of selling. The stimuli for the move to competitive bidding are diverse; some companies are trying to get a foothold in an aggressive market while others are forced into it by the way their clients' purchasing policy operates, and still others are taking an opportunistic approach to growing their business. Whatever instigates a competitive bid, there is usually only one reason for continuing, and that is to win; very little benefit accrues to the losers. It is therefore surprising how little attention is often paid to making the bid successful, and how much money is spent on lost causes.

Practised bid managers, whether they are dedicated to the task or only taking responsibility for specific opportunities, will recognise that success requires much more than just submitting their best offer. They will apply sound business techniques to make sure their bid is the winner, or limit the costs involved in bidding, perhaps by withdrawing or declining to bid. This chapter concentrates on the characteristics of a winning bid, both in its management and production and emphasises how effective bid management techniques can help you to increase your own bid success rate.

MAKING THE BID DECISION

The starting point in winning your bid, and the foundation of effective bid management, is selecting the right opportunities in the first place.

Think of your decision to bid as if you were an athlete considering entering a race. First, you will decide if the prize is worthwhile and one you want to win: you will want to know if there is sufficient reward to justify the time spent training and preparing for it. Or you may have another reason for entering, such as qualifying for the next round, building up championship points, or making a name for yourself. Then you will need to look at your physical and mental condition to see if you are fit enough to run. Next, you will want to assess your strengths to decide whether this is an event you are good at and whether you have prepared well enough to do yourself justice. Assuming that you are in good shape, you will need to look at your opponents to find out who else will be competing and what condition they are in. You will have to assess whether you are likely to beat them, or what race tactics you will need to employ in order to gain an advantage. Another consideration is the risk involved and the commitments you will have to make if you are to win. For example, the chances of injury may be high and its potential consequences will need appraising; you may have to decide whether you can recover in time to race again soon. As an astute performer you will want to look at other races to see if by committing to this one you will have to forego another more lucrative or prestigious, opportunity. Once these factors have been considered and answered, you are ready to race to win or to withdraw or to enter another race another time. No world class athlete enters a race to lose; and so it is with bidding.

Selecting the best opportunities

Before going on to look at some of the factors around which a winning bid may turn, it is helpful to review the prospect selection process itself. You need to select the best opportunities for your company, and some process is needed to figure out which these are. The cost of bidding in terms of labour, time and money can be high and you must meet the cost of every bid you lose from the next one you win. There is little point in submitting bids that you know will not win, unless, of course, you have a strategic purpose in mind. You need to be selective in bidding, only choosing those opportunities which meet your strategic objectives, which you can deliver and which you can win. This selection process, often known as qualifying the prospect, is the situation in which you apply a set of common criteria and assess the risks and chances of success. More often than not this is an iterative process. Assess the opportunity early to decide whether you want to go on, then monitor and reassess as the bid progresses and circumstances alter.

The initial assessment, to see if the opportunity matches the criteria set, can be listed as in Table 1. This checklist represents some areas you will need to look into for a typical bid. The risk associated with every factor and the priority or rating that you give them, serves to highlight the most important aspects of the prospect. It cannot represent every company and every opportunity, but you should aim to develop something similar that you can use for the purpose.

Category	Criteria	Rating	Risk
Prospect Sources	Established internal source (e.g. account channels, business manager)		
	From external source (e.g. EC journal, newspaper, merger)		
	From company business plan (e.g. account strategy, development plan)		
Client Factors	Is the opportunity real? (supporting evidence)		
	Are funds available? (from what source)		
	Credit worthiness (for estimated budget)		
	Is project approved? (at what level)		
	Internal politics (within client or funding organisation)		
Cultural	External politics (status and stability)		
Cost of Bidding	Design		
	Site surveys		
	Performance measurement		
	Bid team		
	Travel and subsistence		
	Subcontractor costs		
	Production costs		
Value to the Company	Profit margin (meets expected level)		
	Contribution to overheads (overheads recovered)		
	Strategic positioning		
	Cash flow (positive)		
Competitive Threat	Competition (strong or weak)		
	Market position		
	Success record (with this client)		
	Technical capability		
	Pricing strategy		
	Time scale record		
	Quality record		
	Strengths		
	Weaknesses		
	Opportunity		
	Threats		

Table 1 Opportunity assessment checklist

The purpose of such an assessment is to provide a foundation for your bid and a basis for going ahead or withdrawing. You could argue that you do not need to go through such a process, but there is a strong tendency within many large organisations (particularly those for whom cost of sale is not an overriding consideration) to bid for all and everything, irrespective of the chances of success. Many companies go blindly into bids that are not only too difficult for them to win but which also require inordinate amounts of time and effort. To justify this kind of high expenditure the rewards must be high, but even so the chances of winning are often low. To win regularly you have to remain focused, so it is worth repeating that you should not bid for opportunities that you clearly have little chance with. Look first for the bid opportunities that are easy for you to win, those involving established clients or using well-known technology or perhaps using your regular suppliers.

Preliminary assessment

You never have all the information you would like at the outset. Information builds as the bid develops and so does your assessment of the opportunity. However, before embarking upon a bid and incurring what could be high costs, a preliminary assessment is recommended. This checks certain aspects of the prospect and provides reassurance that it is worth bidding for. Of course, circumstances change, so you will need to monitor developments carefully.

Your first task should be to check whether it fits with your company business policy or a defined business strategy. There are three broad areas that you need to look at: the work, the client and the location. When you assess the work, try to answer these questions: is this a project that you can undertake? Can you deliver the products or services required? Are the technical skills and facilities available in your company? Is the level of risk within that which you are prepared to accept? Do the size and value of the opportunity fit in with your abilities to do the work?

Look next at the client. Are they new, or existing? If they are existing, then decide whether you wish to develop the relationship further. If they are new, decide if they are the type of client you are seeking. Some clients may not suit your style of business and may act negatively on the way the remainder of the market perceive you. Also, becoming a supplier to one client may jeopardise your relationship with another, particularly if they are competitors.

Finally, see where the client is located and where the project is to be carried out. This may affect your decision. Some third world countries may not be targeted within your company's current thinking. Does your company want to commit itself in volatile areas? Does it have a multinational dimension? Which regulatory and legal factors need to be considered?

In answering these questions, you have narrowed the field and attempted a first-cut assessment of the prospect. If the prospect meets acceptable criteria in these areas the next phase is to refine the qualification process, and this requires much more detailed and accurate information. You must delve deeper and pull out some key factors. A positive preliminary assessment normally suggests the prospect is interesting enough to take to the next stage and that it is worthwhile investing some time and money in exploring it further. It should not represent your final bid decision. That comes later.

Detailed assessment

A positive preliminary assessment will have established that the prospect represents the type of business opportunity that your company wants to win. The next stage is a more detailed assessment of the prospect to find out whether you can win it and what the risks are if you do.

Your starting point in this process is the source of the prospect. This is important, as you have to consider the amount of effort that may already have been expended in influencing the client. Prospects can come from many sources. Internal sources are your regular sales channels, account management or territorial directors. Leads from these can be the result of much hard work with the client or simply bolts from the blue. External sources include the Official Journal of the European Union, newspaper reports, results of mergers or acquisitions and so on. The source of the opportunity will influence the way you assess it. Perhaps the most attractive prospects are those that have developed as part of an account strategy, where your company has provided a lead in deciding what shape the opportunity with the client might take.

PIVOTAL FACTORS IN YOUR BID

You will have seen from the above description of a typical assessment process that in any bid there are four distinct areas that you have to focus on. Each of these has factors that affect your chances of success:

1. Your own position in the marketplace and your readiness to bid.
2. The position of your competitors compared with you, and their influence upon the client.
3. The client and the environment around which the opportunity is based.
4. The element of risk, acting as a modifier on these factors, enhancing or reducing your chances.

Fig. 1.1 shows how these factors come together.

The mix of the factors in each category is complex, varying with every prospect. Thus, the relative importance of each and the interaction between them has to be viewed within the context of each opportunity. Resolving these factors into a winning bid is what bid management is all about. For every bid, and in each category, there are pivotal factors around which winning and losing swing. Finding them is not always easy but these are the areas where you need to concentrate hardest. Start by looking at these pivotal factors as they relate to your own bids, before going on to explore the rest of the bidding process.

Fig. 1.1 The pivotal factors in winning a bid

YOUR WINNING POSITION

A successful bid begins by establishing a winning position for yourself and for this you must decide what it is you wish to achieve. Decide first what your objectives are and why you are bidding. Although many managers tendering for business define their targets and success criteria, others are unclear or uncertain. There are frequent instances of bids being made for prospects that bear no relation to stated company policy, or being pursued without a coherent bid strategy. One large multinational often receives bid invitations with insufficient time to furnish an adequate response. They are completed regardless, usually in a rush, with tempers frayed and with the response poorly prepared. Inevitably, they lose. So why were these bids submitted? There are bid managers in some of the largest corporations in the UK who have submitted many proposals with almost no successes. Why are they continuing to submit losing bids? Where are they going wrong?

Decide what you want

Examining your company's motives for bidding brings valuable information that you can use to put yourself into a winning position. Why do companies like yours submit bids? Are there always valid and legitimate business reasons? Certainly, you will want to win the contract. Maybe you want to establish market position by gaining a foothold in a new or emerging market or geographical sector. The most obvious reason is that you want the profit that you expect the contract to generate. Business is all about profit and it is often said that without profit there is, quite simply, no business. To remain viable, your company must continue to make a profit and a sound reason for bidding is the desire to win profitable new business.

Unfortunately, too often the reasoning is not so clear and the purpose behind bidding becomes obscured. Equivocal rationale may be presented as solid argument. The prime example of this is the strategic bid, perhaps the most hackneyed phrase in the bid manager's repertoire. Sometimes there really are strategic business reasons for submitting bids, occasions where success or failure in a particular opportunity will have profound repercussions upon your future success. However, the camouflage of the strategic bid is frequently used to mask inadequacies in the way the business chooses its opportunities. These are opportunities where you have little or no chance of success but you bid anyway. The reasons for going ahead are frequently complex: internal company politics, external competitive pressures, market or customer influences, lack of information, apathy, inadequate decision making capabilities, each makes a contribution. Whatever the reason, or lack of one, the outcome in such circumstances is disappointingly consistent. These bids do not win.

Apply focus to your prospects

It may sound facetious but when you are bidding to win, you have to take every precaution not to lose. This means overcoming any tendency to submit bids just for the sake of it. Crucially, it means carefully selecting every opportunity, foregoing those where you cannot justify the effort, expense and time needed and concentrating on those opportunities that you really want. Adopting this discriminating approach means you begin to turn down the more fruitless opportunities and become focused on the ones with the greatest chance of success. The benefits are immediate. For a start, you free up resources that would otherwise be wasted chasing hopeless cases and consequently you can pursue the better prospects more vigorously.

Applying focus means you can concentrate on the opportunities that you want to win and then go all out to win them. This encapsulates all your selection processes, first ensuring that the opportunity is one that you want to win and then confirming you have the necessary capabilities to do so. It also includes setting up appropriate processes to help you manage and control the bid. Although these formal bid processes do not win bids on their own, they do have an extremely important function in enhancing your chances of achieving consistent success. Correct bid focus also helps ensure that you have all the resources you need; once you have decided that the bid is one you want to win, then you must make use of all the resources available to you. After all, doing everything that is necessary to win good business includes making best use of your assets. Winning will recover the costs involved, but failing puts a burden on the next bid to finance your lack of success.

When you bid to win, you develop and apply a range of management techniques, disciplines and skills that sharpen your focus. Inevitably you will encounter resistance and pressures to bid where the focus is blurred. But stick to your guns, and in the longer term your success rate will improve, and those bids you do win will be more profitable.

Use structured bid processes

Your winning position is greatly affected by your readiness to bid. Becoming ready to bid and to win, really needs processes in place to help prepare the ground and prime your company resources for the task ahead. Setting up a typical bid process is described later, but it helps to first decide if you need procedures and why.

The first function of an effective bid process or procedure is to provide guidelines to encourage a common level of discipline throughout your company. Good bid processes encourage you to consider all aspects of the bid and prevent any important factor being overlooked. By providing a framework for this analysis, they give a degree of protection to your company and the individual manager within the bid team. The company is then assured that all managers involved in the bid are applying consistent selection and management criteria in line with company policy. Moreover, the individual is protected against overextending the bounds of their authority without recourse back to the company. Setting approvals at the right level within the company will ensure that the full implications of the bid get considered. Finally, instilling a common culture and philosophy throughout the company will help you achieve consistency, develop a house-style and get policy carried out.

However, slavishly following the rules will not win good business. The bid manager is responsible for winning the bid and must use the processes accordingly. If you have concerns about procedures then challenge them; they may not be right for your particular bid and might need to be modified.

Reliable bid processes also form an important part of quality management. Quality systems will help you to control and manage bid opportunities, introduce effective document control and simplify the bid processes and project accomplishment. Your aim is to win profitable business consistently and using quality systems is a major step in achieving that.

Discern the reasons for failure

Why is it that some bids can be successful while others fail miserably? You will have encountered bids where your content and structure are almost identical. Even the market position and competitive forces are the same. Yet, one will win while another will fail. Some bid managers put this down to luck or simply that it was not their turn. Neither of these is a very logical explanation for why a competitor's bid succeeded over theirs. No doubt there are some buyers who operate a rotation system, giving an opportunity to different suppliers in turn, but these are rare. In the prevailing spirit of open competition this is becoming less likely and may only be symptomatic of the failure by any supplier to understand fully the needs of the client. It may simply be very difficult for the client to distinguish between these bids, so in such a rotation system, any supplier who fully meets the value expectations of the client will receive the lion's share.

Many bids can become an exercise in regurgitation. Previous proposals, some good, some bad, are raided for appropriate morsels. These fragments are then compiled into a new bid. Although this technique is a sound one, essential sometimes if you are to complete a bid within timescales, it will fail if you give no thought to what the client's value expectations are. After all, what is good for one client is not necessarily good for another, and simple repackaging is often insufficient.

Although bad luck, fate or divine intervention may play a part, in general bids fail because they have not achieved the value expectations of the client and your competitor has. Unless you are very fortunate, you will not win every bid; there will be times when it is impossible to match completely the client's consolidated value expectations. Sometimes these expectations may not be feasible and in such cases you will need to establish a stronger relationship with the client so that you can displace the ideal with something more realistic. However, by embracing the idea of value engineering, taking a view not only on your competitors, but on the value that the client places on each aspect of your bid, you will improve your success rate.

Deal with specific problems

In every bid you will encounter problems and some efforts falter simply because of failure to manage the bid properly. Some problems are an inherent part of the iterative bid cycle. However, by far the majority of problems arise from lack of foresight, lack of planning or lack of resources. Consider for example, the bid opportunity that suddenly appears taking your whole organisation by surprise. Effective bid organisation can reduce the risk of being caught off guard. Make a point of carefully selecting your prospects, register and control them at an early stage and alert your bid and line management that a tender invitation is imminent. Keeping a careful watch on the account plan will help you to monitor developments within the client's organisation; takeovers, acquisitions, buy-outs, and world events, can all serve as early warning indicators.

With this surprise invitation, you can be certain that your client will not have kept their plans totally secret as it is not in their interest to do so. At least one supplier will have been kept well informed and this is the one likely to steal the game. Again, you must think carefully about whether to bid or not. It is unlikely that you are in a strong position with the client and you may be wasting your time.

Another problem often encountered is the bid invitation that arrives dog-eared and tattered with scribbling and notes all over because it has been through so many different parts of your company. You will have lost valuable time, so your chances of taking early initiatives may also have been lost. This is symptomatic of many large organisations and again it is a bid process or management issue. The solution lies in setting clear reporting lines, in establishing proper and early prospect registration and in making best use of available resources. Too often resources disappear the moment the tender documents arrive. Professional resources are always at a premium and constantly in demand. Your problem is to ensure that essential resources and support are not diverted to other jobs. Commitment is everything, so if you have correctly selected the prospect, ensured that it fits within your company strategy and established that you have a strong chance of success, then you should not allow the resources you need to disappear. Make sure that you confirm the commitment from line management, book common resources well in advance and plan ahead.

Some problems arise from a breakdown in management communication. A perceived reluctance by your management to commit to bidding may be due to a clash of interest. You must try to find out why they are reluctant and make sure that you understand the fit with your company strategy. If you can affirm that the means are available and that you can win, then maybe there is an issue of priority with someone else making a stronger case for the required resources.

It always helps to have a plan for success, as without an effective business strategy you are very likely to meet with failure. Keep your bid strategy in line with your company business strategy as anything else will be ineffectual. You probably can use short-term tactics to enable you to gain a good position with the client, but make sure that it supports your longer-term objectives.

Know the real cost of bidding

It is important to know the real costs to your company of bidding; not just in the stated bid expenses, but in all the less-obvious costs that affect the profitability of your business. Do not assume that all bidders will incur the same costs, they will not. Much depends upon the way in which your company is structured and your total base cost. However, the important fact is whether the potential rewards from the bid justify the risk and costs you will have to spend in winning it. You have always to bear in mind that mostly these costs will not be recovered if you lose. It is all or nothing.

So, the cost of bidding for the opportunity is a key factor in deciding whether to bid or not. For many large contracts, particularly in the public sector, these costs can be extremely high. Many smaller and medium-sized enterprises without the massive financial resources needed, find the cost of bidding for public and government contracts prohibitive and now refuse or are unable to bid. The effects of this are to limit the choice of the client, restrict the price advantages that competition can bring and reduce their chances of finding the right solution to their problem. Organisations in both the public and private sector are beginning to realise this. The European Community directives on public procurement introduced since the single market came into effect, are aimed at encouraging small and medium businesses to bid for public contracts.

On the other hand, you will have opportunities for which it will cost very little to bid. You may have already produced very similar proposals for the same or a different client, completed all the design and production work and only a little effort is needed to tailor it for a new bid. Because the costs are low, you may consider a speculative bid, submitting a proposal even if other factors weigh against you. After all you have very little to lose. However, always consider the risk in winning, as well as the risk in submitting your bid. Make sure that you have taken everything into account and conducted a proper risk assessment.

As the cost of every bid that fails must be met by the next successful bid, you must attempt to quantify and build them into your prospect assessment. For example, there are the costs associated with people (which will vary with the amount of design work needed), such as site assessments and travel, whether you have to derive and provide information not normally available, the size of the bid and assignment teams and so on. Then the production and financing costs need to be considered, particularly if a detailed finance package is needed. And you also have to consider costs associated with selecting subcontractors, partners and suppliers. To these must be added the cost of client meetings, post-tender negotiation, presentations, reference site visits, all of which may extend over several months.

All of these expenses must be appraised in order to assess whether they are to be recovered from the sale price. If so, then you must ensure that by incurring high bid costs you do not submit a very high price that cannot win the business. In the event that bid costs are low, you may be inclined to bid even if certain other factors do not weigh in your favour.

Quantify your gain

The final aspect to consider is what you expect to gain from the contract. Your assessment of the value to your company of the prospect should answer that question. Your usual criteria for judgement will be the anticipated margin on the sale which is determined by the price that will win the business. You need to know your costs and the margin that your company is expecting you to make.

Your margin could be the simple difference between your costs and the winning price so if the margin is insufficient, or even negative, you would probably decide against bidding unless, of course, there are factors other than profit at issue.

As a general guide, the greater the demand on your company's resources for meeting the requirement, the greater the contribution and profit you can expect. You may wish to negotiate hard with any supplier or subcontractor; a hungry supplier might be prepared to provide their services at low margins. You should also look at the cash flow, as a positive cash flow may enable you to earn interest while a negative one may require you to put your own money into the project.

There are likely to be other things that you can expect to gain from the bid, such as an enhanced reputation, improved track record, client goodwill, or a foothold in a new market, all of which contribute to your assessment of the prospect. These are often intangible items that are difficult to quantify. However, try to put some value upon them when you are weighing up all that you expect to receive. For example, client goodwill may bring extra orders, so estimate how much they are worth; an enhanced reputation could bring in new clients, estimate what their spend would be with you; gaining entry to a new market may allow you to diversify, put a figure upon the new net growth. By quantifying as much as possible, you can get a better picture of the value to your business which will help your decision process.

THE POSITION OF YOUR COMPETITORS

Once you have taken stock of your own position and looked at some potential problem areas, it is time to broaden your vision to include your competition and the threats they pose. As most bids are competitive, you can be assured that rivals exist, and that they will be trying just as hard as you to win the business. How do you propose to handle them? Competitive analyses can be valuable and this is covered in depth later, but take a more lateral view in the first instance; look beyond the contentious nature of business to see if there are any lessons to be learnt.

Go beyond competition

In business winning has traditionally been summarised as beating the competition. This view is frequently valid and often you only need to be the best of those invited, to win the bid. Unfortunately this does not always hold true. There are many examples where the most competitive bid does not win the contract. Sometimes it does not get awarded at all and the client subsequently invites other suppliers to tender or looks at alternative means of procuring the goods or services it requires. So the definition of winning as being the best of those competing, does not necessarily hold true. Even getting the contract may not give you the best possible deal, if the client is inherently dissatisfied with the solution.

There are two ways then to view bidding to win. You can aim just to beat the competition and be the best of the bunch or you can aim to satisfy the client totally and beat the competition into the bargain. Winning bids consistently is about achieving client satisfaction. Going a further step beyond competitiveness is often what will give you the edge. How are you to take that step and what will it cost you? The approach and direction will be dictated by many factors: the type of client, the type of product, the market forces operating, the economic environment, and so on.

In the 1980s the global market saw massive growth and expansion, while the recent recession saw a further turn in the cycle of business dynamics as businesses began to contract their operations; scaling down, right-sizing and re-engineering of the business processes has resulted in them becoming leaner and more responsive. Technology has further fuelled this contraction. The introduction of powerful computing capability distributed throughout the organisation, integrated networking, and communications infrastructures have allowed companies to change their ways of operating. Decentralisation is becoming more common as enterprises begin to move from being largely intransigent organisations and focus more upon the smaller operational unit.

Consolidate values

In this changing business environment you must consider the way in which bids are perceived. Cost cutting is critical when a business is in recession and to grow during these periods requires value to be added to the business while containing costs. Adding value through your bid is therefore paramount.

Your bid has a value to the client not only in terms of price but also in terms of the benefits that your proposed solution gives them. Each aspect of your offer will have a specific value which may be high or low depending upon the client's unique requirements. Part of successful bid management is understanding the level of value that your client places on solutions to each need. Some needs are more pressing than others and your solution to these will therefore have a higher value. You should structure your bid so that these high value needs are satisfied fully. This is sometimes termed value engineering: ensuring that the most important issues for the client are dealt with effectively.

During the assessment of bids the individual values of all the bid elements will be added together to produce a consolidated value to them. To win, therefore, your bid has to have a consolidated value to the client that exceeds those of your competitors.

The value elements in your bid include the traditional competitive areas of price, product and quality as for any market segment. But they will also include other areas, such as giving a competitive edge to your client through providing technical innovations that their rivals may not have, or having dominance in technology, market position or industry sector. These value elements also embrace brand recognition and geographical benefits such as being a local company or having a worldwide presence.

What, then, is value engineering within the context of bidding? The client has certain expectations and values specific aspects of their requirement over others. The key to value engineering is to find out which are the high value items and emphasise them within your bid. By concentrating on these and manipulating them, you will reach the threshold of a consolidated value that exceeds those of your competitors and meets your client's expectations.

To understand these value expectations you must put yourself into the position of your client. Perform a value analysis on your offer as if you were the buyer. Ask yourself if there are any extra elements in your bid that the client does not really need but that you see as a benefit (when they assess your offer, they will give no value to those extras, perceiving them only as additional cost items). Look at whether you can carry out the functions another way, at lower cost. See if you can use different materials or construction methods and still offer similar performance. Look to use standard technology and keep prices low, in preference to designing new components. Meeting standard specifications such as those of the International Standards Organisation and the British Standards Institution is becoming more crucial in value engineering. If you are bidding under public sector European Union directives, for example, it is now mandatory for the client to specify the European industry standards that apply.

Previously, each country specified their own laws relating to product safety, technical regulation, testing, production methods and so on. This led to technical barriers to trade being erected, with a product made by a manufacturer for their domestic market possibly contravening the product legislation of another member country. To break down these barriers and prevent new ones being created the EU introduced a new approach to technical harmonisation and standards. This directive resulted in a single community-wide regime which replaces the different national laws.

The next stage is to look for ways to enhance the consolidated value of your offer, but at low cost. You still need to differentiate your proposal from your competitors so you need to look at ways in which you can add benefit without overpricing. This is where your creativity and design initiative comes to the fore and combines with your knowledge of the client to get the competitive edge you need.

It is important to try to think creatively throughout the bid. Investigate new ways in which you can apply your company's existing knowledge and experience or develop new ideas and purposes to exploit the opportunity. This does not mean you continually have to come up with breakthroughs in new products; you can make incremental changes to improve many aspects of your existing portfolio or take other people's ideas a stage further to get the edge. Instill innovation throughout the bid, not just in the technical solution but in the commercial response, the financing and pricing, the presentation of your offer and in the bid management process itself.

Value engineering is an essential task in your bid. At an early stage you should involve your designers, engineers and technical specialists. If you decide to buy-in instead of manufacturing, get your suppliers involved too. Try to draw comparisons between what you are planning to bid and what your competitors are likely to offer. If you do this for every component of your bid you could hit upon a different way of doing things, upon which you can model an alternative approach. Value engineering should ideally be part of your ongoing product or service improvement programme. You may find that focusing on a particular bid opportunity provides the impetus for changes in your value engineering programme bringing longer-term repercussions to your bid success rate.

PIVOTAL CLIENT FACTORS

The final area to consider when assessing what makes a winning bid is perhaps the most important; this is the client factor. In a later chapter, the relationship between client and supplier is examined in detail, but you should look first at some basic criteria to help you in selecting winning bids. The client factor divides into two areas; the first is centred on the client organisation, the second on the client's project, representing the bid opportunity for you. In deciding whether you can win the bid, you need to give due consideration to both areas.

Your client's project could represent a small part of their overall business development strategy, such as purchasing of regular supplies, or it could represent a major diversion from the way they do things, such as the outsourcing of non-core activities. The relative importance of the project to the client is therefore critical and you cannot separate the two. You must consider the impact of the project upon the client organisation and the effect that the client's general situation imposes upon the feasibility of the project; occasionally, the client's very viability may rest on the success of the project.

Realistic projects

If you are sensible, you do not want to spend large sums of money chasing prospects that exist only in the imagination of the client. Finding out how realistic and viable the project may be is a pivotal client factor. This is not always easy to do. The client may firmly believe the project will go ahead, even though you may have strong doubts. But just because it has been advertised, or heralded in the press, do not be led into thinking it is settled.

Many projects do not materialise for a variety of reasons. You need some concrete facts to base your judgement upon, so first check the client's financing to see if there are funds available to pay for it. You can do a check on their credit worthiness through a credit checking company. See if there is a budget available for this project and if so how much has been allocated. For many government and European Union projects or where international lending agencies are involved, the available budget is stated within the project papers and is available to anyone who takes the effort to check it. Take the time to do it. Private companies may play their cards closer to their chests and you will have to use your own sources to find out the information.

Another way to validate the project is to check that the project has been given the go-ahead within the client's organisation. If it is still in the formative stages it may never materialise. See if there are any political factors that you may need to consider both internally, within the customer's organisation and externally, in the world at large.

By looking carefully at these areas you will be able to decide a strategy to help you further develop the prospect. For example, if the project is only an idea in the mind of an influential manager you could have the opportunity to help them bring it to fruition and at the same time bring your influence to bear on their thinking.

RISK MANAGEMENT

Risk is all pervasive in business and bidding is no exception. When making a risk assessment, you are evaluating the client and opportunity, your own position and the competitive threat before making a judgement on how these relationships affect your chances of winning profitably. Risk modifies both the factors and your interpretation of them; high risk is usually commensurate with high reward, low risk with low reward. In the bidding business you have to take chances, but it is up to you to decide at what odds.

Pure risk

In the science of risk management pure risk is considered in four areas. Natural risks are those outside the control of man; fire, earthquake, volcanic activity and flood are typical risks. There is the risk from unacceptable social behaviour such as theft, fraud, vandalism, negligence or civil unrest and riot, and personal risk in the form of death, injury, illness or disability. Technical risk arises from equipment failure or breakdown, failure of safety systems, hazards in the physical processes involved and many other mechanical or structural problems that can occur.

You can assess and handle pure risks in several ways and there are four accepted methods: You can reduce the risk, for example by either introducing safety and security measures or by planning and organising effectively to establish contingency and emergency plans. You can avoid risk by taking an alternative approach and bypassing it or you can combine the risk with other factors to reduce the chances of an event occurring and then finance the losses inherent in the risk.

Loss financing is usually done either by retaining the risk within your company or transferring it to a third party. In risk retention your company will absorb all the losses associated with the risk should the event occur. In risk transfer, all or part of the risk is taken on by somebody else, and this includes insurance and other such protection methods.

Business risk

Business risks are more complex and difficult to assess than pure risks. You should consider them in several categories. These could include: technical risks such as inadequate knowledge or unforseen difficulties occurring; project risks arising from failing to complete the task within budget or timescale; financial risks from currency exchange rates, default on the payment schedule, or calling-in performance bonds; political risks such as problems within the client organisation, or external world events. It is wise to break down the business risks into those areas that are common to your industry sector and your company and perform a detailed analysis in each area to decide the risk factors.

Risk factors

Every bid is an opportunity for your company to make a profit but there is also an attendant risk that you could lose money as well. Money can be lost either because you fail to win the contract and incur bid costs and costs of sale. Even worse, you win the contract but have underestimated the costs involved to such an extent that you are unable to recover the deficit within the project itself. The risk of these two scenarios occurring will be minimised by effective bid management. Selection of only those bids that you can win is crucial and lowers the risk.

Every opportunity that comes your way will have both favourable and unfavourable factors. Your responsibility is to quantify them in such a way that values can be assigned to the risks, thereby reducing likelihood of your company losing money and enhancing your chances of success. Although at the outset you will probably have only minimal information to work with, you must ensure that your assessment is as comprehensive as possible. Doing this thoroughly at this stage, will direct you towards the information you need in order to make a more detailed assessment later.

In bidding, as with other aspects of business, there is an element of risk. It may be a high or low probability of an event or sequence of events occurring, but it will always exist. You should be aware of the extent to which your opportunity displays risk and of the courses of action that are available to you for dealing with it. There are systems that exist to assess and handle risk and the science of risk management has emerged to formalise these processes.

The assessment of risk in bidding combines a mixture of approaches. The deductive approach applies simple logic to the situation. If four suppliers have received invitations to bid, a logical deduction is that each has a one-in-four chance of success. This is true only if all suppliers are equally capable. In reality other factors will affect the outcome. So the logical approach alone has little value in bidding. As bids will vary over a period, you can assess the probability of success by observation of past performance, results and experience. This empirical approach is of more benefit in business. Evaluation of past results may show a higher record of success in bidding one product as opposed to another to a particular client type. The experimental approach suggests that the chances of success are therefore higher under similar circumstances. This assumes that each experience is independent of all others and that the business environment is the same. In the real world this is not likely to be the case.

Both the deductive and empirical approaches are objective and it is possible for you to apply probability theory to assess the risk in each case. As each bid involves many variables, such as clients, requirements, products, and competitors, it is difficult to see how you can always make an objective assessment. Individual managers will have their own feelings about particular opportunities and will assess each aspect of the bid individually. There will be uncertainties in the opportunity, such as political, economic or fiscal variables that cannot be predicted. So you will need a subjective framework in which to assess the risk in these areas. In most bids you will have a combination of subjective and objective information.

Risk assessment

When you receive the client's invitation to bid you will usually complete your risk assessment and decide how you can best manage the risk involved. In most assessments you need to weigh up the effect upon the bid of many risk areas. Some you probably can mitigate or limit the effect of by careful management, other risks may be acceptable with adjustment to pricing or with some other insurance. You should be aiming at locating all risk factors, assessing their combined effects and applying sound risk management techniques to reduce them.

In a bid the risk occurs in three areas, the risk of losing, the risk of winning and the risk of not bidding. If you do not submit a bid you may lose further opportunities. If you submit a bid and lose you may have lost your chance of establishing a foothold. If you win the bid and lose money or fail to deliver then this will have repercussions with other clients by damaging your reputation.

Risk of winning

Possibly, this area involves you in the greatest financial risk. In pricing your bid you will consider the profit that you expect from the project. Where risks leave you exposed, you will need to consider taking insurance. You may need to consider uninsured areas and build in additional contingency to protect yourself. Of course, the danger here is that by attempting to cover all risks you overprice the bid and do not win. The bid manager and business manager will usually take advice from the legal advisor, financial and technical managers to decide the level of risk, the probability of the event occurring and its likely financial impact on the project.

The checklist in Table 2 provides you with some broad risk areas that you may encounter and which you should consider when making your risk assessment. Use the table to assign a rating in importance, from high to low, to each factor as it applies to your bid. You can then take into account the probability of an event occurring, consider the likelihood of failure and success in each and thus decide the risk associated with it.

Competitive risk

No matter how comprehensive your risk analysis, the greatest threat to you winning will come from your competitors. Find out who they are and prepare a shortlist of the main threats they pose. You can get this information from several sources. Try the client's bidders list, the attenders at the bidders' conference, local agent intelligence, the client manager and anyone with knowledge of any existing suppliers. Conduct a Strength, Weakness, Opportunity, Threat (SWOT) analysis for each of your shortlisted competitors to help you assess the risk and focus your strategy.

Competitive bidding by its very nature involves uncertainty and the possibility of incurring losses. Assessing the risks and deciding if they are acceptable or whether you can reduce or eliminate them is essential if you are to win profitable new business. You cannot make a balanced decision to bid or to let the opportunity pass without knowing both the benefits that you hope to achieve and the attendant risks you incur if you are successful. The risks you encounter in bidding are either business risks to which you can apply a business management philosophy, or pure risks that require a risk management approach. More often than not you will meet both types and should be aware of the basics of risk management to allow you to assess the prospect effectively.

Assessment Category	Criteria	Probability	Rating	Risk
Regional	Economic stability of region			
	Country's political situation			
	Electoral position			
	Government and opposition policies			
	Taxation issues			
	Environmental issues or legislation			
	Foreign ownership laws			
	Labour and social legislation			
	Regional politics			
	Religious or cultural problems			
	Local labour skills			
Environmental	Natural (seismic, volcanic or flood etc) or man-made			
Client	Finances sound			
	Supplier relationship good			
	Payment record			
Contract	Length of commitment			
Finance	Hard or soft payments			
	Hedge against recession			
	Currency protection			
	Agency funded			
	Letter of credit			
	Payback period			
	Bid bond amount			
	Performance bond amount			
	Likelihood of client retaining bond			
Project	Familiarity with type of work			
	Experience and expertise available in-house			
	Accuracy of technical information in specification			
	Performance criteria understood			
	Uncertain areas within bid			
	Timescales reasonable			
	Contingency within project plan			
Design Factors	Compliance against specification			
Subcontracts	Second source available			
	Financial position sound			
	Delivery schedule met			
	Penalty clauses adequate			
Competition	SWOT analysis reasonable			

Table 2 Risk assessment checklist

SUMMARY

Bidding is all about winning, there are no prizes for coming second.

- *Start by selecting the opportunities that are best for your company in terms of the technology, the type of work, the client, the location, price and profitability.*
- *Conduct an early assessment to provide reassurance that the opportunity is worth bidding for.*
- *The deciding factors which determine your likelihood of winning are your own position in the marketplace and your readiness to bid. Make sure you know what you want and why you should bid.*
- *Avoid bidding just for the sake of it. Focus on your chosen opportunity and do everything you can to win.*
- *If you cannot win, then consider not bidding.*
- *Apply a structured bid process that supports innovation and creativity.*
- *Always find out why you lost and why you won and use this information to improve your future success rate.*
- *Quantify the costs you will incur and the profit you expect to make. If this ratio is inadequate either change it or consider withdrawing from the bid.*
- *Go further than just doing enough to beat your competition by attempting to provide complete client satisfaction. Understand the values that your client places on each aspect of your bid and make sure you can provide achievable solutions.*
- *Getting a solid understanding of your client's structure, motives and targets will help you assess how realistic the project may be and will influence your bid strategy.*
- *The level of risk affects the way you asess a prospective bid. Understand and quantify the risk so that you can make decisions from a position of knowledge.*

2

THE STRUCTURE OF BIDS

From your examination of the pivotal factors that dictate success, you can see that a great deal of information and analysis is needed. You need to weigh up all this information before you can make a judgement to bid or even decide what your approach should be. Because of the inherent complexities, it helps if you have a framework to support your thinking. This chapter outlines the progress of a typical bid to allow you to develop your own ideas and adjust such a framework to meet your own needs. By viewing the bid both from the suppliers' perspective and from the buyers' position, you can gain a deeper insight than you might from a simple analysis of the opportunity.

However, knowledge is redundant unless you can apply it. Once you have developed an understanding of the structure of the bid, you need to use it in the most effective way to gain you success. The pressures on time and resources that are prevalent in most bids often work against you, forcing corner-cutting and snap judgements. Applying your efforts within an organised bid process will help you to cope with these pressures, and regularly achieve better results than if you continually create the process afresh. Setting up a systematic bid process is discussed later in this chapter.

THE STAGES OF THE BID

Any business process can be considered as a series of inputs which are acted upon to produce an output. Each stage that the process goes through, modifies the inputs and creates an output to the next stage. The bid management process goes through six major phases and many minor ones, which together form the complete cycle of activity. The cycle runs through the identification of an opportunity, its development, the translation of that opportunity into a commitment, the carrying out of that commitment and then the identification of further opportunities. The order in which the stages are completed varies from bid to bid and upon the client's procurement method.

Significantly, your bid cycle encompasses the buying cycle of your client, and should not be separated. Synchronising the cycles allows you to empathise with your client and meet their needs through the various stages of the bid. The buying cycle varies from client to client and within different market sectors but typically it consists of a series of linked decisions, each having an effect upon your bid. During every stage and before proceeding onto the next you should be asking whether to bid and checking that you have enough information upon which to base a decision. The diagram in Fig. 2.1 shows the relationship between the buying and bid cycles.

Identify the prospect

Buying cycle

Perhaps as part of their corporate business strategy or because they have identified deficiencies in their operation, your client identifies an area where some development or change is necessary. They start by examining the problem in some detail, defining its scope and extent and generating ideas for possible solutions. They will probably consult with

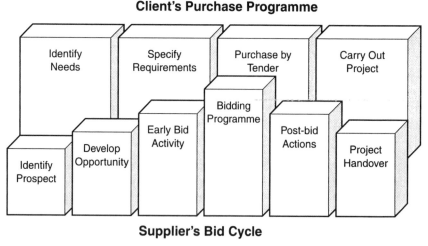

Fig. 2.1 Bid cycle matches buying cycle

many people, both internally and outside the company, to elicit their thoughts or add substance to the concepts they are developing.

Bidding cycle

In this preliminary stage you have to identify the prospect and assess its viability. You clearly need to be close to the client, hopefully operating in a consultative capacity. As you become aware of the prospect, check it against your corporate strategy and decide whether this is one that you want to win. If it is, you need to find out whether sufficient resources are available within the organisation not only to bid, but to carry out the project if successful. The differentiation between business which is good for your company or bad for it, is critical during this stage. Now is the best time to decide to abandon the bid if you are going to. Continuing through the bid cycle and abandoning it at the last minute has only wasted your time and money as well as that of your client. Nevertheless, it is unlikely to be clear cut at this stage and it may not cost you very much effort to go on. You will start generating questions and building a portfolio of relevant information that will be valuable later.

Develop the opportunity

Buying cycle

Solutions will begin to take shape through the various consultation processes. The project is defined, with preliminary budgets being set. The client begins to research trends and developments that are relevant to their needs, perhaps doing a search for potential suppliers of a suitable solution.

Bidding cycle

At this stage, the viability and feasibility of the prospect have been established. Internal and external relationships, with the client, the internal account team and other resources in your company, including senior management, start to form. The prospect begins to take shape. Your influence on the client's thinking is important here and you should try to find out the key commercial issues. Now you begin to assess the competitive threats. This stage can be a long one and yet it is probably the most critical one in the bid cycle. Many bids are won or lost here. It is often the supplier who established the closest relationship with the client now who can exert the greatest influence. They will have the best understanding of the client's value expectations and will be engineering these around what they can provide.

Preliminary bid activity

Buying cycle

The client's review of trends extends to technology, to allow them to produce a complete specification of the solution. The client now sets timescales alongside the specification, chooses the best procurement method and begins production of the necessary documentation.

Bidding cycle

The client is preparing an actual bid invitation. By now you should have identified the members of your bid team and ensured their availability. Do not neglect your client as you still need to develop solid relationships at various levels within their organisation. For larger bids you will probably draft a bid management plan. This will include an overview of the opportunity, its value, bid strategy, sales plan, team responsibilities and other key issues.

For total quality management you should ensure that you have established quality procedures and document control systems. Revise and reissue the bid management plan as this stage progresses. Remember to alert your senior management to the bid and enlist their support. Ask key team members to begin to formulate their ideas and proposals to emulate the client's requirements and to test alternative solutions.

The bidding programme

Buying cycle

With the documentation now complete, the client finishes the search for potential suppliers and invites them to tender. They have set their evaluation criteria to provide an objective assessment of the responses. For fairness and impartiality they will put into effect any formal procedures to ensure that all tenderers have the correct information and are similarly treated.

Bidding cycle

You receive the client's invitation to tender. There may be a bidders' conference, to which all tenderers will be invited. This is a good opportunity to complete your competitive analyses and risk assessments. The client's invitation is likely to throw up many questions and the answers to these will impinge upon your bid strategy and bid plan to reflect the actual requirement. The bid team should continue the design process with reviews and checks made against the client's specification. Once completed, get all approvals including those of your senior management and set the bid price. Prepare and submit your proposals to the client. Retain as much contact with the client as you can during this phase, if allowed under the terms of the invitation to bid.

Post-bid activity

Buying cycle

After all proposals have been received, the client will commence their adjudication based upon the evaluation criteria they set previously. One or more suppliers will be shortlisted. Any concerns about their offers are quantified so they can be resolved or form items for negotiation. Details are negotiated with the shortlisted suppliers and they make a final selection.

Bidding cycle

Using the relationships you established earlier will help you to assess how your bid has been received and to look at alternatives where difficulties may be arising. Use the possibility for a presentation of your proposal to cover any potential problem areas. If you have an opportunity for a site visit then you should plan it well. At the end of the adjudication the client will either prepare a shortlist or announce a winner. They will then begin to negotiate a contract. Your bid will either win or lose. Prepare a bid closure report to help you in future attempts.

The project programme

Buying cycle

The client finalises the agreement with the preferred supplier and a contract is drawn up and signed. A delivery schedule for the work or supply is set and the project commences. The client monitors and reviews progress with the supplier against the agreed schedule and performance criteria.

Bidding cycle

Each successful bid is followed by an assignment. This may be a project to build and deliver the products you tendered or the supply of services. You should ensure that you hand responsibility to the project manager with all the contractual, technical, design and commercial information he will need to be able to carry it out. Ideally, the project manager should have been a member of the bid team throughout the bid cycle. Do not neglect your client at this stage. You should continue to provide support and assistance to both the project team and the client. Bidding is cyclical so you should now be looking for potential new business and maintaining the good relationships that you have already established.

ORGANISING FOR BIDDING

Your organisation will have its own ideas on the structure and philosophy behind your bid strategy and the way in which you manage bids. Planning your bid strategy is covered in depth later. Achieving successful results with bids is made more difficult without a well-structured and documented bid and tendering system. Even smaller businesses will benefit from establishing a consistent approach to their bids. Such a system should not be a rigid and inflexible set of rules, but one that is adaptable and allows you to learn from experience. Any bid and tendering system must be able to feed back into itself the best and remove from itself the inadequate elements. Whether you are setting up a bidding system from scratch, or looking for ways to improve your current system, using the following guidelines will point you in the right direction.

Build an effective bidding system

The most important aspect of any bidding system is its ability to evolve and learn. A system that continually allows you to make the same mistakes is worse than none at all. Effective bid management systems require constant attention.

Total quality management has emerged over recent years to help businesses streamline the way they do things and to compete more effectively for new business. Instead of simply controlling people, managers need to consider what people do and how they do it. Most businesses consist of many processes; the sales process, the accounting process and the production process are examples. Each process is designed to take information, perform some action on it, and produce a result. While some of these processes may be considered minor, others will have a significant effect upon how well the overall business performs. These are sometimes referred to as mission-critical processes. The quality of these processes, how well they are designed and how effective they are is often fundamental to the profitability of the company.

The ideas of total quality management and business process design can be applied to bid management as effectively as any other management system or organisational issue. They can assist you in looking at the benefits of a particular approach although they will not overcome the resistance to change that people will feel. When people have done the same thing in the same way for some time, they may become adverse to any change in the status quo. Although modern quality management techniques may change the process they may not alter the ingrained attitudes of the people performing the tasks. So an effective bidding system must not only consider how the process will be carried out but also the reactions of the people expected to do it.

Setting up the bid management process

Almost every organisation goes through stages where it either needs to improve existing business processes or introduce new ones. The growth in business process re-engineering or redesign is evidence of that fact. In many ways the better approach is to aim for continual improvement without having to make widespread and radical changes in your operation.

The bid process in your business defines the set of tasks that takes you from first receiving information, through some linked actions onto delivery of the bid and beyond. In beginning the redesign you need to establish some baseline objectives. First you have to decide what it is you are trying to achieve by reorganising or setting up a bid process. Then you need to understand the way in which your organisation does things now. Only then can you look at ways to improve or carry out an effective bid management process.

There will be many different people involved in the bid throughout your organisation and Fig. 2.2 shows how they and the resources at your disposal come together to perform the bid process. At each stage these people will provide an input into the process by perhaps providing information or acting upon information they have received. Each will generate an output that will be consolidated into the final output of the bid process which is your proposal, the award of the contract and its realisation.

Objectives for the bid process

Your principal aims for the bid process will centre on ways of improving how things are done in your company. So when organising for improvement, consider what you are trying to achieve. There are probably three main reasons which have stimulated your thinking:

- to reduce your costs
- to maintain position against increased competitiveness or
- to achieve a stronger market position by adopting the best practices.

With these three possibilities in mind you can establish or reorganise the business processes that will best support your bidding strategy. Once you have assessed which combination of these stimuli is most appropriate, you can develop and enhance your bidding system to fit the rationale behind your decision.

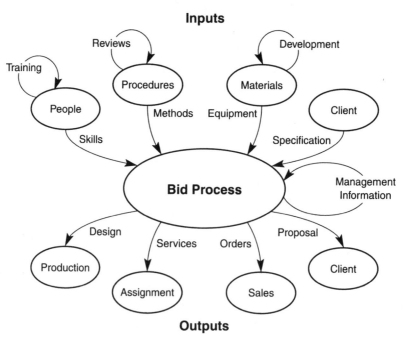

Fig. 2.2 Typical bid process

Organising for cost reduction

To bring about improvements in the bidding process within your company, you will need to look carefully at the processes that your organisation goes through, from the identification of an opportunity through to the bidding and winning of the contract, then onto its accomplishment. The key issues to look for are inherent delays, redundant or duplicated processes, dependencies on critical systems or personnel, and information and decision flows. Try to identify where the bottlenecks occur in the workflow. When you come across duplication or repetition, do away with all the unnecessary steps. To improve throughput, introduce scheduling for key resources. Putting in place fall-back measures for critical events will reduce dependencies. Setting up preliminary and prompt empowerment at various operational levels will help you to get things done quicker. Your intention should be to get a simplified bidding process so that costs are reduced and effectiveness increased.

Organising for improved competitiveness

Leaving aside cost reduction as a motive for change, you may want to organise to achieve *best in class* performance so as to be on a par with your competitors. Why bother with this approach? In your market position you may be finding it difficult or impossible to compete on costs. This could be the case if, for example, you are supplying products or services of a higher standard with a larger underlying cost-base. The cost-reduction approach while improving the cost efficiency of your bidding, will not help you win more, so you require another differentiator. You therefore need to organise the bidding system to take advantage of that differentiator. First, you must know what it is that your client will be willing to pay more for. It could be higher reliability, a superior design, or excellence in project achievement. When you have identified what it is, you should focus on that activity within the bid process. Organise the bidding system around it so that this aspect of your operation becomes central to the bid itself. For example, if you excel in rapid project execution, ensure that the project manager is on board throughout the bid. When preparing your response, structure the proposal to take advantage of the benefits this gives you. You can achieve better project focus by making sure you use the assignment team wherever possible to check contracts or to plan the proposal. Extend this activity throughout the process, by designing handover procedures that are smooth and easy and documentation systems that are tailored to meet the needs of the project team. The same approach should be adopted whatever the competitive differentiator might be; always try to maximise your strengths.

Organising to set the standards

The final reason for organising is to become the market leader and set the standards that others will follow. This is otherwise known as becoming *best in class*. Your reasons for wanting to do this should be clear. You may believe that the market in which you operate is one where price and quality are similar among your competitors. Cost-reduction is inappropriate and effecting a differentiator is difficult. You then need to make a radical change in the way you do business and the bid system should be organised to support that change. You may be using the same ideas and technology as your competitors, but you need to take it that one step further to create a new competitive advantage. This is the most risky way to approach the process. First you must decide what you perceive to be the strategy for market dominance and look at the processes to support that. In other words you are deciding where you want to be. Next, you organise around the new processes and set up the new organisation.

Look at how you do it now

With your objectives for redesigning the bid process firmly fixed, the next stage is to analyse the way in which you bid now. This means examining not only the core activities around the bid process but also the peripheral and supporting functions. The bid process usually involves many people and redesigning it will require you to look at the way in which they interact and the systems they use in doing so.

You will find that there are more people involved than you first thought: there is the bid team itself, the bid manager, the client or sales manager, the commercial department and the technical or services manager. But dig down another level and you will find many other supporting functions which are often overlooked: the taxation department, the legal department, the information technology department and so on. These roles and responsibilities are critical to your process so take time to look at how the people come together for a bid and when. Find out what are their levels of involvement, what are they charged with doing, and whether they do it well. Search out the best practices and those that are deficient. Remember that bidding is about people so seek their co-operation and support throughout the redesign. To improve the process you need to look not only at what they do but at their potential for improvement. Most people in any organisation have their own ideas about how the process can be made better. Listen to them and get them to participate. You need to understand exactly what goes on during the bid process even though this may mean setting aside any existing guidelines or procedures and analysing what actually takes place.

Redesign the bid process

Your redesigned bid process should take your best practices, incorporate other necessary methods and routines, and form the framework upon which you will construct winning bids. It should also define the management information you need in order to control the bidding process and to build synergy between the people and the enterprise structure for all bid activity.

There are clear benefits arising from providing the most essential and often used processes that define and delineate the bidding activity. A structured framework for your bids will help you to maximise the available skills. By adopting a common discipline you should improve bid performance which will give you a higher win rate. A sound process will give more effective use of premium bid resources that will result in lower bid costs. Through objectively assessing each opportunity, you will be better able to focus on your strategic aspirations. Aim to standardise your approach and methods as this will improve the timing of your bids and reduce your overhead costs. Better guidelines for bid planning undoubtably lead to improved performance from the people involved. Making sure that you all use the same assessment criteria means that you will minimise the risk to the company. Put in place authorisation procedures that give you better management control.

Your redesigned bid process should map out the path from the starting point of the bid to its finish, from identifying an opportunity and alerting the business through to the contract decision. On the way it should clearly identify and define the processes for making your bid decisions and submission approvals.

As with any complex management function things do go wrong in bids. A critical part of bid management is ensuring that the bid is resilient, can withstand problems and that the process continues. People do go sick and accidents do happen but the process should allow the bid manager to retain an accurate record of the status of the bid at any time; who is doing what and when it is required. This record of progress will enable anyone to pick up the bid and continue, minimising wasted effort and time.

Remember though, that interaction with and between people is critical. Your process should not restrict or stifle the creativity that every successful and winning bid requires. Set the boundaries within which the bid management tasks will take place. By alleviating the need to reinvent the mundane processes and controls you will reassure the people involved that they are acting with the approval of their management. This will encourage creativity and enable you to maximise your efforts in winning the bid.

Your process should enable bid managers to perform at their optimum while defining the limits within which they must operate. It should encourage innovation, analysis, decision making and the use of skills in the best way possible yet manage and control work within the constraints that the business imposes.

Typical key objectives from an effective bid process include the following points.

Establishing a quality system for bidding

By building quality into your process it will come through in your bid, and into the delivery of the project. Your clients now expect quality and recognise it. Some will insist upon bidders complying with recognised quality standards. Quality objectives from the bid process should typically include:

- document control systems
- formalised processes and procedures
- BS 5750/ISO 9000 standards.

Providing guidance to the bid manager

Your bid process should aim to provide answers to most of the issues that are commonly raised during the bid. This will help you to achieve consistency and enable other bid managers to learn from your experience. In this respect the bid process should state:

- your company's way of managing bids
- consistent bid quality standards and
- your standard approach to proposals.

Defining bid control mechanisms

For large bids exercising effective control can be problematical and even small bids require a touch on the rudder from time to time. The bid process should support this by advising on company policy and procedures so that you overlook nothing during your hurry to complete the bid. Typically, this should include:

- concurrence and authorisation level
- accepted winning disciplines
- resource planning controls

Providing effective management information

Gathering and consolidating information, keeping the bid and management teams informed and feeding back information into future opportunities is critical in achieving consistent wins. Your bid process should include a management information system. It need not be complex or computerised but it must be effective and up to date, as out of date information is worse than none at all. Later in the book the basic outline of a bid information system is described. Essentially provided to help you decide strategy, it needs to be integrated with your company management information system.

Both line and bid managers need information. Line managers need status reports, resource allocations, financial data and so on, to plan strategy and set out operational plans. Bid managers need to have constant feedback on developments to go into strategy reviews and bid planning. The bid process should facilitate this by providing:

- status report processes
- financial forecasts and projections
- business benefit reports.

Keeping the process relevant to your needs

Designing the bid process to meet your precise business needs relies upon the full co-operation of the people involved at operational and management levels. For any process to be effective and achieve its objectives, it must be useful to the people who need it. If it fails in this respect you will not enhance the bidding process but add to the burden on the team during critical phases of the bid.

Aim for simplification and not an increase in the bureaucratic overhead. Keep the process relevant and pertinent to the bid and management teams alike. Careful analysis of the management information that your company needs will give you the flexibility to respond to changes and be proactive in anticipating developments and trends. By keeping management informed and alert to developments, the process will retain its relevance. Your bid process should incorporate items and objectives such as:

- check-list approach for a comprehensive bid
- prospect assessment processes defined
- guidelines for bid team structure
- approval processes detailed
- release resources for creativity
- risk defined and quantified
- assistance in decision-making process
- improved scheduling and bid planning
- comprehensive management reports
- early notification of prospects
- facilitation of resource planning
- bid registration and control systems
- up to date progress reporting
- enhance management input into winning
- complementary total quality system
- BS 5750/ISO 9000 document control.

Documentation control

Documentation control should be a component of your company's bid management system. Bids and their resulting projects will often result in your creating many documents. Some of these are commercially sensitive or critical to the bid and need to be kept under controlled conditions while others are less sensitive and can be openly circulated. Contracts, specifications, memoranda of understanding with your suppliers and priced proposals are examples of controlled documents. Standard terms and conditions, capability statements and descriptive literature are open documents that are readily available and can be included in other bids.

If you are the bid manager, you will normally decide the classification of a document and inform the proposal manager responsible for the document control system.

Opening a bid file

You will need to open and control a bid file containing sufficient information to rework the proposal, if necessary. This is an important consideration as you may be called upon to rebid against a revised specification or revalidate your bid if the client is unable to make a decision within its validity period. As a guide you should retain all the core data that you have used to prepare the proposal for one year after submission. This gives you the best information to rebid, if required, undertake negotiations and carry out the project on the award of the contract.

If you are bidding frequently, you should allocate to each bid a unique identification number and keep the key documents in a working file carrying that unique bid number. To help you in controlling the bid file, include a summary sheet that notes the key documents that exist within it, their titles (or other identifying features) and their dates or issue numbers. If a key document is not in the file, for example a master framework agreement, then the file should show its location. Fig. 2.3 gives a list of the type of information that you would normally expect to keep in the bid file.

Controlled bid documents

For security and management reasons you may want to define certain key documents as controlled. This means that you will know whether it can be copied and who holds the master and duplicate copies and can therefore manage updates or revisions easily. Use the bid file summary sheet to identify them as controlled documents and list who holds the circulated copies. You can then circulate any alterations or revised versions to those people on the controlled list.

You should control all master documents such as the bid guidelines, authorisation forms and proposals by a simple change control procedure. Identify master documents by title, issue number and date of issue. They should also carry the initials of the manager who approved their issue.

When you make changes, revise the documents, mark with the next issue number, date again and get it approved by the appropriate manager before use. Use a control page in each document to carry this information. You may also need to hold the obsolete copy in a suitable master file for possible future reference. Other obsolete copies should be withdrawn.

When fully operational, the system described above comes some way towards establishing a simple ISO 9000 Quality Management Systems requirement for document control. To comply with this standard, you also need to store documents correctly and securely. When the bid is completed, the file summary sheet should show where you filed the proposal hard copy and its file name and location within your computer systems. Always protect electronic files so that they can be copied but not corrupted.

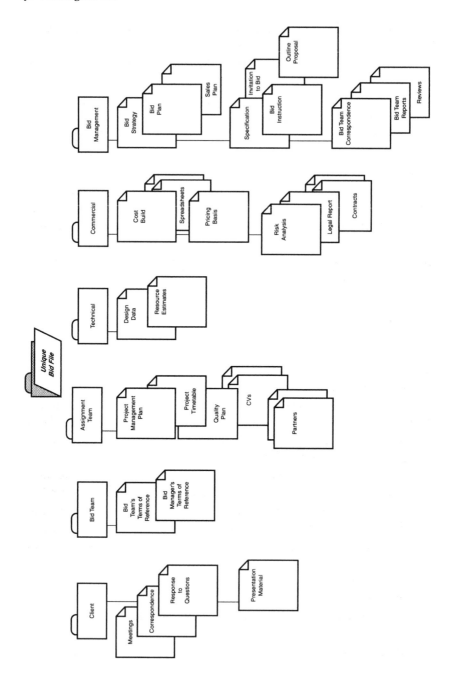

Fig. 2.3 Typical bid file

Accountability and ownership

A well-structured bid plan, with regular bid reports and running action plans will make accountability easier. Keeping an audit trail will also help you in assessing and analysing the bid at a later stage.

During the bid you will have plenty of good opportunities to develop your knowledge and establish a sound information database that you can use on this bid and others. Table 3 (overleaf) charts some areas where useful information is generally available. Do not keep this information to yourself. Other members of the bid team probably could use it now, or on future opportunities. If there are other people managing bids in your company it will be useful if you establish a single library or repository for information, with copies of anything that may be relevant for the future. You can use the bid closure report as an easy way to ensure that you retain summary information.

Time is always short during bids and there are usually many people and tasks to be co-ordinated. The bid manager can ease this task by planning the bid in advance and circulating a bid plan to the team. The bid manager should consider the basic planning information in Chapter 10.

Later, in Chapter 7, the roles and responsibilities of the various members of the bid team will be identified. As the person leading the team, you must delegate responsibility with the authority to make necessary decisions and accountability for actions taken. In defining who does what, it is useful to refer to ownership of the bid. Ownership confers possession and control. The client manager owns the relationship with the customer, the business manager owns the bid and project budgets and is responsible for the profitability of the project. The owner of the bid is the bid manager who is responsible for it meeting the objectives decided by the project owner. Each team member owns their contribution to the bid.

SUMMARY

The bid process does not just consist of preparing and submitting a tender; successful bidders start early and have a structured bid system.

- *Bids run through several stages: identification of a suitable prospect that you can win, developing the prospect and enhancing your position within it, preparing for the bid by setting up the processes and people you will need, responding to the client's invitation to bid by preparing a detailed proposal, following up once you have submitted your offer to maximise your chances of success.*

General Research Sources		Value Rating	Check Date/File	Specific Direct Sources	Value Rating	Check Date/File
Financial Analyses	Financial Times			Credit agency check		
	Client reports			Funding agency check		
	Finance report services			Auditors		
	Interim statements			Your financial services		
	Report & accounts			Your operations unit		
	Previous reports & accounts			Other customers		
Market Research	Market intelligence			Your business unit		
	Marketing analyst			Your strategy database		
	Marketing databases			Regulatory body		
	Current market reports			Marketing department		
	Future reports			Library		
	Other			Marketing consultants		
Products & Services	Product literature			Your strategy database		
	Directory (name)			Consultants		
Cultural	Company briefings			Regional controller		
	Country reports			Previous bid file		
Current Status	Your trade journal			Recent press coverage		
	Client trade journal			Recruitment adverts		
	Press office			Client account reports		
	On-line database			Current bid reports		
	Information services			Colleagues		
Competition	Marketing data			Your strategy databases		
	Press coverage			Your operations unit		
	Ex-employees			Regional controller		
	Consultants			Bidder's conference notes		

Table 3 Information sources checklist

- *Establish a bid and tendering system to help you reach a higher standard of bid management and quality.*

- *Constantly monitor the process that supports the bidding activity to identify where you can make improvements, reduce costs, remain in a competitive position and build your market share.*

- *In larger organisations, the bid system can support your quality systems and provide sound management information that will enhance the entire business function.*

3

THE BIDDING SPECTRUM

Each bid is different and rarely will you be bidding under the same circumstances twice. At the very least the client will change, the terms and conditions change or the scope of the project changes. So, it is no good approaching each bid in the same way; the client's value expectation will be different, as will your requirement from the resulting contract. You need to deal with each bid in the most appropriate way. This is often dictated by the type of response that the client wants and the circumstances under which you are bidding. This results in a wide spectrum of bids, tenders and proposals covering the full range of business opportunities: supply of works or products, supply of services, project management, turnkey systems, build-own-operate, investment projects, consultancy assignments and so on. In practice, you will probably be submitting several different documents to your clients during the bid cycle and each of these must be fitted to the purpose you want to achieve. These have to represent your company to your client and sell them on your offer. Do not forget that the bid or proposal is essentially a selling document designed to influence and inform. No matter how complex the technical or commercial nuances are, you have to show that the client will gain benefit from selecting your offer above that of your competitors.

Your actions during the bid cycle will give rise to a variety of documents produced for your clients. These will range from unsolicited proposals to responses to bid invitations. Of course, there should be a single purpose behind all these documents and techniques, and that is to win good business. Therefore, the ideas and precepts of successful bidding apply to the whole range of documents, as they do for other types of procurement or contract opportunities. As the manager responsible for some or all the bidding activities, you must select the methods that are most useful to you.

Perhaps the most important point to remember is to be consistent in every bid, applying the same methods to each. You need to go through the same assessment process for a small project as for a large one. What will vary will be the time you have to respond and the resources that you will need. Clearly, for a major, multi-disciplined, million pound project you will need more people and have to cope with more complex logistics than for a smaller project. But you should use the same bid management principles for both. The complexities of unravelling the politics of a multinational corporation, or government agency will need certain appraisal and commercial skills. For smaller bids you may not need these, but you may require someone who understands and empathises with the smaller business and its problems. It is how you go about discerning the differences and dealing with them that will give you the better chances of winning in each situation.

BID CLASSIFICATIONS

The spectrum of bids covers a variety of tenders, proposals and responses. These range from the very informal, for example a letter or presentation, to the very formal. You should even consider non-competitive situations, such as single action tenders or preferred supplier arrangements, as bids from a management perspective. Your responsibility is to deliver a response to the client that is in keeping with what they require and which also meets your company's objectives. It is worthwhile considering in which category your bid sits to decide the best response. Table 4 summarises some often encountered proposal types.

Usually you will be submitting a formal bound proposal, although this may not be always needed. For example, if the proposal is to an existing client, for a change or addition to current work or for a very simple project, you may consider a letter or a presentation. Of course, you have to be aware of what the client wants, so seek advice from someone close to them, such as the business or client manager. If you are still in doubt you should submit a formal proposal. As a guide, you will generally submit formal proposals for new and high-value opportunities where you expect competition, or where you are responding to a client's invitation. Moreover, always consider a formal response whenever you need to present a good image of your business to the client. The proposal will set out for the client the details of the offer you are making which will either form the contract or provide the basis upon which you will negotiate. Usually you will present the proposal in written form, typed and bound.

Category	Typical Document	Characteristics
Prequalifying Proposals	Request for Information	Informative, outline benefits, interesting
	Qualifying Statement	Express competence, ideas, emphasising personnel and approach
	Capability Statement	Benefits from previous work, success stories, show expertise
Unsolicited Proposals	Preliminary Proposal	Concise, exciting, visually appealing, gains interest and avoids negatives
	Feasibility Study	More detail, careful about commitments, exclusivity benefits, indicative pricing
	Design Study	Develops solution, firm price, often part-funded by client
Informal Tenders	Offer Letter	Price critical, short timescales, benefits from ability to respond
	Presentation Material	Visually appealing, stimulates interest and answers questions
Formal Tenders	Sealed Bid	Multi-section targeted to readers, price, technical content and people are critical
	Budgetary Proposal	Formal style but estimated price, careful with contractual commitment, not an offer
	Negotiated Tender	One or two preselected suppliers. Formal offer
	Open Tender	Open invitation published in journal, press. Formal response and selection process
	Selective Tender	Invited suppliers only. Shortlist critical
	Single-action Tender	Negotiated tender with one selected supplier

Table 4 Some examples of different proposal types

The way you structure your response is very influential; an informal response in a formal bid is inappropriate and may act against you. You could be seen as too lightweight or insignificant. Similarly, preparing a very formal response in an informal bidding situation may portray you as stuffy and inflexible. You need to understand the bid environment and a review of some different classifications will help you get a better understanding of what is required and when.

Formal bids

For major competitive procurement it is most likely that the client will adopt a formal procurement process. This is almost certain to be the case for government and European Community bids. Large multinational companies with projects of high value will also tend to take a more formal approach. If the project has a high profile, is high in value, or has sensitive issues at stake, then the likelihood of a formal procurement process is greater. Business circumstances are rarely straightforward, so stay aware of what each client is trying to achieve.

Formal bids normally take a longer time to complete and consist of several procurement phases. This usually requires the client to put in place controls and checks to manage the relationships with suppliers, to ensure fairness and to help with the assessment. The costs to you in preparing your bid will invariably be higher, if only because of the greater time you will spend on managing and preparing your proposal.

A typical formal government procurement may last from six months to several years and often it is only the largest or most favoured suppliers who can afford to commit the time and money required. This trend has resulted in many companies being unwilling to bid. The private sector cannot normally afford to spend as long on procurement as the public sector, with the result that timescales are often shorter. Even so, bid cycles that exceed a year are still common for significant projects, even in the private sector.

The reason for formal bids taking so much longer than a more simple, informal bid is usually attributable to the complexity of the procurement cycle, as illustrated in Fig. 3.1, which is indicative of the relative importance of the project. You may find formal bids beginning with a prequalification process of some kind, designed to identify likely candidates to supply. Selected suppliers may then be invited to respond within the context of the client's operational requirement and to supply further information, often on a questionnaire. The client may use this stage to refine his thinking and may incorporate ideas from various suppliers into their final specification. Your response at this stage should be directed towards showing that your company is a suitable supplier, aiming to move you onto the shortlist. You should also try to introduce your company's thinking on the project with the intention of influencing the final requirement.

If you are successful at this stage you may make it to the short list. It is not unusual for the shortlist to be common knowledge. Depending upon the specific need, shortlisted suppliers may need to build and demonstrate products, systems or services to the client and to benchmark these against a detailed specification. Successful suppliers in the demonstration stages may then enter an agreement with the client to set out the ground rules for the contract.

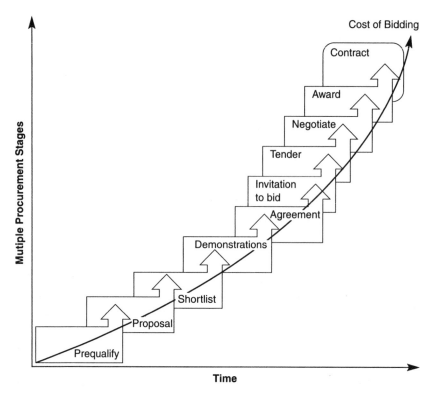

Fig. 3.1 Costs rise with progress through the stages of a complex bid

Two or more suppliers may now be invited to compete head-to-head for the contract. The client issues an invitation to tender with all their technical, commercial and operational requirements laid out. Rebids may be invited if any changes to the requirement are warranted. You will prepare your tender document containing your response and your offer to the client. The client evaluates the tenders and will probably enter negotiations with one or more supplier before awarding the contract to the winner.

You can deduce from the complex nature of the formal procurement cycle that the client needs to apply some quite structured control procedures to ensure that the process does not degenerate. They will often specify strict guidelines on communication between suppliers and themselves, the format of the bid documents and what details you should include in your proposal. They may impose a formalised assessment stating their mandatory and desirable requirements. These allow the client to adjudicate the proposal objectively. They may separate the document into component volumes to allow different parts of their organisation to assess it on a weighted scoring system. Technical, commercial and pricing assessments may be made by different people.

The client's aim is to ensure that they achieve clarity in the resulting contract for all commercial, technical and management aspects. Their procurement method will strive to enhance that clarification process. The way in which they elicit bids, receive them and adjudicate their contents is fair and controlled and can be audited and checked. The client may use a recognised procurement institute's criteria in the assessment of your bid. These will look at the general capability of the supplier, assess compliance with the technical requirement, analyse the commercial context and see what management systems are employed. There are many tools and disciplines available in these areas to help them in their evaluation of tenders.

From all this you can see that the costs involved in bidding for these types of contract can be enormous. Several large corporations have announced that the cost of bidding for UK government contracts is prohibitive and have withdrawn from these types of procurement. Obviously, the rewards for this type of contract need to justify the cost involved. High bid costs are a major factor influencing your decision to bid. You must assess continually how much you are spending and whether you can justify any further spend. Just because you have already incurred high bid costs is no reason for spending more in chasing business that you are unlikely or unwilling to win.

Informal bids

Fortunately for most suppliers, not all procurement is complex and formalised. Informal bids take place over a shorter period and with fewer stages. The client's rules are less demanding allowing greater innovation and creativity and the cost of bidding is significantly lower.

The client's timetable can often be flexible and quite short. He may reach a decision in days or weeks, not months. As the schedule can be critical you must make sure that you can respond within the period allowed. Consider everything that you will need to put in place if you are going to meet the deadline. Timing can also be a major consideration so try to discover the client's motives for a quick decision. They may need to commit the expenditure within their current fiscal year, or have a deadline of their own to meet. By structuring your bid correctly you can probably support their motives and improve your chances.

Informal procurement usually does not have as many phases. It often consists simply of a few discussions with suppliers and presentations leading to a request for a proposal by your company, followed by your bid. The client's invitation to tender may not be a formal document at all and he may well have no stated requirement. This is when your proposal effectively decides the route that your client takes. Exercise caution, though, if this happens, as your practices must be faultless. No matter how informal the client's procedures are, you should make sure that your processes are meticulous. Follow your company procedures making sure you document and confirm in writing everything relating to the bid. Clients can and do change their mind, and you could come unstuck if you have failed to take proper precautions. Changes and alterations to the requirement can happen all too frequently under these circumstances; a simple conversation can affect thinking and influence the client's opinion and consequently, their requirement. Try to ensure that there are no misunderstandings.

In these informal situations it is often the viewpoint of the client that is most important. These bids are won and lost on the relationships that your company establishes with them. So, influencing the key decision-makers is critical.

Because the timescale is shorter and procedures less complex, informal bid costs are lower and as a result, the expectation of reward in these types of purchases can be high. Bear in mind that you have been selected to tender and could therefore be in a very strong position but that the risks can be high and that you should take every step to minimise them.

Unsolicited proposals

Least formal of all types of bid is the unsolicited proposal, which is the converse of responding to the client's requirements. Here, it is up to you to take the initiative in submitting a proposal. Opportunities for unsolicited proposals often take time to develop. You need to know the client well, develop strong relationships and raise their awareness of potential improvements to their business. The key to success lies in becoming established with them so that they heed and value your opinion. This process often begins with a preliminary proposal that interests the client and reassures them that you can carry out the project. The danger is that by doing so, you may alert them to a need while not having the capabilities to deliver a full solution to it yourself, making it difficult to secure a contract. So beware of providing a proposal where your ability to respond to the identified need is limited.

Your preliminary proposal should be short, concise and exciting; use your imagination to produce a visually appealing document and make it stand out. The tenor of the document should be positive, selling benefits and facilities to the client and avoiding any negatives or qualifying conditions. Above all, you must express confidence that your company can meet the stated aims and provide client satisfaction.

If your preliminary proposal has achieved its objectives, the client may hand you an order. More likely, they will want to look at the project and your proposal in greater detail. This is the time to be very careful about any commitments you make, so seek commercial advice now. They may ask you to conduct a feasibility study, sometimes possibly paying you for the work and at, other times expecting you to do it for nothing. An in-depth feasibility study may be used as free consultancy by the client and he could employ this information to go to competitive tender. If you can, it is better to get commitment from the client for some exclusivity or a single tender action before commencing the study. Within your study you will need to propose a plan that takes your results and migrates them into a firm project and orders for your company.

Keep your costs well under control during the study. Split the work into separate stages, obtaining further commitment and authority from the client to continue as each stage is completed. When the study is completed and its finding accepted by the client you will progress into the final stages. Your aim here is to move the study forward into a firm project.

Even with a well-planned and executed unsolicited proposal, you could end up having to go through a tender stage. With any hope, you will have engineered a single action tender and all that remains is to submit prices and negotiate a contract. Generally, where an invitation comes from the client to tender, the contractual relationship is specified in the commercial section. This can often be excluded from an unsolicited proposal where no formal tender exists, so you must be sure to include all aspects of the commercial relationships in your negotiations.

Submitting an unsolicited proposal is an exciting and profitable way of gaining business. Companies who succeed at this, have worked hard to keep out the competition at every stage and will have gained a thorough understanding of the client organisation and their business. It can be difficult though and there is no guarantee that at the end of the feasibility study the client will go ahead with the project. You must be sure of their commitment to the venture.

Budgetary proposals

You may have to submit a qualified offer, estimate or quotation, which although you should still manage as if it was a bid, requires some special treatment to prevent the client from considering it as such. Your intention behind a budgetary proposal is to give the client all the information they need but without committing to supply them at the price you have given. In other words, you have reservations or uncertainties that you have been unable to resolve before submitting the proposal, but still wish to be given consideration.

Whether this is good or bad can only be judged on individual merit. However, the important commercial aspect is that it is not considered contractually binding. You need to include certain clauses to make this clear. Typically, you should include statements to the effect that the prices are for estimating a budget. Avoid giving project delivery dates, relying instead on lead times from receipt of an order. You may wish to exclude a comprehensive response to the client's terms and conditions, substituting instead your own standard terms and conditions. Always say that the proposal does not constitute a formal offer.

CONTEXTUAL CATEGORISATIONS

Besides categorising bids by timescale, procurement complexity and bid costs, you can view them from a contextual standpoint in either commercial or technical terms. Sorting bids by context allows you to refine your bid method further. For example, the opportunity for which you are bidding could be an investment project, a consultancy assignment, the supply of products or services, the design of a system, the digging of a tunnel, or any other task within your business remit. You will need to vary your approach to these bids to reflect the technical or strategic complexities inherent within it, as some of the following examples show.

Technological complexity

Your approach to the supply of a standard portfolio product will differ from the design and construction of a customised item. In general, the more complex the technological requirement the higher is the cost of bidding. Procurement timescale and complexity also increase. So the bid for simple, standard technology or portfolio products, is likely to be quicker, less complex and less costly than the bid for designing a high technology system as is illustrated in Fig. 3.2.

Standard technology items tend to have a limited range of facilities and client benefits; they suit a specific purpose. Take for example, a requirement for a consumable product such as stationery. This is relatively low-tech, purchased in bulk, with multiple repeat orders. It is also a highly competitive market. The items are tangible and can be examined and tested, so the buying decision process is unlikely to be lengthy; detailed benchmarking is usually not necessary and neither is a complex contract. Your bid will most likely focus on price and value for money, with quality, availability and product range being essential. In preparing your response, you will draw from earlier sales, standard product literature, standard contract conditions and previous bids. So standard technology tends towards a standardised approach to bidding. This accelerates the process, quickening the turnaround between bid and order, and limiting the costs to both the buyer and bidder. That is not to say that you should exclude any other win factors when making your bid, you should still seek a competitive edge, through innovation and creativity.

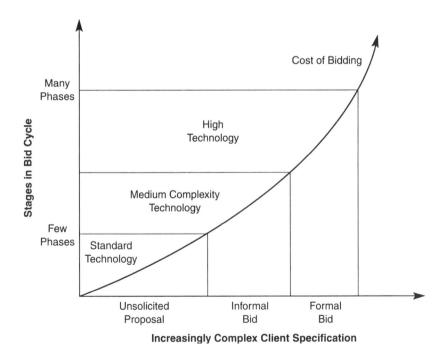

Fig. 3.2 Relationship between bid and cost

More complex technology normally needs a more complex buying process. The range of choices is usually larger, as are the facilities and benefits associated with the product or service. Take a design project for instance, say for an office or house interior. This often requires complex technology in the products incorporated within the design, an understanding of ergonomics, mechanics and architectural engineering, as well as creative flair. The product is intangible until it is completed and cannot be readily examined until then. So, the buyer has to seek reassurance during the bidding process that he will get what he expects at the end. The bidding process is therefore more involved, with many more stages. Typically, the buyer prepares a brief for several consultants. Once the brief has been agreed, they will ask for a conceptual design. The resulting designs are reviewed and the design concept agreed. Detailed drawings may be drawn up, demonstrations sought and other benchmarks of design elements gone through before the client is ready to invite tenders. They may short-list two or more suppliers, each to produce pilot implementations, before making the final selection. You can see that this involves the bidder in much more effort and cost.

Value criteria

Another way of categorising types of bid, is to consider the value of the end contract. A conjectural analysis would suggest that higher value contracts require more difficult decisions, resulting in more complex bids and therefore higher bid costs. This is borne out by experience, up to a point. In absolute terms, higher value projects do have higher bid costs, but expressed as a percentage of the total project value, bid costs tend to reduce as value increases. The reason for this becomes clear once you consider the inherent overheads in people and equipment which have to be funded from the bid costs. Using typical figures, the diagram in Fig. 3.3 shows how the percentile bid costs reduce as project values rise.

This is all very well, but high value projects still need more funding, even if the rewards are greater. This is one reason why often only the very largest corporations can afford to bid for very large contracts.

Large companies will usually respond to high value bids by dedicating resources to the opportunity. This often means putting a large bid team in place, giving it high-level management exposure and providing it with a substantial bid budget. In these situations, it is more necessary than ever to be sure that you can win and to put into effect the bid management and control processes described later. The cost of failure can be very high

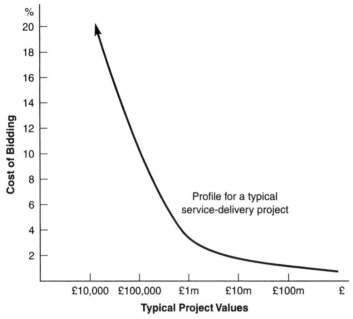

Fig. 3.3 Percentile bid costs reduce as contract value rises

indeed. Smaller companies cannot always sustain dedicated resources and often cannot afford the funds needed to bid on their own so their response to larger value bids tends to be to seek partnership arrangements. This may be by forming a consortium to bid with other smaller companies with each bringing their own expertise or it may be by becoming a subcontractor to a larger company acting as prime contractor.

Strategic bids

Perhaps one other way to classify bids is in terms of their tactical or strategic objectives. In most bids profitability is paramount, but there will be some which have a strategic purpose meaning that the value of the opportunity is not the overriding consideration. A bid with a strategic objective does not mean that you should ignore the profit element in your offer, but it does mean you must be more diligent in the attention you give to the selection of opportunities and in getting the bid right. The chances are that your strategic objective will be intended to gain you future higher rewards and getting the offer wrong could adversely affect your long-term plans.

In many ways your approach to a strategic bid will be the same as for any other, but more stringent. You may find it necessary to put more effort into the bid and spend more; if winning is truly strategic to the future of your business, you do not want to let it slip because of skimping. You will have motives outside the direct context of the bid which have to be built into your bid strategy and this alone causes strategic bids to be more complex and difficult to manage.

SUMMARY

Knowing the type of bid you are dealing with will help you fashion the most appropriate response.

- *More formal bids, such as those in the public sector, take more time, have complex procurement processes and incur higher costs, so ensure that you are able to see it through to completion before starting.*

- *Informal bids and unsolicited proposals occur more frequently in private industry and tend to be quicker and are often simpler to control; they are also usually less costly than public sector bids. Success here depends upon you being able to provide a complete response rapidly.*

- *The technical context of the bid also impinges upon how much you have to do to win. Bidding to provide highly complex or bespoke technology usually involves greater cost whilst bidding to provide standard technology is less costly but generally encourages greater competition.*

- *The financial value of the opportunity is also relevant to the bid. Higher value contracts tend to require more difficult decisions to be made and also incur higher costs. Often, only very large corporations or consortia can afford to take the risk.*

- *Look careful at the strategic implications of each bid. Although profit is usually a prerequisite, you may have other motives which increase the degree of difficulty inherent in managing it.*

4

CONTRACTS

An understanding of contract law is a necessary part of the bid manager's function and is valuable in deciding the appropriate strategy. It is important that you should have a grasp of the legal implications when submitting your bid and there are many good books available on the subject that will give you the necessary insight. In England, the commercial position of companies doing business together is governed by private law. However, in the global market, it will not always be possible or advisable for English law to apply so you should make sure you are familiar with applicable law in the countries into which you are bidding.

When bidding, as with all contractual matters, you should exercise caution and restraint. It is easy to slip up by neglecting or overlooking some contractual detail so be wary of the commitments you make. For example, oral statements made to the client can also constitute an offer and a contract could have been established. For practical purposes, you should always make the contract in writing, it saves much time and argument later. Confirm any oral agreements or amendments in a letter and incorporate them into the contract. If in doubt, always consult the experts in your company on any contractual matter.

The contract for which you are bidding can take many forms, dictated often by what the client is trying to achieve. However, the contract formalises an agreement between you and the client and as such it should also represent your objectives. Nevertheless, it is the buyer who usually has the upper hand in dictating the style of the contract and you clearly need to position your bid to take advantage of what they are trying to get out of it.

This section briefly touches on some more pertinent aspects of contract law as it affects the bidder. Different contract types and their uses are explored to give you further insight into your client objectives. Using the contract effectively is extremely valuable in bidding. If it is done well the contract can be an asset, but done badly it is a liability.

ENGLISH CONTRACT LAW

Although some basics of English contract law are discussed here, you may be required to contract under the legislation of another country. Make sure that you know where the differences lie and seek appropriate professional advice. Although there may be broad compliance between the law of two countries, it is the subtleties that often cause the problems.

Reaching agreement with the client

To reach a legally enforceable agreement is quite simple. You put an offer to a client and they say yes or no. For the agreement to be valid and enforceable, there are some important elements to consider. These are the offer and the acceptance, the intention of you and your client to enter a commercial relationship and the consideration or payment. Consideration usually means a price, but it could include any benefit that is economic in character, something of worth or value to the client. Furthermore, to become a contract, the agreement must be for something that is both possible and legal. You cannot have an enforceable contract to do something that cannot be done or that commits an illegal act.

Finally, the people creating the agreement must have the capacity to contract. This can also be a cause of some perplexity. Because of the commitments you give to perform a service or supply goods and the liabilities associated with failure, your company may only allow nominated individuals to negotiate and sign contracts. This is designed to safeguard your business from entering into undesirable contracts. There can be problems when tendering even when these safeguards are in place. Any formal tender response or a letter on headed notepaper referring to the invitation number, or other official communication, even though not from an authorised person, can effectively commit the business. This is why you should instigate a tendering procedure, which will formalise the bidding process from the contractual position. Within this process will be the requisite levels of authorisation that you will need for your bids.

Remember that the contract relies upon agreement between you and the client and encapsulates your rights under the arrangement. The client has a right to expect you to supply what you promise and if you act in good faith, you have a right to expect compensation or payment for what you supply. Accordingly, it is important to gain concurrence from your business at the right level. It may be difficult to extricate the company from an agreement even if the persons signing were not authorised by the business.

Rejecting your bid

Your bid comprises an offer providing it meets the criteria stated above and does not modify the terms and conditions stated in the client's invitation. A modification of your offer or counter-offer suggested by the client, is in effect a rejection of it. This counter-offer sets up a fresh offer to bring about a commercial relationship. If the customer rejects your offer, the offer no longer exists.

This works both ways. If you respond to a client invitation with other than a fully compliant bid, you are rejecting their invitation and setting up a counter-offer to buy. The client is under no obligation to consider such an offer. This could have serious implications if, for example, you are submitting a formal bid for a major contract where full compliance and lowest prices are the main criteria. You could be ruling yourself out by a technicality. Similarly, if the client comes back to you asking you to modify the terms of your bid, this is a rejection and you are under no obligation to accept such changes. Of course, you are unlikely then to get the contract. It is at this stage that pragmatism usually takes over with negotiation over the final details and terms of the contract being agreed after the bids are submitted.

Withdrawing your bid

Under English law you can withdraw a tender any time until it is accepted. Although allowed, in practice this is rare unless you have clearly made a mistake in your offer that would jeopardise the project viability. Usually, you should be prepared to live by what you have offered. Withdrawing a tender is unlikely to endear you to the client and they may well have no further dealings with you.

Bid bonds

To prevent offers being withdrawn clients may insist on you lodging a bid bond. This is usually a sum relating to a percentage of the total contract value as tendered in your offer. This attempts to guarantee that suppliers will accept a contract based on their offer within its validity period.

Budgetary quotations

Take care when submitting proposals that you do not wish to have considered as offers; these include budgetary quotes, estimates and indicative prices. Unless you make sure that your proposal says that this is not an offer you may find yourselves with a contract in place, possibly on unfavourable terms to you.

COMMERCIAL TERMS, CONDITIONS AND WARRANTIES

There are some areas that tend to crop up frequently in bidding which cause difficulty, either because they are not fully understood, or because they attempt to place onerous responsibilities on the bidder. Dealing with these terms and conditions is part of the bid management function, but you need to respond so that you do not jeopardise the acceptability of your offer. Start by grasping what it is that the client is trying to achieve in placing particularly difficult conditions upon you. There are several possibilities: they could be uncertain about what they want and are seeking to provide some additional protection; they could have had a bad experience with a previous tender and are imposing conditions that they believe will prevent it happening again, they could be forced to go back-to-back on conditions imposed upon them by a third party such as the funding agency, they may be using model contracts which are inappropriate for the type of procurement they are undertaking, or they may be testing the supplier's willingness to acquiesce. There are probably many more reasons, which you will have to discover in your bid.

Begin by getting a practical, commercial definition of the terms. The terms of the contract make up the contract, as they specify the detail of your agreement and are either expressed or implied. Expressed terms are those you and your client agree between you, while implied terms are not stated. Implied terms may relate to other legislation, such as the Sale of Goods or Misrepresentation Acts, or Product Liability legislation, or they could be terms upon which some legal interpretation could be made through the courts. Implied terms cause problems simply because they are not written into the contract and because your client has a legal right to expect you to comply with them; you must therefore know about any legislation that may be relevant.

The terms then divide into conditions and warranties. The distinction between these is that failing to meet a condition of the contract will normally give a right of termination. Failing to meet a warranty will normally give rise to the payment of damages only, not termination. For example, in a simple supply contract the supply of the goods will be a condition, while the monthly production of quality assurance reports would be a warranty. So, the effect between failure of a condition and a warranty can be vastly different; one can revoke the contract, the other causes a penalty to be paid. Decide your response to the terms by assessing both the risk and the consequences of any failure. Some specific terms that can be disconcerting in bids are listed below:

Limited liability

A recent ruling by the High Court under the Unfair Contract Terms Act 1977 has sent suppliers hurrying to check out their contracts for limited liability. It has previously been common to set a limit on the amount for which a supplier will be liable in the event that the products or services fail to meet the terms of the supply. This ruling concerned faulty software and deemed that the limit of liability stated in the contract was unreasonable and too low. This could mean that any such clause inserted in your contract may not be enforceable. Clearly, you should review any limitation of liability in the light of this judgement as you could become exposed to a high greater risk than you originally envisaged.

Liquidated damages

Another way of limiting liability is through liquidated damages. In this, the contract may specify a fixed sum or percentage of the value to be forfeited by the supplier if the supply of goods or services is not completed on time or is inadequate in some way. The sum is agreed in advance and represents a reasonable amount. The client gains the assurance of eliminating supply delays or contract non-performance from the payment of compensation. When considering liquidated damages bear in mind that these can be either damages or costs. Damages could be the profits your client expects from the resale of goods that you were contracted to supply. Costs could be those arising from relying upon the contract, such as the need to buy alternate goods at a higher price to meet other contractual commitments. Limitation of damages depends upon whether the losses could have been foreseen. You are deemed liable if you could have foreseen the event that caused non-performance or delay in the contract.

Consequential loss

Your client may wish to seek restitution for losses arising out of non-performance. Here the liability for losses incurred due to the supplier's failure is not limited. Failure of, say, a gas turbine or pipeline system could result in millions of pounds of consequential loss making this a particularly onerous condition and one that you need to consider very carefully.

Penalties

This is a sum inserted in a contract designed to force the supplier to fulfil the contract. The amount to be paid may increase with time. Penalty clauses are difficult, if not impossible, to enforce in law.

Product liability

Under product liability legislation the victim of a defective product need no longer establish negligence by the supplier. This legislation does not apply to businesses supplying other businesses or to individuals who get your product through their company. However, it will apply if your product is either resold directly or used as a component in a product which is then retailed to a private individual. Any clause related to government legislation has to be thoroughly researched. It is better to have an expert review the contract from this perspective than rely upon inadequate knowledge.

Force majeure

A supplier may wish to exclude liability for delays they consider to be beyond their control and that they cannot insure against. These usually include the areas of pure risk in your risk assessment and other factors that the buyer believes should be under the control of the supplier and vice versa. Make sure that this term is specific; it is better to resolve these issues early than wait until an event occurs which is disputed by both parties.

Timescales

Your client may impose a tough completion date for any number of reasons. Draft your contractual response so that it gives sufficient detail to convince them that you can meet it. Of course, you must then devise ways to carry it out within your strategy so that you can be confident in your statements. Schedules are often a point for negotiation once agreement has been reached in principal. Be careful, however, to ensure that any penalties or bonds associated with timescales take into account only those areas where you have direct control. You do not want to be liable for delays caused by other persons, for whom you are not responsible.

Local content

Some overseas bids often require local contribution. You will need a strategy that goes further than just meeting the minimum requirement. You will need to consider joint ventures, acquisitions, local agents and subcontracts. These are requirements that take time to put in place and so must be considered early in your strategy. Local content is very important for international aid-funded bids and you must be sure to address it fully in your bid strategy. This is covered in more detail later.

Training

Training and the transfer of technology are common potential problem areas. Your strategy must consider how you will undertake training needs and development. In overseas bids the training requirement can often be a major component and influencing factor, particularly if training takes place in the UK. You may need to set up training in your client's location and in their language. Although at first sight the training and technology transfer terms may appear uncomplicated and easy to comply with, make sure that you look into all the implications. Foreign language training, work permits, visas, health and medical insurances, documentation production and premises, can cause problems if your strategy has not been well thought through.

Intellectual property rights

The ownership of intellectual property rights can be a source of conflict, so make sure you develop your commercial strategy so that you are able to consider your position on ownership and the value that you assign to that ownership. The intangible nature of intellectual property makes it a difficult area to deal with. You must first reach a definition, before deciding how to treat it. Intellectual property is primarily the ownership of ideas, inventions or innovations. The value in these can be high, as in software development with multiple licenses or the introduction of new technology. To realise the value of your intellectual property you can sell the product derived from it direct to your client while retaining your rights or you can transfer the rights themselves for your client to use as they wish or you can license your client to use the intellectual property while you retain ownership. The law pertaining to this area in the UK is principally the Copyright, Designs and Patents Act 1988. Long and bitter (and expensive) legal battles have been fought over intellectual property. It is worth the effort to establish the ground-rules with your client from the outset. Use professional legal advisors who specialise in this area.

Performance bonds

The client may want to retain a percentage of the contract value as leverage on you to reach an acceptable level of performance. This is usually tied to certain mileposts within the project timetable, at each phase of a construction project for example. In a supply contract the performance will usually relate to delivery schedules, suitability of the goods or services supplied, conformance with quality standards or some other transient performance measurement. In a service contract, it is possible that some ongoing service performance may be asked for over a specified period. This could be response times, availability targets or any other continuing factor. The buyer will want to retain as much as possible so as to have a stronger hand in enforcing high performance. You will want as much of your payment as early as possible to keep your cash flow positive. Usually, some compromise position is reached. Be careful of not allowing too high a bond for too long. Of course, if you believe that there is some doubt over your performance it is better to deal with the root cause of the matter, than rely upon bonds to overcome the difficulties.

EUROPEAN CONTRACT LAW ON BIDS

The introduction of the single European market abolished internal borders between member states and harmonised many trading practices. Customs controls disappeared, easing the movement of goods while broader recognition of professional status is helping in the supply of services. Although there is now a single market, the legislation under which individual states operate for contracts is still subject to variation. The only sure way to reach an agreement under foreign legislation is to seek professional advice from a local lawyer or contracts specialist.

Besides the local law under which the contract is deemed to exist, you will also have to comply with European Community directives, where these apply. You will therefore need to be fully conversant with the appropriate European legislation. These fall into several broad areas. Implemented and adopted measures will probably feature in the forefront of your analysis. Implemented measures are those that have already been sanctioned and are now in force and adopted measures are those that have been agreed by the European Parliament Council of Ministers and have been given dates when they are to come into effect. You must be cognisant of both these categories of measures and how they will affect your bid.

There are also two other categories of measures, which although not yet in force may affect the longer-term viability or achievement of your business project. These are proposed measures, which are detailed propositions still under discussion in the European Parliament and projected measures, which have yet to reach the detailed proposal stages.

The subjects covered under European legislation are extensive, particularly covering the removal of barriers to trading within the European Union. Although physical barriers to trading have been removed, you will need to know about the control of certain goods and people. Directives covering the removal of technical barriers include technical harmonisation programmes and the free movement of goods. If you are bidding for public works you must be aware of the public procurement directives in the traditional sectors and in the utilities areas. If you plan to provide services in Europe, using your people in the client's country or a local agent, you will have to comply with the freedom of movement directives. These include agency law, recognition of professional qualifications and social securities measures. Opening up the market for services has resulted in directives covering financial services, information technology, transport, post and telecommunications. To help businesses work together, there have been agreements reached on company law, intellectual property rights and taxation. And, when you are deciding upon appropriate payment methods for your bid, bear in mind that the areas of capital transfer, excise duties and the removal of other fiscal barriers have also been variously addressed.

TYPES OF CONTRACTS

Your client is likely to supply contract terms and conditions within their invitation to tender. Buyers are becoming more aware of poorly managed projects, inadequate specifications and are mindful of how much money can be lost as a result. The trend is towards more professional purchasing and greater attention to the contractual detail, with increases in the range and variety of contracts that you will encounter. As with all aspects of bidding, you should have a very good understanding of the basis upon which the client wishes to contract well before the bid and any subsequent negotiations.

The market sector in which you operate will also influence your approach to the contract. Construction and engineering have well-established methods for handling large and complex contracts. Information technology, systems integration and facilities management are relatively young market sectors that have yet to lay down solid guidelines.

Standard contracts

Standard contracts are generally acceptable for simple supply, but different clients have different needs that cannot be met under a catch-all contract. Be wary of signing a standard contract if the project is complex.

Quite often, there are standard contracts printed on the back of purchase orders, invoices or sales orders. They are easy to use where a regular relationship exists between you and your client but you should not use them for bids. As standard conditions, they are designed to eliminate the need to negotiate for tenders and contracts and are only appropriate for simple supply contracts. They are unlikely to reflect the practicalities of your bid situation. Another common problem is the well-known battle of the forms where the buyer and seller exchange purchase order, sales invoices, receipts, each trying to get their contract terms accepted. Usually the last contract terms exchanged will be considered the ones that will prevail. Be very careful not to enter such a conflict with your client by avoiding standard contracts. It is always better for you to obtain full agreement by negotiation in the bid context.

Model contracts

Model contracts are those produced by an independent third party available to the two contracting parties. They seek to be impartial and cover the needs of both the client and the supplier. As a result they are better than standard contracts but tend to try to be all things to all people. They are very thorough and very complex and cover every eventuality. Use a model contract if you and your client are willing to accept it without negotiation or change. In most bids you should not take model contracts on their face value. They will frequently require a degree of amendment or modification to suit both your needs and those of your client. Consequently, this can lead to extended negotiations and contract amendments. It may be better to negotiate a contract from the outset. Typical model contracts are those published by the professional institutions.

You will also find model contracts used for aid-funded bids such as the Model Contract for Community Activities in the Fields of

Research and Technology, used for European Community Framework Programme contracts.

Negotiated contracts

More often than not, you will negotiate a contract with the client. Each of these will be different, varying with the client and their needs and your supply. You will encounter some degree of categorisation, usually on price. In negotiating the contract it is worthwhile considering the basic benefits and drawbacks of each type.

Firm price

A firm price contract is one where the price tendered is immutable and will apply irrespectively of time or resources required. The risk to the client is low; they pay the agreed price and no more. Your risk is higher as you must fund any difficulties you encounter in meeting the contract.

Fixed price

An alternative to this is a fixed price contract that allows for a variation in price fixed to a cost or other index. This would usually include a variation of price clause, defining the variable factor and when it applies. The variable element usually only applies to part of the contract price. This will allow you to reduce the risk on, say, inflation or exchange rate by linking to the appropriate indices.

Fixed quantity

In a fixed quantity contract you deliver the materials over a specified period at set dates. Usually the price will be fixed over the period as well. This is often used for supply of raw materials where the quantities are already known. There may be a variation of price clause included but usually such contracts are inflexible.

Time and materials

You may negotiate a Time and Materials Contract. These are common in consultancy projects or software development contracts where you provide an estimate of the time required to complete the total project and you charge at a daily or weekly rate. The client's risk is higher. They run the risk of going over the budget or suffering an incomplete project. You are on safer ground as your costs are met plus an element for profit.

This is an example of a cost-plus contract, where your costs are paid plus a profit margin. Sometimes these can be more explicitly defined and the client will pay your costs plus an agreed profit margin. Consider the basis of the profit margin. Where it is a percentage of costs, your profit will increase as your costs increase. Where it is a predefined sum, your profit percentage decreases as your costs increase. You may look to this type of contract where the risks to you are high. It clearly requires you to be up-front and open with your client.

Incentive contracts

Incentive contracts have become fashionable of late. Several major incentive contracts based upon outsourcing of services have been awarded by some of the largest companies in the UK. Typically, these lay somewhere between cost plus and fixed price contracts in terms of risk to you and the client and motivation to achieve the aims of the agreement. They can be considered another variation of cost-plus contracts. Typically an incentive contract is based upon costs. You agree a cost budget and share any savings or losses against this at some predetermined ratio. The financial risk to you is reduced if you feel that the chances of not meeting the target are high. You also have an incentive to come in under budget so that you take a share of the savings. Similarly, your client gains reassurance that you will try your hardest to achieve the budget figure thereby improving your profit margin. Both you and your client then see the benefits when you hit your target.

Incentive contracts can become quite complex. Some will require you to open your accounts to the clients showing your precise cost breakdown. This may require detailed analyses and careful controls and monitoring. This can be difficult and time consuming and make some suppliers uncomfortable. Generally, the benefits are higher and risk is reduced or ameliorated.

Call-off contracts

Call-off contracts are those in which you agree the price and terms of the supply, but delivery and payment are deferred until some time later. When the client requires the goods or services, it places an order under the call-off contract and receives delivery and makes payment under the specified terms. Quantities are rarely fixed, but they often specify upper and lower limits based upon estimates agreed during negotiations. These

are common for commodity items where precise requirements are difficult to specify and less common for more complex systems and projects.
Your client has the advantage of knowing in advance what their costs
will be without having to commit to spending that amount until later.
The supplier is vulnerable because the client is not obliged to call-off or
order any of the goods. This type of contract requires sound relationships and trust between the parties.

Catalogue contracts

Another development in bidding originating in the public sector and now
spreading to the private industry, is the use of catalogue contracts. In
these, the client is selecting a single supplier to provide a portfolio of
products or services. This means that the client does not have to invite
open tenders for each procurement. Ordering under the catalogue contract itself is simplified. Users within the client organisation use a price
list to select the products they need and place the order with the selected
supplier. Sometimes termed blanket contracts, these are generally only
employed by large organisations, government departments and multinational corporate giants, where the volume of supply is high. They are
usually for the supply of commodity, packaged items rather than complex
systems and the client can negotiate massive discounts.

From the client's point of view they have eased their procurement
burden and therefore lowered their costs and they have achieved significant equipment savings. One drawback is that such contracts do not
provide expertise or guidance. Users may not be able to select solutions to
meet their precise needs from within the catalogue. For a successful bidder
they offer a guaranteed volume of business over the fixed duration of the
contract. Once established they are easy to administer and can result in a
long-standing relationship between client and supplier.

Infrastructure contracts

When projects become more than just simple equipment supply, clients
are generally seeking longer-term relationships with their suppliers.
Typically a government department will develop a framework for its
operational strategy and then invite bids for the supply of equipment,
services, operational support and maintenance to put into effect that
strategy. There have been several such contracts awarded in recent years,
all of them being of very high value. Infrastructure contracts will often
incorporate catalogue and call-off elements.

When maintenance is at issue, the downward trend in certain equipment prices can create difficulties in recouping your costs because third party maintenance contracts have traditionally been based upon a percentage of the value of the equipment being maintained. In some areas, particularly computing, and with other high-technological equipment, prices have fallen dramatically in real terms as production technology advances and products become more universally available. With values decreasing and quality improving third party maintainers will find it difficult to make the returns that they would have expected in previous years. If you are bidding for a contract that involves third party maintenance you may well have to review the basis upon which you provide the service.

Outsourcing contracts

Because of the recession, many large companies focusing on cost control, have resorted to the outsourcing of some or all of their peripheral activities. This leaves them free to concentrate on their core activities. In an outsourcing contract, responsibilities for non-core activities are contracted to a third party. It is usual for a service level agreement to be effected which specifies the precise nature of the outsourced service and how it will be accomplished. Many companies, for example, have taken services such as travel, catering, reprographic services and cleaning, for which they used to employ people and contracted these out to other companies, thereby making savings in staff costs.

CONTRACT NEGOTIATIONS

Although activities after submission of the bid are covered in a later chapter, it is worth mentioning one or two aspects of contract negotiation now. You can enter contract negotiations at any stage of the bid, before bids are submitted, after they have gone in but before the award, and after the contract has been awarded but before starting work.

Successful bidders tend to negotiate and agree the basis of the contract before tendering. This means that there are no surprises for you or your client when the invitation is issued and tenders submitted.

In most formal bids the invitation to tender will contain terms and conditions that will form the contract. You need to know whether you have bid on these terms in the past and if they are acceptable. As part of the risk assessment the bid manager will have assessed the legal and commercial risk. Any major areas of concern and exposure should be listed for discussion during negotiation. Legal department resources are always in demand so it may help if you can carry out the basic assessment before referring the bid for specialist advice. Always alert legal advisors as soon as the invitation is received so that the full commercial response can be prepared in good time and a negotiating stance decided.

Pre-bid negotiations

The important point to note from a legal position, is that pre-bid negotiations rarely result in a contractual agreement. These discussions tend to focus on setting the scene, laying out the ground-rules and smoothing the way for future negotiations. This is where many decisions are made on the terms and conditions to be included in the contract. The client will want to emphasise what they see as the most important areas in the bid; these could be delivery schedules, pricing or quality of services for example. They will also set out for the supplier the basis upon which they will make their decision. Suppliers will be trying to justify their own likely response in these areas and to get their conditions accepted. There is much to be gained from this phase of contract negotiation. Both sides can learn a great deal about the other. You should take any information you get and apply it early so that you can respond quickly when the bid invitation arrives. For example, if you find out that the client is set on using a model contract, you can prepare your own response to it immediately.

Post-tender negotiations

This is probably the most critical time for contractual negotiations. You will be aiming to fine-tune your offer, after you have submitted it, to reach agreement with the client. There will often be terms in your bid that either you or the client is unhappy about, and this is the stage when these are resolved. Of course, if you have submitted a non-compliant bid, there is a chance that you will not be invited to negotiate at all so it must be clear in your bid strategy what approach you are planning to take. Some clients and opportunities preclude any post-tender negotiation and while this is still practised in public sector bidding, it is becoming less common in private industry.

Post-contract negotiations

An area of contract negotiation which is often neglected occurs after the contract has been signed or an order placed. Quite often these post-contractual negotiations are carried out by the project manager, who is responsible for carrying out the assignment. These negotiations would typically cover such areas as delivery, quantities, quality assurance testing, benchmarking and service support; rarely does it cover the actual price content of the contract. From the bid manager's perspective, these negotiations represent ways to enhance the value of the original contract, either by negotiating changes to the actual supply or by identifying additional work that the client wants accomplished.

SUMMARY

The outcome of your bid is a contract which formalises the agreement between you and the client and specifies what each of you will do.

- *Submitting a bid normally contractually commits you to delivering products or services contained within your proposal. It is important to understand the basis of contract law and use the contract to your advantage to win the business.*

- *Contractual terms and conditions can be burdensome and a barrier to winning so try to eliminate potential problem areas by understanding what your client really wants to achieve with the contract.*

- *Foreign and European Community legislation may place different requirements on you than those you would normally encounter in your domestic market. Make sure you understand their implications and seek advice from specialists if necessary.*

- *Standard and model contracts are often too rigid and inflexible to be of use in complex bids. It is usually better to negotiate a mutually beneficial contract that meets the specific needs of the bid.*

- *Incentive contracts are becoming more popular, often with a risk and reward component linked to performance. These may require open-book accounting, so make sure your company is comfortable with this approach.*

- *The supplier can be vulnerable in a call-off contract as there is little or no commitment from the client to buy anything. Catalogue contracts on the other hand, guarantee a volume of business and are easy to administer.*

- *Infrastructure and outsourcing contracts often incorporate components of both call-off and catalogue contracts. These types of contract are usually driven by the need of the client to contain and reduce their costs. As a result they are often high-risk to the supplier.*

5

PUBLIC SECTOR BIDDING

Procurement by the public sector accounts for an estimated 15 per cent of the gross domestic product in the UK. When you consider spending by national government departments and agencies and local authorities in the rest of Europe this amounts to nearly £500 billion. It is difficult to estimate the amounts spent worldwide but it is significant. Not surprisingly, bidding for these opportunities is vital to many businesses.

The public sector market has traditionally been the realm of the larger company able to afford the high costs, long time-scales and complex procurement processes involved. Various government departments and successive administrations have tried to address the problems associated with public sector buying, with some success.

What distinguishes private and public sector bids, are the formalised processes involved, the heightened political profile and the cultural difficulties encountered with government departments. Success in public procurement opportunities relies very much upon knowing and manipulating the rules and regulations that govern the process. Bids are often rejected for failing to comply fully. Once the hurdle of the bidding regulations has been crossed, bidders fail because their knowledge of the local, regional and national political situations is inadequate. The final challenge is in recognising and overcoming the cultural barriers. Global public procurement is a vast and complex topic and cannot be fully addressed here. However, some of the more frequently encountered situations are analysed with some recommendations on how best they should be approached. Much of this holds true for all bids and some is relevant only to specific lending agencies.

This chapter looks in detail at public sector bids in the UK, the European Union and globally, through world aid-funded organisations. These three areas represent probably the most common areas for bidding. In the UK and increasingly in Europe, there are also bids for the privatised public utilities and former state enterprises which, although not public sector, still share many of their characteristics.

BIDDING IN THE UK PUBLIC SECTOR

The public sector in the UK is not restricted to central and local government departments. It also includes a wide range of other authorities and agencies, such as the police forces, education authorities, emergency services, housing associations and many more. Through the application of the European directive on utilities, many former state-owned enterprises are also dealt with under the public sector banner. These are companies that have special or exclusive rights and include the water, electricity and power companies, British Rail, British Telecom, British Petroleum and British Gas. The types of contracts for which these organisations invite bids are equally diverse and numerous and, what is more, the single European market has opened up these opportunities to competition from elsewhere in Europe.

There are some central planks to the UK government strategy on public procurement that separate it from public buying in the rest of Europe. In many ways the UK leads the way in opening up this sector to private companies, a model that may be followed elsewhere. It is worth looking at some current initiatives, which could set future patterns for bidding outside the UK.

Government initiatives

In June 1994, the UK Government published its white paper 'Competitiveness: Helping Business to Win', in which it analysed the economic performance of the UK compared to its main rivals. Its purpose was to highlight areas where improvements are needed and to set out plans to make those improvements, spotlighting the effectiveness of businesses, including those in the public sector services. In this document the government sets out its policies for improving the competitiveness of UK businesses in the world economic markets. It considers Europe and the General Agreement on Tariffs and Trade (GATT) nations and sets its sights on evenhanded enforcement procedures in a fair and open market. In the public domain specifically, it sets out to improve the management of companies who win contracts in the public sector and make it easier for both large and small companies to bid for these contracts. Included within the white paper is the introduction of standards and best practices in procurement. By 1996, key posts in central government procurement should hold professional qualifications or have completed a rigorous training programme. The effect of this initiative has been difficult to discern. Clearly some of the more practical measures will begin to have an impact quickly while the consequences of others may take longer to emerge.

Other government campaigns include the Private Sector Initiative (PSI), in which all work is offered to tender to private sector suppliers. Work under this initiative includes UK government information technology purchases, and offers little risk to the departments concerned. In-house bids are not allowed under this scheme. Private suppliers agree to fund all the development costs associated with the production and delivery of the systems required. Once developed, these systems are then benchmarked against departmental acceptance criteria and if they pass, the supplier's costs are met in full. The department therefore reduces the risk in developing its own systems or in paying for software that does not come up to scratch. The benefit to the supplier is that, while the resulting system continues to meet the benchmark, they will get full payment for development and associated costs. In addition, they have a guaranteed client and reference site and a system that they can sell on elsewhere. The only losers in such an arrangement are likely to be the in-house personnel as their jobs could be at risk.

Compulsory competitive tendering

It is nearly six years since the government introduced compulsory competitive tendering in the UK. Many aspects of local government, such as refuse collection and catering, have been reviewed under this scheme and it will be applied to a much wider field of activity over the coming years. Future compulsory competitive tendering in local authorities will extend over the next two to three years to include housing, library services, legal, financial and personnel services, and information technology. As central government plans for the reorganisation of the local councils and as the introduction of more unitary councils takes effect, more and more local services will be targeted for provision by the private sector. Local councils are resistant to changes and will fight to retain their roles. They argue that the issues have not been fully addressed and not enough time given to the preparation of tendering schemes, which will result in increasing overheads and soaring costs. Whatever the motivation behind compulsory competitive tendering it is unlikely to disappear. The issues are complex and are still not fully resolved. Whether you are bidding in-house or privately for compulsory competitive tendering projects you need to proceed cautiously, there is still a long way to go and much can change.

Market testing

Market testing was introduced to allow services provided by government departments to be opened to the competitive marketplace. In this, activities carried out by internal government departments are subjected to fair and open competition aimed at achieving the best value for money for the customer and taxpayer. At the start of 1994 the government offered over £1 billion worth of civil service operations for market testing against open competition.

The distinction between market testing and privatisation has become blurred since its introduction. Implicit in the privatisation of nationalised industries or government services is that no internal bids are permitted, with the service being contracted out to the private sector. Market testing on the other hand allowed the incumbent department to bid in direct competition with the open market. However, recent market testing initiatives, such as the contracting out of information technology services within the Inland Revenue did not allow any internal bids. Before market testing starts, the department undertakes a Prior Options Review which can recommend that the department bypasses market testing completely. The options being full privatisation, in which case no internal bids are allowed, or retention of the unit as a semi-autonomous agency. This trend seems more prevalent. It is outside the scope of this book to pass judgement on the benefits and savings that are currently being achieved through market testing. Pundits have spoken at length on the subject and it is still very much a matter for debate.

If you intend to bid under market testing you should be aware of trends. Some government departments are rethinking their strategy; the Department of the Environment has recently abandoned plans to market test its computer services after incurring large sums in early, preparatory work. In November 1993, the Lord Chancellor's Department was left with only the internal bid for court services development technology when three short-listed private sector bidders withdrew.

One view of market testing is that it imposes restrictions which limit the freedom of potential bidders to be innovative. Indications of this are displayed by the client's propensity to over-specify the requirements or oblige the contractor to carry out the operations of the department by retaining the existing set up. Analysis of recent results seems to support this view. There is a lower success rate for the winning of contracts by external bidders than when operating in the private sector. Roughly 60 per cent of market testing contracts have been awarded to the internal bidder. The cry of partisan market testing is being shouted. Several large system contracts have been placed in jeopardy as suppliers refuse to submit bids, judging that their chances of success are small.

Sound advice therefore is to enter with caution into market testing bids especially as the assessment rules and accounting principles being used are still being defined. You should be wary of incurring high bid costs unless you are confident that you understand the basis of the evaluation. If you are leading an in-house bid then you should make sure that you have sufficient skills to compete with the private sector challenges. It is unlikely you will have the full range of sales, marketing, bid management and commercial expertise at your disposal within your department so you will need to recruit consultants or colleagues with the necessary skills.

TUPE

Recent rulings in the European Court may have a dramatic impact upon future government market testing and privatisation initiatives. The Transfer of Undertakings (Protection of Employment) Regulations known as TUPE, prevent the successful bidder from imposing worse pay and conditions when they take over the operations than previously existed. A statutory duty is imposed upon employers to consult with employees and to take into account all reasonable concerns when contracting out services. It is possible that this will discourage suppliers from bidding in market tests and because of the ambiguous wording in the TUPE directive, courts have ruled that the regulations apply to all outsourced services, even when only a single person is involved. Companies that have won contracts under market testing, now face being sued for unfair dismissal, because they assumed that TUPE did not apply to them. The Confederation of British Industry (CBI) advises all its members to be wary of bidding for contracts without taking full cognisance of the TUPE directive. A revised or replacement directive is planned. However, it is too early yet to know the full implications. As bid managers you should be aware of the ruling. If bidding under market testing, it is possible that failure to give sufficient consultation or notice to existing staff could result in your being sued for compensation, even retrospectively.

WORLD AID-FUNDED BIDS

Bidding where international lending agencies are involved can be very complex and time consuming. Knowing your way around is critical, as the inexperienced or ill-prepared bidder can become lost in the bureau-cracy and entangled in the processes, and waste much effort finding a way through. Each agency has its own rules and regulations for tender-ing and there is no substitute for fully familiarising yourself with these before considering a bid.

There are several main funding agencies: The World Bank Group, The European Bank for Reconstruction and Development (EBRD), The Asian Development Bank (ADB), the African Development Bank, the European Development Fund, the Inter-American Development Bank (IDB), the United Nations Agencies (UN) and the European Structural Funds (EC). In addition there are other agencies and funds covering spe-cific geographical sectors such as the Caribbean and Arab states.

These banks and agencies lend funds to public bodies to allow them to buy products or services on the open market. Each of the lending agencies operates their own procedures for tendering and selection. But you should note that in nearly every case, the selection of the winning bidder is entirely down to the borrower of the funds, not the lender. So the borrower, your client, should remain your focus of attention during the bid. The lender still has considerable power as they are of course holding the purse-strings and you must still address yourself to getting all the information you can from them, including their adjudication and selection methods and details of the client project and related development programme.

The important factor about aid-funded bids is to remember why the client is bidding in the first place. They are not inviting you to bid so that you reap financial benefits to pay your shareholders' dividends. Neither are they inviting you to bid so that you can benefit from the experience. There are usually many factors underlying the reason for inviting bids through international competitive tendering. These will probably include: to provide products and services which are not available locally, to pro-vide some supporting infrastructure that is necessary to enable the region to develop culturally and economically, to encourage the development of local industries, manufacturing or service sectors, to provide employ-ment, to gain hard currency for other capital projects, to meet some tactical objective, to transfer knowledge and technology, to build self-reliance, to build relationships for further development, to set up ventures to allow growth outside the domestic market, to supplement existing resources, and to complement services where a perceived deficiency exists.

Developing a bid strategy in these circumstances requires you to shift your focus. To be successful you need to place the emphasis on what your client will get from your bid, not on what you stand to gain. This is, of course, fundamental to all bids but it assumes greater importance in aid-funded projects.

Advance notice of bids

Information on aid-funded projects for all the above institutions is published twice a month in the United Nations journal, *Development Business* which contains information on new projects, notices of prequalification, bids and tender invitations, awards of contracts and other newsworthy items. Companies that subscribe to *Development Business* can also get access to an on-line database which gives the same information but much earlier, usually several weeks ahead of it being published, thereby allowing you to get a head start in your prospect assessment. The World Bank operates the International Business Opportunities Service which provides similar information as *Development Business*, but is specific to the World Bank and with fuller details on how and when to bid.

Smaller contracts could go through an accelerated process but unless you have people on the ground ready to respond quickly you could lose out.

Tendering and selection processes

As each lender is different you should obtain full details direct from them on how they operate their processes and procedures. Do not assume that conditions will be the same for all projects with the same lender. Variations will occur during negotiation between lender and recipient, making the terms of the bid different for each project. Even if the general conditions remain fairly constant, special conditions, that state the requirements particular to the project, will not. Check the terms out carefully in every case.

The World Bank has various procurement methods; international competitive bidding that is open to anyone, limited competitive bidding by invitation only, domestic competitive bidding open only to local companies, and international or local shopping for buying low-value commodity goods. Interestingly, the selection of consultants is not subject to a bidding process. Consultants need to register and those who are competent and capable are short-listed for particular projects. For other products and services they will use the most appropriate and cost-effective method of procurement. This will normally be International Competitive Bidding. Bids under these rules are advertised in the United Nations publication *Development Business* and in local newspapers in the country where the project will be carried out. You will find that local suppliers are often given preference so it may be advisable to seek a partnership or joint venture with a domestic company. You are allowed to bid and receive payment in your own currency. Hard currency is frequently a highly valued commodity and it is worthwhile looking at ways in which you can maximise this without affecting your own cost base.

The contract is awarded to the lowest price-evaluated bid, but as in all bids, consideration is given to other factors such as service, performance, quality and support, so do not overlook these when they are called for in the tender.

Bidders' guidelines

There are some aspects of bidding for aid-funded projects that deserve special emphasis. Although they apply equally to all bids, they have greater importance in these scenarios. Guidance on some of these is listed below.

Get in early

Advance notices are always published, giving you the opportunity to start your assessment process early and begin planning your strategy. It may be worthwhile subscribing to the relevant publications where the notices are placed or to another service which alerts you to forthcoming tenders. These often operate a filter system allowing you to specify particular industry sectors and geographical locations that you are interested in cutting out much that will not be of interest to you.

In aid-funded bids there is frequently an earlier study done to assess the feasibility of the project. The client may reveal this information to you or they may not, there is no obligation for them to make it generally available. Check with the lending agency whether they have had any preliminary studies or work carried out and try to get copies of the reports. The project may be part of a much larger development programme with some detailed studies already completed. You can usually get valuable information on your client and on your competition by doing some desk research at the lending agency offices or local government departments. There will usually be information on the budget available for each aspect of the programme, including your prospect, which will put you on track for assessing how much the client has available to spend.

Pre-qualification

Complex projects may go through a pre-qualification process and invitations to pre-qualify are advertised in the same way as invitations to bid.

If you are successful in pre-qualifying the client will certainly invite you to bid. The aid-funding agencies view any decision not to bid after pre-qualifying extremely unfavourably and you will have to justify yourself if you want to pull out; you may have prevented another potential bidder from qualifying or involved the agency in additional and unnecessary administration. Commonly they will not invite your company to bid again which is hard if you see this as a major strategic direction for your business. So be very cautious when assessing the opportunity and be very sure that you can bid.

Clarify uncertainties

Abide by the rules. In aid-funded projects as in most other public sector procurement, compliance with the bidding rules and regulations is vital. Your bid can and will be eliminated from the assessment if you contravene any of the rules. Remember that you are operating in a global market with tough competitors who will assess every threat and look for ways to eliminate them. Even seemingly trivial rules must be followed. Late bids, contravention of packaging and labelling rules, evidence of attempts at illicit communication are all reasons why the agency can refuse to accept your bid. The agencies are keen on effectively operating their complaints procedures, so if your competitor objects to a perceived contravention of the rules it may be impossible for them not to dismiss your bid on a technicality meaning that all your months of effort will be wasted.

Establish a network of contacts

It is most important in international bids of this type to set up and maintain good contacts. Without them you may miss chances to capitalise on any opportunity because waiting until notices are published is unlikely to give you enough time to get your name and credentials established. Aim for a broad but influential network of people with whom you keep in touch regularly. This normally operates at three levels. Your prime focus will be building affiliations with the client directly (see Chapter 6). Avoid appearing arrogant and try to show empathy with them and their culture. Although you may be a large established company in the UK, your name alone will not win you the bid. Secondary support would typically include appropriate government officials in the target country as well as your own consular or embassy staff. It is also of use to hire a good local agent if you do not have direct representation. Cultivate associations in the export agencies such as the Exports Credits Guarantee Department, the UK official export credit insurer, and country-desk in your government export support section, such as the DTI World Aid Section. These organisations will often have their own in-country contacts and get advance warning of anything that might be coming up. You may find it worthwhile attending or supporting any trade missions to the target country or meeting with delegations visiting your base.

Tertiary connections are those that may be useful in indirectly supporting your bid. This would encompass the lending agency or the bank's regional officers, field staff, or task managers. If you can justify it, appoint a local agent to keep in regular contact with bank officials. Most of the funding agencies arrange organised visits every so often and you should attend at least one of these to get your name known and to get to know them. If there is no organised visit planned, you can usually arrange an informal meeting at the bank headquarters.

Project financing

As perhaps half the overseas aid projects are financed by two or more lending agencies, knowing where the client is getting their funds from is critical and will help you focus your bid correctly. There is a proliferation of lending sources, including aid funds, banking and commercial institutions, governmental aid, export credit agencies, and charities. Pay particular attention if a multilateral agreement exists between the client, the funding agency and another national government. In such instances the aid is nearly always linked in some way to the country supplying some of the funds. Usually there will be a condition that all or part of the contract is let to companies within that country. If this includes you it will work to your advantage and against you if not. The government and lending agency will normally review projects to identify which aspects will be suitable for shared financing and is readily available from the agency concerned.

Tender documents and specification

Because of the nature of the recipients of aid-funding in undeveloped or developing countries, consultants are sometimes used to supplement local technical expertise. Lending agencies will usually appoint them to research the project and independently assess the bids received. Although tender documents and specifications are drawn up in the country carrying out the project, it is with the assistance of the lending agency and consultant. You need to establish contact with the consultant if this is allowed. If there is any doubt at all about any aspect of the documentation you should seek early clarification. Price plays such a significant role in the evaluation that, if your interpretation differs from that of the consultant, it could result in price variations and lose you the contract.

Compliance with the specification is strictly enforced by most agencies. There are several reasons for this. There will often be a formal financing agreement in place between the recipient of the funds and the lending agency that stipulates the precise technical nature of the project. Another reason is that the client will have established formal evaluation criteria and any divergence away from the specification may make your proposal difficult to assess. Any alternative proposal, which although meeting the perceived needs of the project does not comply with the technical specification, will be given short shrift. Do not reject it out of hand though, there is still a place and an allowance for alternative solutions in most formal aid-funded bids. You should make sure that this is kept separate from your main compliant response.

You will encounter technical specifications designed to allow you to use your initiative in deciding the best approach and method to carry out your proposal. These set out objectives for the project that you have to attain.

Preparing your proposal

When you are preparing your proposal always remember to emphasise the local content of your offer. This is worth repeating often, but make sure that your client is happy with the company you have selected. If they are not your chances of success are radically reduced. Finding this out is not always easy. Depending on your relationship with the client you could just ask them. Alternatively, you may have to undertake some detailed research to establish how your chosen local support is perceived by them.

Compliance to the terms and conditions is critical, so avoid submitting a conditional response with reservations or caveats simply because you have not obtained sufficient information. This can complicate your proposal which is then viewed less favourably than a more simple response. Remember that you may be able to negotiate on critical issues later.

Pricing is perhaps the most important area to prepare well. Most aid-funded bids are price sensitive so they will consider the most cost-effective or economically favourable bid within the budget and funding available. Pricing techniques will be discussed in detail in Chapter 9 but for aid bids there are one or two particular points worth noting. You will have to submit prices according to the specified schedule. Try not to omit anything, even if you do not believe it will be used in the general assessment. Do a double check on the pricing spreadsheets because you will be more restricted in the degree of financial innovation you can apply than for other bid situations. For example, your proposal may show significant benefits over the long term by having lower ongoing costs for a higher up-front price, but such economies over time may not be considered in the price assessment or, if they are considered, may not be given the same weight as the initial capital spend. You will find that most lending agencies insist upon ignoring anything other than what the invitation to tender specifies. You then have the task of trying to massage your prices to fit most advantageously with the required specification, which may not always be possible. You should, however, still include the economic advantages even though they may not be considered in the main assessment; it could become the deciding factor between two finely balanced bids.

Where there is little difference between the lowest priced bids, perhaps only two or three per cent, they may be considered equal. Other factors then come into play such as technical innovation, local content, training and support issues that are given more weight. Many agencies will give a preference to bids from local companies. The European Development Fund for example, gives a 10 per cent preference to such a company for any works valued under five million European Currency Units (ECU) and a 15 per cent preference for supplies of any value. This puts you at a distinct disadvantage if you are a foreign company and the only way to avoid losing the bid is to prevent a tie happening. This is why local content can play such a critical part; by having a high element of local support you can gain an advantage of up to 15 per cent if two or more bids are adjudged to be equal.

Finally, unless it is specifically asked for in the tender documents you should avoid any price escalation clauses.

TENDERING IN THE EUROPEAN ECONOMIC AREA

The European Economic Area (EEA) comprises those countries of the European Community (EC) and the European Free Trade Association (EFTA). EFTA comprises Austria, Finland, Iceland, Norway and Sweden, with Liechtenstein joining soon. Switzerland, which is also an EFTA member has not agreed to co-operate in the EEA.

The EEA agreement completes the European internal market and introduces commonality for competition across Europe by adopting standards similar to the European Community competition rules. Now that the European internal market is complete with a single market in operation, legislation is in effect aimed at harmonisation and at ensuring fairness in competition. In some areas of public operation utilities such as water and electricity, telecommunications and transport, the EC has recognised that a closed market operates. This is due in the main to the contribution each member state government may make in these sectors and the influence they bring to bear on these services in their own countries. Not all states have advanced as far and as fast as the UK in the privatisation of utilities. So the purpose of these new directives is to keep potential suppliers better informed of buyers' needs and to open the decision process to analysis and review.

Previously, and some say it still goes on, preferential treatment of local companies was a problem. The contracting authorities developed many ways to get around the legislation including dividing large contracts into several smaller ones so they fell below the value threshold, failing to advertise the opportunity correctly in the Official Journal, applying local standards and discriminatory selection processes. All were used to ensure that the market was kept closed and favoured the domestic suppliers.

The new directives tighten the procedure and close the loopholes and aim at making this market sector more accessible to small- and medium-sized companies. Open access to this market has long been a major objective of the single European market and since January 1993 the legal and political framework has existed to facilitate this. All companies in the European Community have the right to compete on equal terms for all public contracts, except where a strictly defined closed market exists.

General tendering procedure

In keeping with the spirit of the open market, open tendering is now the preferred procurement method. This means that any company in the EC can submit tenders for any opportunity with no restrictions or pre-qualifications necessary. Restricted or selective tendering is allowed in some specific cases where it can be justified by the contracting authority. Such instances will also include projects which need products or services that are not available on the open market. This method allows the contracting authority a certain latitude in selecting which suppliers they will invite to bid and will probably involve some pre-qualification activity. The contracting authority must first advertise for suppliers to apply for consideration and can only invite to bid those suppliers who do apply.

Normally, at least five bidders must be invited. Another tendering method exists through negotiated tendering. In this method the client can select the suppliers they wish to invite to bid. As in restricted tendering the contracting authority must justify their choice of the negotiated tendering method and provide regular reports on progress.

Negotiated tenders could be open to misuse unless properly controlled and so the legislation provides rigidly enforced rules for when it can be used. The negotiated method can be used when open or selective tendering fails to find a suitable supplier; either because no-one responded or they were all unsuitable or there was an irregularity in the procedure that rendered it void or, for an urgent requirement, there was insufficient time to comply with the rules. Projects where only one or a few suppliers exist or for pure experimentation, research and development can also be considered. Finally, contracts for repeat work or carrying some other exceptional high risk factor may be contemplated.

Which projects apply?

Not all procurement need go through this process. There is a minimum value above which the procedures apply so anything coming in below the stated figure is exempt. For most public works projects the limit is five million ECU, and one million for each component of a larger project. This component value was applied to stop the contracting authorities dividing large projects into several smaller ones to circumvent the legislation. Even call-off contracts, with supplies over a longer period have to be tendered again if the total accumulated value of orders exceeds the original estimated value.

The limit for supplies of goods before the tendering rules need be applied is 200,000 ECU. Some agencies, who are buyers on behalf of central governments, and GATT bodies, are required to operate a lower limit of around 125,000 ECU. This threshold of 200,000 ECU also applies for service contracts with some defined exceptions such as insurance and complete turnkey projects. The limits in the utilities sector are slightly different. The threshold for supply of goods here is 400,000 ECU (600,000 ECU for telecommunication supplies) and the same for services. The works limit remains at five million ECU.

Note that the limits are converted into local currencies and announced in November of each year and then apply for the following year irrespective of fluctuations in currency exchange rates. So the actual sterling rate is stabilised over the period.

Official notices

All conforming opportunities have to be advertised in the *Official Journal Supplement* and its electronic equivalent *Tenders Electronic Daily*. Adverts have to conform with a concise model format. Where it is necessary to advertise in the Official Journal there is a considerable increase in the time-scales of the tendering processes.

The directives make official notices mandatory, even specifying set models for time limits on the invitations to tender being made. Clients must give proper notice, issue periodic notices on product and work groups and provide information on any qualification systems that they will apply.

The *Journal* contains preliminary information, invitation to tender notices, results of contracts awarded and advance notices of larger supply purchases exceeding 750,000 ECU. Advance notices are given at the start of the financial year in which the procurement is planned and usually not less than six months beforehand. These are particularly valuable to the alert bid manager who can begin planning a bid strategy six months ahead or longer.

Notice periods and time limits

The limits on advertising the bid and closing dates for bid submission vary on the type of tendering method used. Open tenders have to allow 52 days from the date of the invitation to bid notice until the closing date for receipt of bids. The minimum is 36 days if there has been an advance notice published. Invitations to participate in a selective or negotiated tender must allow 37 days to receive application. Once invited to bid, you are given at least 40 days to submit your response. If an advance notice was previously published this is reduced to 36 days. In urgent bids, the accelerated form of selective tendering allows 12 days for receipt of application from the time of the invitation to participate, with 10 days allowed for bid submission once you have received the invitation to bid.

In all methods, when you respond to participate or request an invitation to bid, the contracting authority has four days to send you the details. If you request any further information or documentation these must be sent to you at least six days before the bid submission date, unless it is an accelerated selective tender in which case the limit is four days.

Use of standards within specifications

There is a requirement to make use of European standards wherever they exist or a harmonised national equivalent. The exceptions to this are when no standards exist or the project is innovative. Exceptions are also made if there is a risk of incompatibility with existing systems or if the supply to a standard would render the existing system obsolescent. Otherwise technical specifications will refer to any existing European standards and will force their mandatory use.

It is possible that use of standards may widen the clients' choice of products and services but it will almost certainly limit the amount of co-operation and collaboration between supplier and user. Probably, clients will need to show evidence of their compliance with these rules.

Such rules include the use of quality standards ISO 9000 or EN 2900 or BS 5750. It is becoming extremely difficult for any company to compete to supply in the European public sector or to sophisticated purchasers in large private organisations, without having compliance with this quality management standard. The ISO 9000 standards cover a wide range of quality elements.

You can comply with the ISO 9000 standard by setting up a company-wide quality management and control system which meets the requirements for documentation control, procedures, policy, change-control, monitoring and review. There is nothing to prevent you stating that you comply with ISO 9000. Most purchasers however, will require some evidence of your compliance and this is generally done by obtaining certification by a recognised quality accreditation organisation.

Decision criteria

Transparency in the selection and award of the contract is intended. Although the purchaser can use quality-based selection criteria, they must be objective and freely available to anyone who is interested. At the most basic level, selection will consider the lowest or most advantageous priced bid. But they can take other price factors into account such as any cost savings that may accrue. Other objective criteria can include technical innovation and originality, and exceptional quality of performance by any tenderer.

Bidders must be technically competent to carry out the task, financially sound and of good general standing, which means that they are neither bankrupt, nor guilty of committing grave misconduct such as tax evasion or deception. The contracting authority will usually request checks to be made in these areas before inspecting the content of the bid or issuing an invitation to bid in a selective tender.

Control measures

It is for the contracting authority to ensure that suppliers are treated fairly, that there is no discrimination and that bids were selected using agreed criteria. The threat hanging over them is litigation by potential suppliers who feel they may have been unfairly treated and are now able to pursue their case through the law courts.

Selective and negotiated tenders require reports to be submitted in writing to the Commission giving a justification of the reason for not choosing open competition. This can be audited by the Commission, the management of the authority concerned and the public. Any supplier rejected in a selective tender can ask for a reason which has to be supplied within 15 days.

An interesting situation arises when bids are judged to be equal. Under German legislation for example, the winner should be chosen by a lottery. However, there have been recent cases where the German courts have placed injunctions on the client preventing them awarding the contract because they have failed to follow this route, although there was a court ruling that the bids were equally competitive. This throws into question the whole issue of objective decision making. If the courts are now factors in making the decision, the bidders' function of satisfying the client's expectation while eliminating the opposition is called into doubt. One has to question whether this is what businesses want or whether bureaucracy and legislation is taking over from common sense.

For the client engaged in procurement, the requirements of the new directives will add greatly to their burden. While tendering provides for fair treatment of suppliers, this additional burden of proof may inhibit the client from developing the close relationships with them that modern procurement methods are intended to encourage.

Other directives

Beyond those encouraging fair competition, there are many other directives covering all industry sectors that are seeking to engender harmonisation across the member states. You need to be aware of those that are used in your bid and industry sectors. Directives are now in place covering health and safety, data protection, copyright, rental rights, product liability and so on. There are many good treatments on the subject to which you should refer.

Guidelines for a European bid strategy

For many companies Europe represents the largest single market and the most accessible. On size alone it outstrips the USA and Pacific Rim regions and there are perhaps closer cultural ties which make expansion desirable. Developing a European strategy for bids becomes an important consideration. Be prepared to submit your proposal in the language of the country to which you are bidding and in their currency. The scale of aid available to assist businesses in exploiting these markets decreases with the degree of development.

There are a few basic precepts to bear in mind when considering a European bid strategy. First, target existing or latent volume markets, not forgetting that in Europe this requires a large amount of money to do effectively. Always ensure however that you protect the home base market; a liberalised single market means there is increased domestic competition so do not leave yourself exposed. In targeting your area of operation, the degree of market development will have a great effect. Europe is divided into three parts; the developed markets of north-west Europe, including most of the EC and EFTA countries, the developing markets in the south, including Spain, Portugal and Greece, and the emerging markets in the east, such as Russia, and the CIS. Of these, the developed markets are sound and established, procedures and processes are clear and funding is available. The developing markets are higher risk, whilst the emerging markets represent probably the highest risk.

You can develop strength in Europe by building a network of alliances but ensure that you ally yourself with someone who counts. Your fiercest competition will come from the domestic companies in a developed market and it is here you will need to build strong local support. If you expect fierce competition, you will need to generate the capability to retaliate and in Europe this really means being big enough to inflict some damage on them. Often this will come about from the effectiveness of the allegiances and alliances that you develop. You will make the greatest impact by concentrating on areas where your competitors do not want to compete. Providing you are satisfied that you can achieve adequate returns for your efforts, this will be the most effective way of becoming established.

When selecting a geographical area for bidding, examine some basic factors: the economy should be attractive with no impediment to repatriation of funds. It helps if it is a safe area having a competent legal framework and an ethical business ethos. Look for areas where your involvement will be welcome; you are unlikely to be successful if you are seen as a threat to local companies. There should be skilled and professional people available with associated training and development opportunities for them. Finally, you will need to separate out your cost–price relationship. You must be able to withstand losses in one area to make money somewhere else and this usually requires strength in depth within the company.

SUMMARY

Procurement by the public sector accounts for around 15 per cent of the UK gross domestic product so winning bids in this sector is vital to many businesses.

- *Public sector bids tend to be formal, complex and quite costly and sometimes only larger companies can afford to bid. Initiatives aimed at facilitating bids by small and medium-sized enterprises should make it easier for these groups to win.*

- *Compulsory competitive tendering and market testing in the UK presents many opportunities for in-house and private bidders to win public sector contracts. There are still many unresolved issues in the tendering processes, so be circumspect in these deals.*

- *Aid-funded bids are those in which the client's funds are provided by one of the international lending agencies. Each of these has their own processes which are strictly enforced so when bidding for these contracts you must play by their rules.*

- *It is advisable in aid-funded bids to make an early start, set up a broad network of contacts to support your efforts, understand the rules and aim to get the lowest price. Look also for ways to add local content which adds value to your bid.*

- *The European Community internal single market presents the whole of Europe and the EFTA countries to open competition. Open tendering is the norm, but negotiated and selective tendering rules can also apply.*

6

UNDERSTANDING AND INFLUENCING THE CLIENT

The most important aspect of effective bid management is the client relationship. Yet it is so often the one that is most neglected. Many companies bid for opportunities knowing nothing at all about the client; their wants, needs or aspirations. Perhaps the rules and regulations for competitive tendering in the public sector share some responsibility for this. Advertisements in the European *Journal*, newspapers and magazines all invite open competition, as they have to. Getting the invitation in these circumstances is easy; the payment of a fee or a letter normally suffices. Winning is a different matter all together. Winning means getting to know and understand your client better than they do themselves. Get under their corporate skin. Empathise with them, putting yourself in their shoes. Only then can you hope to begin to understand the consolidated values that they are looking for. You can then go on to develop ways to engineer your solution to meet their expectations and beat your competitors.

This chapter explores various aspects of the client–bidder relationship. The starting point is gaining a firm understanding of tendering from your client's viewpoint, finding out why they have selected a particular method and what they wish to get out of it. By getting to know some of the problems they may have in tendering, you can alleviate them. You will need to develop your knowledge in specific areas so you can understand the dynamics of their business and their needs. Knowing where to get the right information will enable you to build a comprehensive client profile. All these factors contribute towards your plan to influence them and deal with them face to face.

MOTIVATION FOR BUYING BY TENDER

Tendering is the process of requesting suppliers to bid or present their offer containing unequivocal prices, terms and conditions that, upon acceptance by the client, will form the basis of a contract. There are probably any number of reasons why a business decides to adopt competitive tendering in preference to buying on the open market. They may well have no alternative; if it is a public sector client then they may have to conform with compulsory competitive tendering procedures or another form of open competition. If the client is in the private sector commercial reasons may dictate that they take this approach. In some larger organisations, the client must go out to tender if the value of the procurement is above a set limit.

Other reasons which might influence the client's decision could be a restricted market or difficulties in finding what they want to buy. This would be the case where there is no off-the-shelf product so they must have a tailor-made solution. Take a telecommunications network design, for example. Telephones, being almost a commodity product, could be sourced from many suppliers. However, the design of a data network linking all their branches and providing enhanced facilities has to suit the client's precise needs and they would probably go out to tender. Similarly, if they needed an individual design for a product, a building, or packaging, they could invite tenders. In these situations the client is hard pressed to know what the right price is to pay; if what they want does not yet exist it is easy to see their dilemma. By tendering, they achieve a better idea of the right price from a range of suppliers and are better able to make an informed judgement upon which to select.

Conversely, the supply market for the products could be very wide. Prices in such markets may vary considerably. Take the personal computer market as an example. Similar products performing similar functions cover the whole price spectrum, low-end easily affordable machines with basic software installed, to top-end high performance systems with sophisticated software. Although still categorised as personal computers these vary greatly in what they can offer the client in terms of performance, reliability, facilities, processing capability, support, training and so on. By going out to tender the client can specify closely what they need from the product and allow the manufacturers to interpret those needs and put a price against them.

The advantage of tendering is that the client gains an objective assessment which they can review and audit. The administration of the tender, although often lengthy, is relatively straightforward unless circumstances, such as an overly-formal assessment process, impose a higher degree of complexity. However, there are often guidelines and models that the client can use to help in the process.

In every tender situation the client will want to know precisely what suppliers can deliver and within what time-scale. By inviting tenders they gain an understanding of the quality that the supplier can achieve.

Disadvantages of inviting tenders

Despite the benefits of fairness, impartiality, objectivity and accuracy that the tender process purports to provide, it rarely proves to be the procurement panacea that the client hopes for. There are familiar disadvantages that regularly appear, stemming from a fundamental dilemma.

The tender dilemma

There are two ways that the client can initiate a bid: they can either start from the point where they have a very good understanding of what they want to buy and produce a detailed specification telling the suppliers what to bid for, or they can state the problems that they face and ask suppliers to come up with solutions that meet their needs. The former option has disadvantages in that the cost and involvement of the client are high in producing the specification and tender documents. Furthermore, it restricts the amount of initiative that the suppliers can take in interpreting the specification. In the latter option, the client spends less on tender preparation but is likely to receive any number of diverse solutions that will vary in price and content, so decision making becomes extremely difficult.

From your perspective, the rigorous specification will be easier to respond to. You will quite simply have to design a solution against the client's stated requirement. Of course your chances of success are reduced as you will be hard pressed to offer any key differentiators over your competitors, so price will often be the deciding factor. The second option of the client, to provide a statement of the need and allow suppliers to offer solutions, gives you greater scope for innovation and creativity. This is where price will often take less prominence than design, innovation and creativity. Unfortunately, far too many suppliers fail to take advantage of these types of invitations. They misinterpret the specification thinking that the client does not really know what they want or does not have the competence to prepare an adequate or precise definition. What they fail to understand is the basis of the dilemma and why the client has decided upon their chosen approach.

One way that a client will get around the dilemma is to combine tendering with a pre-selection process and negotiation after tenders have been received. They will pre-qualify certain suppliers, perhaps by issuing a request for information, or eliciting a statement of capability. This will often state the problem areas and ask for solutions. Based on the responses received the client then prepares a more detailed specification around the solution that they prefer and invites tenders. Once they have completed evaluating the bids, they then negotiate on price and other conditions with the preferred suppliers.

Price disadvantages

Knowing the right price to pay is critical for the client and may be the main reason for them going through the process. Suppliers could quote prices too high for their budget or a price too low that could lead to dispute or failure of supply or even to the supplier going out of business. Clients may be uncertain of the profit margins of any bidder and whether that company can survive at that margin. They have to decide either to go for what appears a good deal, with the risk that performance, support or maintenance may suffer later, or perhaps pay a higher price and get better after-sales service. They may have to decide between an established supplier and one who can undercut their price. The risk of the unknown is quite high. They could find sudden and unexpected increases in prices later or suffer other performance compromises when the supplier attempts to recoup low profits. Low prices could be the result of low costs or low margins and the client may have no means of knowing which it is.

Delays in buying

The procedures for tendering are often slow and therefore the client has to plan the requirement thoroughly. If the subject of the procurement is urgently required then inviting tenders may cause unacceptable delays. Public procurement procedures specify mandatory time limits which are usually strictly enforced, thereby causing delays in the delivery of the final project. If the client attempts to accelerate the tendering process they run the risk of putting off potential suppliers or of receiving ill-prepared responses. Thus, tendering may not be possible for rush jobs even though other factors would suggest that it is the better method.

Past performance ignored

On bids where the lowest price wins, the client may not give consideration to past performance and quality of supply. Strict interpretation of bidding rules would preclude factors other than price being a differentiator between technically compliant proposals. Although perfectly happy with the incumbent supplier, the client is forced into taking a risk by going with a cheaper alternative.

Expensive procedures

Tendering procedures may be expensive to set up, particularly in the case of open tendering. Costs are incurred in the preparation and submission of notices and the buying of advertising space. Tender documents also can be extremely lengthy, running to hundreds of pages. The cost of production can be high, as can the postage and packing needed to get the documents to the tenderers. Then there are the administration costs: collating, copying and checking tender documentation before issues, maintaining an accurate list of bidders, holding meetings with suppliers, answering enquiries. Finally, there are the adjudication costs of checking responses, further meetings with suppliers and drawing-up contracts. As a result, some clients levy charges for the tender documents to offset part of the cost involved.

Unsuitability for contract

Tendering can be unsuitable for some types of contract. If there is only one supplier of the product or service required, going out to tender is pointless. Similarly, contracts that are of low value may also not lend themselves to tendering; the additional costs involved may outweigh any savings that could be achieved. Other contracts for which tendering may not be appropriate are those that could be carried out by an existing supplier or where it is not viable or feasible to bring in another contractor. The client could find it much more difficult managing the interaction between the two contractors than allowing just one to carry out all the tasks. These are just a few examples, there are many more where either the material costs involved or the indirect costs incurred through additional management time do not warrant competitive purchasing. In these situations it is usually better for the client to seek to develop partnerships with a few suppliers and negotiate each contract independently.

Suppliers decline to bid or withdraw

Another potential disadvantage your client may encounter occurs when one or more of the suppliers from whom the client wants to receive a bid, declines the invitation. Their choice is immediately reduced. If too many suppliers go a similar route there may be no choice at all, defeating the whole purpose behind the tender procedure. If only one or two bids are received, the client may not find one that fully meets their aims and aspirations.

Suppliers will usually see similar disadvantages in going through the tender process. This is particularly true of long delays in the buying process and in the cost involved in lengthy bids. Because businesses are dynamic and under constant review it is possible that even while initially accepting the invitation to bid, the supplier subsequently makes a decision to withdraw at some stage before submission. The client encounters the same problems again.

THE TENDERING PROCESS

With the decision made to purchase by tender, the client now has to look in depth at what they have to do to secure the best solution. They have several uncertainties to resolve before completing the tendering process; differences in the type of tender, the assessment method and the selection of bidders all contribute to making this a multifarious management function. It brings benefits to you as a bidder if you can comprehend the client's difficulties. If you can derive additional facts to add to your bid information system you might be able to help the client in some way, simplifying their task and gaining more credence for your own bid.

Type of tenders

There are three basic tendering methods open to your client. The choice will depend on their company procedures, the expected cost of the purchase and the budget available. Selecting the right approach requires some thought on their part. You can clearly influence their thinking where choices exist. If the client is a government department or agency, central, local or regional administration, hospital, health authority, or other state department, the chances are they will have little choice except buying through open competition. But private sector companies can select any method, usually decided by how cost-effective each is for the project. There are three options.

Open tendering

Competitive or open tendering allows all prospective suppliers to respond to a public advertisement of the proposed contract and to submit an offer. In an open invitation any enterprise or company, individual, partnership or consortium can submit an offer. These invitations are frequently advertised in the *Official Journal of the European Community* (for public sector procurement), the United Nations publication *Development Business* (for aid-funded projects), the national press, trade journals and papers.

Selective tendering

In selective or restrictive tendering, the client undertakes some form of supplier selection before issuing the invitation to tender. This may take the form of a public announcement inviting interested parties to respond with supplier information from which a shortlist of tenderers will be drawn. The client may have a list of preferred suppliers from which they operate exclusively, or they may establish a shortlist of suppliers they know can carry out the work. In restricted tendering only those suppliers that have been invited may submit offers.

Negotiated tendering

With negotiated tenders the client consults the enterprises or suppliers and negotiates conditions with one or more of them. Your clients will commonly use this method where there are only a few suppliers that can meet their requirements. They negotiate with each supplier to decide the exact requirement and identify common ground. This type of tendering often comes about where an existing contract is in place and the client requires a variation or addition to it. The client may negotiate with the incumbent supplier and a competitor to source the new service or product. Negotiated tendering with an existing supplier for repeat work could arguably be considered part of project management.

The process of inviting tenders

The client will go through a number of different stages in preparation for inviting tenders and in completing the procurement. Level of detail and duration of each stage will depend on the method they select and the complexity of their requirement. Commonly there are ten distinct phases:

- identify the problem area and the possible requirement
- develop plans to provide the solution
- assess potential solution providers
- decide upon the tendering method
- prepare tender documents, technical and commercial specifications
- invite suppliers to tender and issue tender documents
- receive suppliers' tenders and proposals
- evaluate the responses
- negotiate with the preferred suppliers
- award the contract to the winning bidder

Each stage breaks down into subsidiary tasks. Some could take weeks or months, others just days, depending on the project, the commercial considerations and technical factors. The client is unlikely to go through the complete process in isolation. They will seek advice from solutions providers, suppliers, consultants, and market researchers. During the earlier stages it is imperative that you take every opportunity to inform, affect and influence the client and their advisors.

UNDERSTANDING THE CLIENT

Understanding the reasons why the client is going out to tender for a particular opportunity is an essential part of the bid manager's task; only by doing so can you attempt to influence their decision processes. Your client is the person who will reward your efforts by supplying you with a contract, so it is in your interests to understand them well and know their motives, objectives and their business. You should always attempt to view the opportunity from their perspective first; if they do not like what you are selling they will not buy it.

It is important for you to get a grasp on their strategic objectives by talking to them and eliciting details of their plans. You can try to paint a realistic scenario based upon the information you get. Try to visualise where they want to be in the next three to five years and where your company fits in. Can you see any avenues that you can investigate together? You can attempt to quantify some realistic objectives for the client, such as their need to buy within a given period, budget and quality limits. Other objectives will be to add value to their business and to increase the profits they need to maintain their position or to grow. Your client will need to eliminate or reduce risks within their business and to achieve a measure of business success, however they judge it. Within your visualised scenario you should qualify and quantify each area to uncover secret or hidden motives and ascertain the best way to continue in your bid.

Understand their enterprise

Knowing your client's business may seem fundamental but many suppliers often overlook it. If, for example, a golden bid opportunity falls on your desk from a client you do not know, what do you do? Do you bid? You cannot decide unless you know the client and their business as well as, or better, than they do themselves. You have seen that while preparing to invite tenders the perspicacious buyer consults with as many people as possible to get the best information and solidify ideas. Displaying a thorough and accurate knowledge of the way their business operates, coupled with practical solutions can make you invaluable to them during this consultative phase. This can open the door to unsolicited proposals where you identify both the need and its solution.

Clearly, there is an almost unlimited amount of material and detail into which you can delve. You have to be realistic about it. You only have a limited amount of time in which to bid and you cannot afford to waste any of it. Therefore you must identify the strongest indicators that will give you real and valuable intelligence and that will help you construct your winning bid. Concentrate on the following four main areas.

The enterprise structure

Business structures are constantly changing. The currents of market forces flow inexorably, and successful enterprises change to accommodate them. Your client is likely to be under severe commercial pressures which you can better understand by knowing how or if they are adapting. Scrutinise the way they are organised and structured. For example, have they embraced total quality management or just-in-time philosophy? Many manufacturers have and, if so, they will be trying to use the minimum amount of their resources to get the best value possible. This will be reflected across the board: organisationally, operationally, administratively and financially. Develop your understanding of their business philosophy and structure so you can ensure your bid fits in with their corporate objectives.

Commercial position

Another strong indicator is their current financial position. You should see if there are any constraints under which they are operating which will limit their choices or force them into making a policy change. This could be in the form of a threat from an acquisition or merger, or collaborative venture. A business in a sound financial position is more likely to buy for added value than for the cheapest price. An upward trend in share value could suggest something is about to happen within the company, an increase in anticipated profits or a better than expected dividend, for example.

It is very worthwhile doing a commercial analysis, starting with the company's published annual or interim report and accounts. The profit and loss account will show changes in turnover, costs and operating profit. Pre-tax profits and equity earnings after tax are important indicators. You should check whether dividends are being paid or whether funds are being retained in reserves. Read the notes to the accounts to see if any extraordinary items have been included, either before or after the pre-tax profit line.

The company's balance sheet only shows its position just before the end of its current financial year and may not be an accurate representation of their general condition. Companies will usually try to portray the best image possible. All assets and liabilities are shown, but look closely at the figures for retained earnings, capital reserves and issued ordinary shares. The share figures will be displayed as nominal, book and market values. It is the market value that is most relevant as it tells you what the market thinks the company is really worth.

Finally, on the client's report, take a good look at the cash flow of the company. Even a profitable company can fail because of adverse movement of revenue, an inability to service outstanding liabilities, interest payments or other debts.

Before concluding your commercial analysis, examine the investment ratios of your client to see if there is underlying strength. These ratios must be considered in the context of the market in which your client operates so you will need to refer to sector performance figures. The pre-tax profit margin, derived from dividing pre-tax profit into turnover, will show how efficient the company is compared to its competitors. Their market capitalisation is simply the number of issued shares multiplied by their current price. The earnings per share ratio will show how the company is performing for its shareholders. Evaluate the price earnings ratio, which is the earnings per share divided by the current share price, to assess the company's relative strength compared to its rivals. A low price earnings ratio indicates low risk and the company's current position is relatively secure, while a high one shows potential for more growth, but at a higher risk.

Include a quick but thorough analysis of their market, the current trends and what your client's main competitors are doing. If they are not market leaders, then they could be following market trends which can give you good insights into what your client is likely to do. When you are satisfied you understand your client's commercial situation, use that knowledge to gain advantages in your bid or to review your bid decision, if their prospects look poor.

Procurement policy

Your bid cycle overlays the buying cycle of your client, not only temporally but also in method and style. Some clients are very open with their buying policy freely informing their suppliers while others are more reticent. Take a hard look at everything your client has purchased in the past year or two and see if you can spot a buying pattern. Are they tending to concentrate on core activities by outsourcing support functions or do they favour one or two key companies? Is their method to look for business partners or to operate a hands-off formal interface? Do they encourage collaborations, or competition among suppliers? Do they always buy the cheapest or do they look for added value? Have you had opportunities to bid in the past and taken them? If so find out the rationale and conclusions, good and bad. When you have the answers to these questions you can assemble a procurement profile and contrast it with your current bid. Map the confluences and divergencies within your bid strategy.

The personal level

Corporations are run by individuals; it is people who decide policy and choose what to buy. So while knowing company policy is very important, you need to get down to the working level and build affiliations. You should begin by identifying the key decision makers for your bid and whoever is acting in an advisory capacity to them. Find out what each is expecting to achieve at a personal level. Relationships are not built by corporations with corporations, but *by* people *with* people.

Understand their concerns

Understanding the enterprise is important and all potential bidders will find it difficult to construct a feasible bid without having at least cursory awareness of their problems. Understanding and dealing with the concerns of the enterprise is critical and distinguishes the winning bid from the also-rans. Earlier you saw that consolidated values are the differentiating factors that will help you in achieving success; this is taking one further step away from the ideology of competition towards the philosophy of providing total client satisfaction. Incorporating these consolidated values within your solution is impossible without having cognisance of the concerns that face your client.

Cost concerns

Without a doubt, the recession during the 1990s has caused businesses to review their cost structures. Economic decline has driven them towards cost containment; by controlling cost they maintain profitability. The unstable and uncertain nature of the global economy has exacerbated this position. Even when national economies appear to be growing, cost containment is still likely to be viewed as the top priority. Once the global economy becomes stable, businesses will see cost of ownership issues begin to take higher importance than simple containment.

To understand the cost concerns of your client you must be aware of the economic conditions under which they operate, and your commercial analysis will provide you with valuable information. Most businesses will see costs in raw materials as the primary concern they face. Interest rate rises, even though causing pain, can usually be accommodated by managing the cashflow. When the basic building blocks such as materials and wages begin to rise, this is when businesses really can suffer. You have to understand the effect of this on your client. They will probably find it difficult to raise their output prices, at least until the global economy strengthens, and so rising costs will begin to squeeze their margins. Try to look for ways to help them in your offer; it will be much valued.

Skills shortages

Symptomatic of the recessionary trend is the reduction in staffing levels that many companies have undertaken as part of the cost containment exercise. The inevitable longer-term effect of this will be a shortage of necessary skills and experience needed to help the company grow again. This is a problem facing the whole of industry and one that your client will see as a concern. How can they expand without the necessary in-company skills? They may decide to recruit, outsource or employ contractors, consultants or advisors. Temper their concerns by having a sound understanding of the problem.

Bid concerns

The client's business concerns will come through in the invitation to bid. They are rarely expressly defined but read between the lines and you will spot them. Your client has invited tenders for the supply of products or services, but what they are really seeking is relief from these business concerns. You have to unearth them to be sure that your bid alleviates them. Consolidate your thinking in the main bid areas.

Price issues

Try to allay the cost concern through inventive pricing. One reason for tendering is to allow the client to know what is the right price for what they are buying. Usually they are after the best possible deal, a cost-effective solution that meets their needs at a price that is within their available budget. What factors do you need to consider that will convince them that your proposal can meet that objective? Much depends on the way in which they analyse your bid. They may be attracted by a superficially low bid price in which case you should take every opportunity, no matter how transparent it might be, to reduce your apparent costs.

Consider every available cost-reduction factor. Show that using your products or services will reduce their staff costs, their operating costs or their fixed direct costs. You should always consider the possibility of packaging the price to take advantage of a positive cash flow to make the price more competitive. You can apply a price weighting to the services or products you are providing first or include a separate item for set-up costs paid in stages as work progresses. A revenue package may be much more attractive than a capital investment programme, even if they have allocated funds for the purchase.

Your bid price may be more favourably considered if you can unbundle your prices. This has the advantage that the client can select those parts of the offer that they require now, purchasing any variations and additions at a later stage. Conversely, a turnkey system at a single price may provide the client with significant advantages.

Suitability of the solution

Does your solution meet the stated objectives? If not, why not? The client may well have produced a detailed specification following months of study within their organisation. If your proposal does not meet the specification on the mandatory requirements then it is unlikely to be considered, irrespective of any price advantages. Attempt to be fully compliant with the requirement wherever possible.

Your proposal must be persuasive. For you to persuade you must understand what your client really wants. You should view the opportunity from their perspective, to see if you would buy what is on offer. Understand their business needs by considering factors like budget, quality, added value, growth, risk management and profit. Check your knowledge against the broad areas listed in Fig. 6.1. If your information is incomplete, find out where you can get it.

Suitability of the supplier

The client will look for evidence that your company has a good track record and history in the supply of the products and services they want

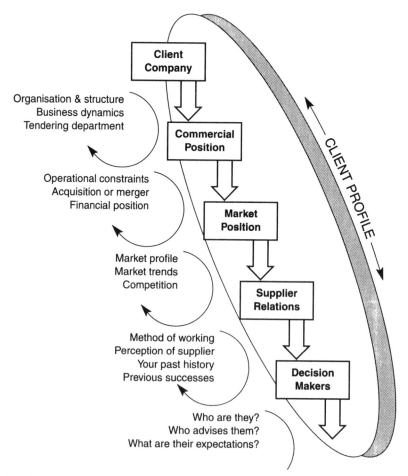

Fig. 6.1 Building a profile of your clients

to buy. Similarly, professional competence in engineering and carrying out the project, and planning for the project life-cycle will be a key factor in their assessment. They will not want the project to founder for any reason.

The financial stability and strength of the supplier is critical to them. So are sound commercial management and a willingness to provide staff of the right level of experience and expertise to support the project.

INFLUENCE THE CLIENT

Having enhanced considerably your understanding of the client, their reasons for bidding, their concerns and their objectives, you have two options: either you have a perfect solution to all their requirements and need only to bid to win or you have to affect the outcome in some way by getting your message across and exerting influence on their thinking and decision making. In most bids, having all the knowledge is little use unless you can apply it effectively in favour of your offer. No opportunity should be lost in trying to influence the client. Plan how best to do this using the resources available.

You now know what the client is trying to achieve in the tendering process and need to consider ways in which you can influence and sway their thinking towards your solution. You may argue that this is irrelevant and that the quality and price of your offer alone should be sufficient in influencing the decision making. You could argue that to try to influence the decision by any other method is morally unsound and is not in keeping with the principle of fair and open competition. You must make your own decision on this. It is a thin line between corporate hospitality and bribery. There has been so much press about corruption, slush-funds and sleaze, that you would be unwise not to give a great deal of thought to it. What you might consider as totally ethical, may be considered by one of your competitors, or an interested third-party, as overstepping the bounds of acceptability.

Whether you are aware of it or not, you are operating in a global marketplace; your competitors are not sitting idly by waiting for the bid submission date to make their play. They are wisely at work, actively influencing the client towards a bid decision in their favour. So what can you legitimately do to gain an advantage with the client? You can begin by establishing the right sort of relationships with their organisation.

Building relationships

The relationship between client and supplier is changing. Recessionary trends have influenced the way in which suppliers relate to their clients. With less money to spend on new projects, clients have become more selective, and with fewer opportunities around, suppliers have had to concentrate on keeping their clients contented and meeting their needs. Traditionally, the roles were clearly defined with the client in a position of dominance, the supplier servicing their requirements. In the area of commodity products this position probably still holds true but when it comes to more complex systems and services, the client has to rely more upon the skills and knowledge of the suppliers. In some areas of innovative technology, computing and communications, the reverse has been true. Suppliers have often dictated what their clients can and cannot have. Neither of these positions brings about a satisfactory relationship. Either the client or the supplier dominates the other. Consequently, a trend towards partnerships is becoming more evident. Clients and suppliers are working in closer collaboration than ever before. Even in commodity supplies this is beginning to prevail.

The benefits to the client are clear. They have a better relationship with the supplier resulting in knowledge transfer and improved pricing, an influence in future developments and improved competitiveness. The supplier benefits from having a longer-term relationship that evolves with the client organisation, a satisfied reference site and steady income streams. This is proving necessary in the complicated business environment that exists in the global market. Developing these partnerships is critical to bidding.

The power that your client has to influence the makers and manufacturers of what they want to buy is becoming greater. More suppliers are consulting with their clients before bringing new products to the market. Finding out what they need and what are their concerns at the development stages, enables them to incorporate solutions into the design. By listening to their clients the supplier improves the design, tests the market and aids their strategic planning. Clients who are given the opportunity to express their views will feel that they are contributing to a better solution. This will greatly improve the supplier's prospects of convincing the client to buy the final product.

Ultimately, the costs to both the supplier and the client in a managed partnership are less than they would be in a confrontational relationship. Clients are less likely to go out to tender if the incumbent supplier is proactive to their needs and responsive to their problems. Time spent in negotiating is reduced. The supplier's costs of sales are lower, bid costs are reduced and their time is better spent looking for business solutions and not haggling over price. This trend has led to the client manager role replacing that of the traditional salesman. In client or account management an up-front relationship is encouraged. Openness and frankness are attributes of a successful partnership and these must prevail. The hard-sell is fast becoming inappropriate. The client will soon know if they have been short-changed and your opportunity for future sales is gone. You should be seeking a managed sale instead; understand your client's needs and develop a close and responsive attitude.

This has never been more true than in the bidding environment. In some areas of industry, clients base the selection of suppliers for tendering and shortlisting upon their ability to listen and respond to their needs. They have expectations from your company as a supplier. They feel they are important and will demand respect and good manners. Consequently, they will expect your interest in them and expect you to show it. It is reasonable for them to want to know how they will benefit from your service or product. You should always aim to empathise with them and discuss each topic from their perspective.

Positioning tactics to exert influence

Building a managed partnership, as opposed to pure selling, epitomises the successful bid. Positioning yourself to develop and take advantage of such a partnership is part of bid management, but not every bid will easily afford such opportunities. You have first to consider whether the client wants a partnership or whether they prefer operating at a distance. You will also have to take into consideration their degree of sophistication in procurement techniques. Whatever the stance taken in your bid, you will enhance your situation by making an early start, gaining the client's backing and winning friends among those who will make the final decision.

Early bid inception

Open tendering can result in many bidders submitting offers. A large, high-profile project could receive 20 or 30 proposals. The client adjudicating these responses is faced with a demanding duty. Often, the assessment process is segmented in order to apply an objective scoring system. Although simplifying the judging for the client, your difficulty is in ensuring all the nuances of your offer are brought out. The danger in large bids is that the client becomes swamped by the sheer volume of paper with the result that the ramifications of your blindingly brilliant proposal are overlooked.

Reliance upon your offer alone securing the contract is therefore a perilous tactic. To give yourself a better chance, it is essential that you have established your company as a major contender at the earliest possible stage in the project. You must attempt to influence the decision in your favour from the outset and there are many ways in which you can achieve this. Consider unsolicited proposals, free consultation, presentations, reference site visits, business lunches, meetings between senior company management and explore any other avenues. Once the formal bid procedure is running, you will have little chance to do any of these things.

Unless your bid strategy requires an element of secrecy, try to avoid dropping bombshells into your bid. There is a well-worn presentation guideline that says you tell them what you are going to tell them, then tell them, and finally tell them what you have told them. Although simplistic, it is good advice for bidding also. Let your client know what you are planning to do in advance so there are no surprises or shocks when they open your offer. Let your bid reinforce and enhance your ideas, incorporating feedback from the client. Follow it up with effective presentations and meetings that emphasise the benefits your bid brings to them.

Some companies argue that all major bids are won or lost before the receipt of the invitation to bid. This is not necessarily true, but you will not go far wrong if you work on that basis. The premise is to establish your business as a major contender as early as you can. The ideal outcome from an early start is a single tender action; you will have established your company as the only serious contender and eliminated the competition. This happens occasionally but it is more common these days to expect competition. Starting early with your bid prepares you better to meet the challenges that your competitors bring.

Finding supporters

Making an early start in the bid is good, but it needs to be with the right people. You will need people within the client organisation with influence and power who you can enlist onto your side. Someone must fight your corner internally; you need someone to spotlight your motives, stress the value that your involvement brings and highlight the beneficial factors within your proposal in the right places.

Undoubtedly, the more influence your proponents have, the greater your chances of success. This is not to say, however, that simply having champions for your cause will acquire you the contract. You cannot allow the consolidated value to be diluted nor ignore the threat of your opponents. However, with a complementary network of contacts and support, you can begin to tailor your bid to meet those values and to overcome advantages that your competitors may have.

Dealing with clients overseas can present its own unique range of activities and problems; many of these could involve you in difficult ethical decisions. You may be required to overcome political resistance either from within the government in whose country you are trying to bid, or from local representatives with their own motives. You will also need to deal with business practices that would perhaps be considered unacceptable in the developed states, but are the norm elsewhere. This is where knowledge of the culture and ethics is essential, and where many bidders come unstuck. The best advice is to recruit external support to help you. You should look to find proponents in local and overseas government staff, embassy officials, lending agency representatives, and local agents.

Other valuable champions, often neglected, are the customers of your client. These can be external customers who are consumers of the products or services your client supplies and they can be internal customers, who are either part of the client's organisation or in some way directly affiliated to them. Your client's key accounts are very important to them and can exert considerable pressure on the way they operate. Find out who are the most influential and target them for support. Your aim should be to convince them that the relationship between you and your client will bring them significant benefits. In a total quality environment, everyone is a customer, including the internal ones. The users, systems operators, utilisers of information or receivers of services, play a major part in the buying decision. Often they are not consulted, so make the effort to bring them into the equation and get them supporting you.

Find the decision makers

Locating the right people is not always easy either. However, you should have identified the enterprise structure and organisation and, with assistance from the business manager, client manager or others with inside knowledge, you can get to know who makes the decision. This is normally more than one person and is sometimes called the decision-making unit. Seek allies in this unit.

In larger organisations the decision to buy is spread across several departments. It is likely to be those involved with commercial and business management who will be ultimately responsible and you should focus your efforts on influencing these people at the senior levels. There is frequently a hierarchy within the decision-making unit. On the lower levels are those managers responsible for technical decisions, the contractual stance and financial evaluation, who will assess the offers and compile the results. At the next level the results are evaluated and a recommendation is made. Above that, the authorisation level approves the recommendation and commits the company to buy.

Build your support from the bottom up by getting to know your way around the organisation and the decision-making unit. When the time is right to go up a level, make sure you have backing from below. It is all too easy to upset people by appearing not to consider them important enough or ignoring the role that they play. This could be felt as a slight against those contacts you have established elsewhere; the technical manager, the services manager, the procurement manager although maybe not final arbiters, will have a great deal of influence. You should try to ensure that the technocrats support your proposal. Help them provide substantiation for your bid to their line management if they are not able to do so effectively by themselves.

MANAGE CLIENT ENCOUNTERS

The encounters between you and your client are fundamental in developing the relationship, exerting influence to help you to win the bid. There are several events which occur during the bid that will pitch you together. How you handle these can often be critical to your success. Client encounters run right through the bid cycle and each will vary, but consider three particularly important scenarios: formation meetings, just between you and the client; progression conferences, with the client, you and your competitors; and the concluding encounter, negotiation between the client and the preferred supplier.

Formation meetings

The first meetings with your client are those that are going to create the strongest impressions. It is in these encounters that you will sound each other out, decide whether your objectives are compatible, whether you can work together and whether there are advantages to each of you in forming a closer relationship. They may be prelude to pre-qualification or part of the process itself but they will always be critical to your aim, which is to win the business. Getting off on the wrong foot or creating a bad impression can sour your association, making it very difficult for you to rebuild it.

In many ways these formation meetings are negotiations and you should adopt a negotiating style appropriate to the client and the situation. The classical theories of behaviour set four styles: compliant, dynamic, collaborative and contentious. The compliant negotiator tends towards submissiveness, probably not a very effective style for most circumstances in business. The dynamic, more forceful approach tends to be more successful, taking the lead and forcing the pace. Similarly, the contentious stance is unlikely to win you friends, and at this early formative stage, creating arguments and being aggressive have no place. The collaborative style is more likely to see patterns of co-operation and mutual benefit emerging. Trying to get a mixture between collaborative and dynamic behaviour is a good technique, but it has to fit the environment of your bid. Only you can make that decision.

Bidders' conference

There are few occasions in a bid that offer you the opportunity to meet face to face with your opponents. A bidders' conference is called usually at the discretion of the client or where required by the funding agency, say the World Bank, under their tendering rules. Typically for a high-profile or important project, the client invites all potential bidders to attend a pre-bid meeting. This is the opportunity for the client to elaborate upon any special needs they may have and highlight various points of the project. It is an occasion for the bidding companies to clarify areas of concern in the invitation to tender. You must use this valuable chance to enhance your knowledge of the client, the prospect and the threat from the competition. So do not approach it too lightly, plan what you are going to do and how you will get the information you want. Look at what the client and suppliers want from a typical bidders' conference. The following outlines will give you some guidance.

The client's approach

First of all, the client wants to impart information to the bidders. They may start with a reiteration of the opportunity plus additional data that was not part of the original specification or tender documents. Any such material distributed to tenderers will usually form part of the requirement so be careful not to overlook it in your response.

It is common practice for the client to request all questions relating to the opportunity to be submitted in writing beforehand. These are then tabled at the conference, so all bidders receive the same information simultaneously for consistency and fairness, avoiding confusion arising from different or conflicting answers. Often supplementary questions raised at the meeting are answered in writing by the client later and sent to all participants. Again, you should expect this data to form part of the specification.

The suppliers' objectives

You should view the conference as an important chance to expand your bid information system and add to your bid plan and strategy. Look upon it as a game of poker; never reveal your hand or expose your intentions. Develop your tactics to elicit information without revealing anything of your own plan and see if you can call the bluff of the other players.

Start by being very circumspect with the questions that you ask, either in writing or in person. A knowledgeable and aware competitor knows your portfolio and pricing policy and may deduce aspects of your strategy from what you ask, so frame your questions such that they will not harm you if they know the answers. You may want to try out some alternatives on the client and gauge their reaction. Be careful not to give away any of your thinking here; you could test their reaction to what you think your competitors will be bidding.

Study your competition to identify who is there and who is missing. On an international bid this may be more difficult than it seems at first sight as they may be represented by local agents. You should involve your own local contacts who will, if they are good, have a first-hand knowledge of these people. Plan the event well so you have a clear idea of what you want from it. It is wise to brief local agents on your plan so that you have a consistent approach and always debrief them afterwards; your local man may have noted something important which you missed.

Negotiation meetings

Negotiation is a skill which every bid manager should practice. To be successful you will probably negotiate with your client throughout the bid cycle. Negotiation is frequently considered to centre on price or delivery schedules, performance or quality, but there are many other factors which are included. You will probably begin early in the bid, before the invitation is made, by trading what you can offer against what the client needs, or by translating the client's wishes into realistic goals through negotiation. The intention at this stage is to get an order or be invited to bid. At the same time, you will be justifying to the client your price and technical position and getting them to bias the final specification in your favour. Assuming you cannot get a single action, the important aspect of this negotiation is to position yourself for benefits later. You are unlikely to reach a firm agreement with the client at this stage but both of you will be better informed and ground rules established. Once you have submitted your offer you may move onto post-tender or post-contract negotiation. These specific aspects of bidding are covered elsewhere.

There is a time and a place for different negotiating stances and you should apply the appropriate technique to the right position. A fundamental rule in winning consistently is to negotiate deals where both you and the client win. This is not usually achieved through adopting an aggressive attitude, but more frequently by taking a conciliatory viewpoint; listening to your client and interpreting their stated, implied and hidden motives.

When you are negotiating a deal for a complex system, try to break it down into discrete and discernible elements. The consolidated values that you established when submitting your bid now need to be studied in detail so that you know the worth to the client of each component. You will need to know what you can give away and what you must retain, so go into any negotiation with an end position already firmly fixed in your mind. Bid negotiations often founder because of too much aggression and confrontation and not enough listening and conciliation. Concentrate on the key issues. Contract negotiations can become horribly messy if every clause, warranty, penalty and aspect of phraseology is turgidly debated. Remember that a good contract is one that is put away in a filing cabinet and never needed again.

SUMMARY

The most important aspect of bid management is your relationship with the client.

- *Clients buy through competitive tendering to get the best solution at the best value for money. Using tendering they can get an objective industry assessment of prices for non-standard or high-volume products and services.*

- *Tendering can bring disadvantages to the client such as high cost and increased management involvement in producing detailed specifications, or difficulty in making accurate assessments when presenting a wider and less-detailed requirement.*

- *The other disadvantages to your client of inviting bids include ensuring that the lowest price is feasible and sustainable, coping with potential delays brought about by the bid process, reconciling past performance with bid price and ensuring that the right suppliers bid.*

- *You must try to understand the client motives: know their business, their commercial and fiscal position, their policy on buying, and their business concerns. Use this knowledge to tailor your solution to their needs.*

- *Influence the client by building solid relationships at various levels in their organisation. Managed partnerships often bring more benefits to both parties than selling by traditional customer-supplier relationships, so try to develop close ties.*

- *Take every opportunity to enhance your position with the client. Start as early as you can and find a supporter within the company who can champion your cause. Find out who makes the decisions and influence the people who can influence decision makers.*

7

PREPARING THE BID TEAM

The phases of the bid cycle which put most strain upon the resources of bidders are the phase immediately leading up to receiving the invitation to bid and the phase from reception of the invitation through to bid submission. The effort required ramps up as the deadline closes in, as illustrated in Fig. 7.1. Careful planning of the expected activity before these phases start is essential in allowing you to cope with these pressures.

This chapter deals with those tasks that anticipate the arrival of the bid invitation, prepare you for it and lead towards constructing a cohesive and persuasive proposal that encapsulates all your bid strategy and hard work. In particular, it focuses on the organisational aspects over the strategic ones, by looking at the people needed to make a winning bid and how

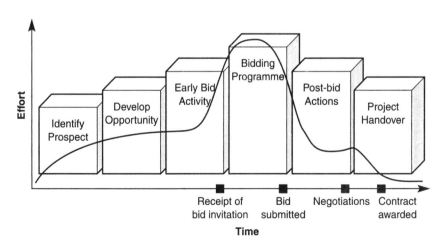

Fig. 7.1 Change of effort during bid cycle

they are most effectively organised and controlled. The members of the actual bid team are perhaps the most important in this process, but you also need to look at partners, suppliers, and collaborators who come together to form the assignment team when carrying out the project.

CONSTITUENTS OF A WINNING TEAM

Your client is not just buying your company's products or services but also the people that make the products or deliver the service. In asking them to accept your bid you are also asking them to admit the people behind it; you, your bid team, your associates and the assignment team who undertake the work in the contract. When applying your focus to the bid, you are selecting the prospect as one you want to win and doing everything necessary to succeed. You therefore have to consider the people you need to bid and to carry out the project. Earlier chapters analysed in some detail the first part, the reason you bid and your objectives for each prospect. You now need to study the structure of the bid team that you will need later. Once you have made the preliminary decision to go with the prospect onto the next stage of the bid cycle, this team will put your bid strategy into practice. Before reviewing the specific requirements for a bid team, it is useful to have a general understanding of team work and what you should be trying to achieve by it.

The essence of successful team work is the transformation of a group of individuals, with their own objectives, motives and purposes into a unit sharing common goals. This becomes even more difficult in the bid environment because of the need to bring together a broad range of skills, talents and personalities, often for a short period and often under tight time constraints. Bids require intensive effort over short periods, with full commitment. Building an efficient team within this framework which gets results, is a challenge that requires a structured approach to leadership.

The bid manager usually assumes the mantle of leadership within the team, taking on the responsibility to effect changes. To take a diverse group of individual managers, each with their own reporting structure, individual motivations, quirks and foibles and build a bid team that has a common objective, works in harmony and achieves results is not easy and requires a great deal of skill and resourcefulness.

The essence of team work

There are some basic distinctions between working as a team and operating as a group of individuals. Individuals work independently, often at
cross-purposes with other group members, while team members understand that they are interdependent, best able to achieve their personal
and team goals by supporting each other. An independent focus is usually the result of lack of involvement in planning the team objectives.
You can overcome this and instil a sense of ownership of the job and
commitment to the team, by getting all members to help in establishing
the goals. You will not achieve this by simply telling people what to do
or by discouraging suggestions; allow each member to contribute to the
team's success by applying their own skills to meet mutually agreed purposes. By encouraging participation much of the distrust in the motives
of others, brought on by failing to understand their roles and responsibilities, is eliminated and members begin to have confidence in each
other and begin to exchange ideas and opinions.

Clear objectives

The first stage in team building is to set the objectives that you want to
achieve. Although it is easy to set generalised objectives, these have little
value in providing clear motivation to the team members. Avoid non-
specific goals such as winning the contract, getting the right resources
for the job and gaining full commitment from each individual. These are
often meaningless. Your objectives should specify exactly what it is you
are planning to do and be constructed in such a way that you can measure success or failure. Setting goals that cannot be achieved is a sure
recipe for demotivation, so concentrate on making them realistic. And
do not allow them to be open-ended; you are working under time constraints and therefore you need to set deadlines for what you need to do.

Clear objectives serve to maintain commitment and focus, so do not
set targets without giving the team the opportunity to discuss ways in
which it can meet them. Imposed objectives with no thought as to
their consequences will result in loss of commitment from the team.
Involve the team in the decision making, the setting of realistic objectives and targets, and of the standards you wish to meet. Similarly, the
team should evaluate its own performance. The bid manager should
express organisational needs and act as a facilitator and enabler in
these processes.

Guidance and organisation

To carry out the objectives, your bid team will need clear guidance on why they have been brought together, what is expected of them, what will be the results of their actions, and who else is involved. You will need to advise them on the direction that the bid is taking and how they are to co-ordinate the activity needed to complete it successfully. This needs effective bid planning and some examples of this are given later. With a plan in place, good organisational skills are essential to ensure that all the bid resources, people, finance, technology, production facilities, and delivery mechanisms are well co-ordinated. Lack of organisation will result in the team becoming fragmented and undisciplined and will reduce its effectiveness.

As you saw in Chapter 3, a valuable aid in organising the bid is the bid management procedure. Devise this so that you establish a common organisational structure that helps you use your resources to their best effect. Scheduling of the bid will enable you to review progress and will ensure that actions are completed on time. Document controls will see that reports are circulated and distributed correctly, and that important documents are not mislaid but recorded and filed according to the document control system. Communication and reactions between and within the team should be allowed to flow freely so that everyone knows what is going on.

Provide encouragement

Motivating people is not difficult when things are going smoothly and the team is working well together; the team will work as a unit providing it shares a common desire to meet the bid objectives. However, people are individuals, each with different reasons for doing what they do. What sustains motivation is often a very personal thing requiring careful treatment. When enthusiasm begins to wane or a team member is apparently losing interest, you have to seek ways to continue motivating them. Recognise the efforts made by each individual and give praise where it is due.

As the team leader, the bid manager must keep in mind the objectives and keep the team focused on meeting them. As the bid develops, rapid and constant changes can easily divert the team from the original bid objectives. You must control the situation and restore equilibrium so that the team keeps its sights fixed firmly on the reasons that brought them together. Regular bid reviews can serve to maintain this focus as will a solid and timely organisational structure.

Select the right people for the job

Finding the right person for a particular role in the bid team is crucial and can decide the success or failure of the team. If you get good people in the right position they will be an asset, the wrong person in the wrong position becomes a liability and a disruptive component within the team. You must make the selection you feel is right for the task in hand. Involve each individual in any area where they can effectively contribute to make the best use of the resources you have.

Often the selection process is outside your control; either there is no choice or someone else makes it. Your task is easier if you are happy with the selection. If you are uncertain, try to anticipate what difficulties could occur and produce a team plan that mitigates them thereby preventing any problem area becoming serious. You should try to establish control systems that will help you in this. For example, if someone is unreliable, build in back-up options to take effect if they should fail to deliver what you expect, or if they agitate others in the team, manage meetings and contacts to reduce the tension. If you cannot plan around or control the difficulty, or severe conflict threatens to disrupt the team, then you must look to remove or replace the disruptive elements.

Continual team development

Just as the bid is dynamic and changes during the bid cycle, so the bid team has to be flexible and responsive to events. There is frequently a need on complex bids with perhaps an innovative product or bid strategy to enhance the team or develop and train people while the bid continues. It is likely that you will often identify problems or opportunities beyond the skills of the existing team members. Try to be alert to any deficiencies so that you can pick them out early; it may be a matter simply of bringing in personnel with the necessary skills or perhaps providing additional technical training on a new product, or maybe cultural and management training to allow greater understanding of a new territory which needs to be understood better. Where there is a deficiency in the team, deal with it in the most effective way to meet your objectives. It is valuable to undertake regular reviews during the bid to see if there are any areas which need additional development. In these reviews, you should aim to identify which team members will gain most from the training and can make the best use of it.

Besides developing the individuals within the team, there may be a need to take the whole team through training to encourage them to pull together. Team-working skills can be learnt in the same way as any other business practice and for major opportunities, where success is critical, they can make or break the bid. If it is justifiable, consider a training course for the team. These can range from outward-bound courses, literally building bridges together, to psychometric instruments such as questionnaires, personal discussions and team exercises which can be used to get people to communicate with each other. Some people believe that a collectivist approach to bidding, where the team dynamic is everything, can cause problems if one team member has to leave. For this reason, most successful bid teams rely upon the individuals having a degree of independence within their own area, but functioning well with others. Moreover, individual training usually brings benefits to the workings of the team as a whole. In all things, you have to decide what is appropriate. A good team has its own sense of camaraderie; help this to develop by spending time together outside the workplace.

Deal rapidly with problems

There will be many occasions during the bid process when problems spring up requiring rapid solution. The process of problem solving must be one that is as simple as the need to complete the job. There are many methodologies used in solving problems, from techniques where you visualise yourselves wearing different coloured hats, to detailed analytical methods. Use whichever approach you feel yields the best results. A simple, structured technique will usually suffice: express the problem in terms that the team understands, get as many facts and opinions from them as you can and then restate the problem to see if it remains the same or has changed. As a team try to find every possible solution, then assess each in turn, to establish the pros and cons of every alternative. From the results of the assessment make a decision on which solution you are going to try and then carry it out. Evaluate the results and reiterate the process if the problem persists.

You will probably have your own methods of solving problems, but bear in mind that time is tight in a bid and you generally need rapid answers. Simple processes often work purely by giving a structure to the task, preventing you latching on to the first offering and thereby missing a better one. You should encourage the bid team to participate fully in the process, as often the solution reached in assembly is more effective than that provided by an individual.

Problems of team conflict

Perhaps the biggest problem you will face is not from outside but arises from conflict within the bid team itself. It is almost certain that it will occur in most bid teams at some stage and can cause negative or positive results depending on the circumstances and the people involved. You have to be sensitive to the situation, to prevent things getting out of control and to encourage a positive outcome. Positive benefits can result from conflict when it causes you to explore new ideas or tests your understanding of the situation. Often by challenging fixed beliefs, you give creativity a chance to flourish. This can stimulate people to greater use of their imagination and may present you with a wider choice of options.

Conflict can and often does work against you, making communication difficult and causing support and trust to evaporate, even leading to open hostility in the team. If you allow conflict to create fissions then it may make completing the bid and the project extremely difficult. It is far better to resolve the conflict as early as you can, either by confronting the people concerned or bypassing the issue at stake. Try to seek agreement on the issue of conflict by inviting the conflicting parties to co-operate in seeking a solution and preventing further disruption. Alternatively, look for a compromise or another mutually acceptable settlement. Whichever way you decide to deal with it, conflict is a problem you must solve, not ignore.

Team definition method

Bid team building is a business process and should be treated as such within your procedures. It is helpful to have a system or model to work from. This assists you to present a common view of the team, get management to release staff for the bid and define the roles and responsibilities that each team member will have.

The team definition model described in Fig. 7.2 shows how such a method operates. This can be integrated into your bid process. In this system there are three levels of structures; the high level structures provide a broad definition, stating strategy and objectives. In this instance this is your bid plan. Below this is the general structure level which describes the building blocks of the function. These are the terms of reference of the teams. Detailed level structures contain precise tasks, instructions and responsibilities; this is the team member role definition.

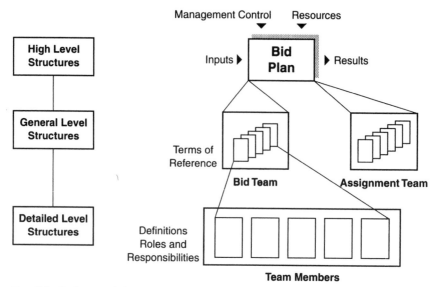

Fig. 7.2 Bid team definition model

Each of these structures has four variables that dictate the way the function is carried out. The first variable is the resource assigned to the function: the person or team who will actually do the work. Then there are the inputs into the process, which will vary with the type of bid, client, competition and so on. The results of the process will always be different and it is necessary to generate progress information at each level: peer, higher and lower. Finally, management controls apply the rules on how the tasks will be done. Although it may seem like a complex method, in reality it is easy to use once the initial system has been set up. Using a model like this helps to ensure that there are no gaps in the team, and generally speeds and facilitates your management of the bid.

THE BID TEAM NUCLEUS

Now you have looked at the essence of team work you need to bring together the right people in the right place to work in unison. Preparing a winning bid requires contributions from many people, and the scope and structure of these contributions is critical. The terminology and titles you use for these people in your own company may be different from those here, but the functions are usually the same. Each of your bids will vary and you should treat them individually, so you might not always use the same people or size of team.

There are two distinct but overlapping teams in any bid. These are the bid team and the assignment team. You cannot construct a successful bid in isolation. The bid team must intimately involve the delivery or supply mechanisms in your company, the design and production facilities, the project team and other internal departments and external companies who will be associated with the venture if your bid is successful.

Roles and responsibilities

In most bids, the bid team will prepare the proposal. Typically, for a large, complex or high-value bid, the team consists of several individuals who are co-ordinated by the bid manager, each bringing with them their specialist knowledge. On small bids one person may play several roles. The diagram in Fig. 7.3 shows the typical roles and functions carried out by the team. For all but the simplest bids, you should expect the team to comprise people able to carry out these roles. The make-up of this bid team typifies most situations and incorporates the key functions. Clearly, you can only determine the precise fabric of any team by assessing the

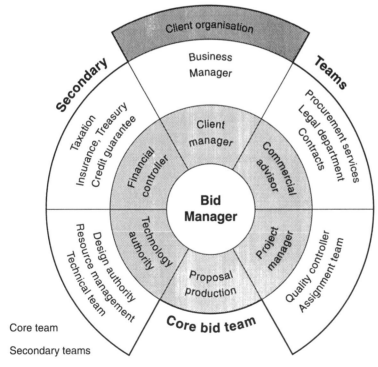

Core team

Secondary teams

Fig. 7.3 Typical bid team

requirement and the resources available. Your decision will therefore be influenced strongly by the opportunity itself, technical complexity and value. The team usually consists of a core of essential individuals who will either manage, or liaise with, the secondary teams whose contributions will be needed at various times during the bid.

In the core team, you should expect to include someone who knows the client well. If you have followed the earlier guidelines on influencing the client, you will by now have an intimate understanding of them. Larger clients or your key accounts may well have an account or client manager assigned and, if possible, you should bring them into your team as well. For overseas bids you may need to include a territorial or regional manager or local agent.

Functional expertise will be needed, so your team should contain a technical specialist with a firm understanding of the technology you are planning to bid. They should also be capable of managing a technical team. Someone with financial knowledge is valuable in calculating bid prices, preparing the project cash-flow and refining the finance packages. They may also act to collect and negotiate the costs with external suppliers and in-house departments. A commercial or legal manager may be necessary to handle the contract. Try to get someone who recognises practical and real solutions and who can use the commercial proposal to help you win. The preparation of the proposal can be a mammoth task so you should include someone to put the bid together, handle the organisational detail and manage the paperwork. Always try to get on board the project manager who has been designated to carry the project through when you have won it. Their involvement is critical in ensuring the bid is profitable. Depending on the complexity of the bid, you may also want functional experts in quality management, installation, design, or procurement.

Defining who will do what can often be a problem and controlling this is the bid manager's responsibility. Under the kind of tight time constraints that you will encounter during the bid, you may overlook some tasks, so it is best to define beforehand the broad areas of responsibility and identify who will be carrying out what. It is impossible here to define precise role models for every bid team. However, the functions that you need to have carried out are often very similar, irrespective of the type of bid, or the company bidding. To illustrate these functions, a typical team bidding for a complex and valuable opportunity would consist of the following people.

Bid manager

The bid manager has responsibility for planning, preparing and managing the production of a high-quality proposal. They have to ensure that it meets the technical and commercial needs of the client while fulfilling the profit and strategic needs of your company. The bid manager is the management focus of the bid and leads the bid effort by co-ordinating the roles, responsibilities and contributions of all of the bid team's members.

In an ideal world, the bid manager will be a dedicated manager with full bid responsibility and authority, commercial knowledge, a broad outlook and a strong understanding of the business. If the size and value of the opportunity justify it, they could be working on the bid full time and giving total commitment to the opportunity. On the other hand, they could be working on several smaller bids simultaneously.

In many companies this function will come from within sales and marketing, or business or technical development, whichever has general responsibility for this activity. There are no fixed rules. However, to make sure no business opportunities or sales efforts are neglected it is advantageous that the bid manager is not the business or client manager. There are drawbacks in making the team leader someone with responsibility for a particular function, such as sales, since their interest and their judgement will be naturally biased towards their own function. Also, they may not have the time available to manage the bid effectively.

The bid manager will continually assess the opportunity and advise the business manager on all aspects of and all the elements that will be included in the bid, such as costs, pricing, resources, strategy and application. Fig. 7.4 indicates the definition model for the bid manager, showing the major tasks that they should expect to handle. Their principal role is to co-ordinate all activity associated with the bid, finding solutions to any deficiencies that the process throws out. They must ensure that the tender response is balanced between technical excellence and commercial viability, and directed at the main objective of winning the contract and incorporating all the winning factors in the bid strategy.

Bid managers often have the unenviable duty of keeping senior management informed of progress and managing the bid upwards should problems arise. The corollary to this is they also have to keep senior management from involving themselves in details of the project that may not concern them. They must also present the proposal to management and obtain all the necessary approvals before the tender goes out.

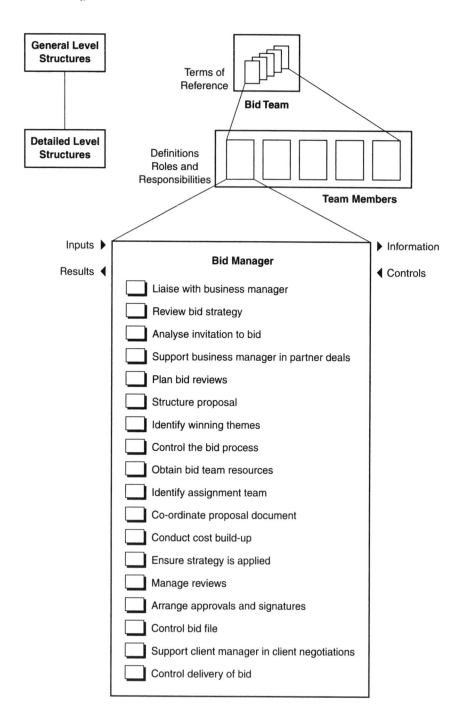

Fig. 7.4 Bid manager's task definition

Business manager

The business managers will generally come from your operational departments with the responsibility for line management and profit or loss on contracts arising from the bid. They will work closely with the bid manager for specific opportunities, but they also need a broader business view. This is because they are probably responsible for putting into effect corporate policy which has been designed to develop new business areas.

In many organisations they take the lead in assessing the prospect, advising on whether to bid and requesting the appointment of key positions such as the bid manager. They will often develop an outline strategy designed to win the bid and you should expect them to summarise this within the bid manager's terms of reference. Carrying out this strategy and ensuring its inclusion in the bid is important. The bid manager usually refines and communicates the strategy to all members of the bid team, especially the authors of each section.

Client manager

Many companies have embraced the idea of account or client management replacing the traditional salesperson. This allies closely to the development of managed partnerships between the client and the supplier. In this definition, the client manager will be the person who has the most intimate personal knowledge of the way your client's business runs. Frequently, this is also the bid manger, although it could still be a sales manager for smaller accounts or the business manager or another regional or general manager. The client manager will usually be responsible for dealing with the client, negotiating the contract and winning the business. This is a critical function often overlooked unless a designated client manager is in place, so find out who is the most appropriate person to take this responsibility.

The client manager establishes and builds relationships with the people in the client organisation who make the decision on the bid with the aim to influence them towards your offer through lobbying, presentations, meetings and provision of general support. Throughout the bid process, the client manager will maintain these contacts, informing the bid team of any changes or developments. They will monitor the progress of the bid when received by the client and deal with problems, negotiations or other post-submission activities.

Before the invitation to bid the client manager would expect to have a thorough understanding of the needs of the client and of the opportunity, stated, implied and hidden. They will gain information on the position of your company and that of your competition and understand the basis upon which the client will be making their decision. Such information is invaluable in preparing the bid and deciding the most effective sales strategy.

Commercial advisor

You will normally need one or more persons to deal with the commercial, contractual and legal aspects of the bid. The commercial advisor will provide recommendations and advise on how to respond to the terms and conditions contained within the invitation to bid. They should be aware of the standard responses required by you and any variations agreed on previous bids with the client. A commercial proposal is usual within the bid and you would expect them to contribute much of the necessary detail. In dealing directly with the client, they should provide support to the business manager in negotiations and the bid manager on commercial matters. Fig. 7.5 lists some of their main tasks.

Finance manager

Usually this would be someone with a good accounting or finance background in practical business situations, such as a management or financial accountant, or other suitably experienced person. A good idea is to involve someone who manages the finance of your successful contracts. Because they will be responsible for co-ordinating and advising on the financial issues relating to the project, they will be interested in endorsing the bid effort. Working under guidance from the bid manager, the finance manager will liaise on all aspects of the financing, costing and pricing of the bid. They will also handle the accounting tasks such as raising bid and project codes when appropriate, dealing with tax issues, liaising with the banks or treasury department, arranging bid and performance bonds and ensuring compliance with exchange rate controls. Where auditing of financial figures is needed they can co-ordinate the activity with external auditors

The finance manager can be a neglected part of the bid team and yet can provide valuable support to the bid manager during the hectic final stages of the bid. Involve them as early as possible so that you can make best use of their contribution. Fig. 7.6 summarises some support tasks they would typically undertake.

Technology authority

You will require someone who has a thorough understanding of the technology you are bidding to provide. This could be a designer,

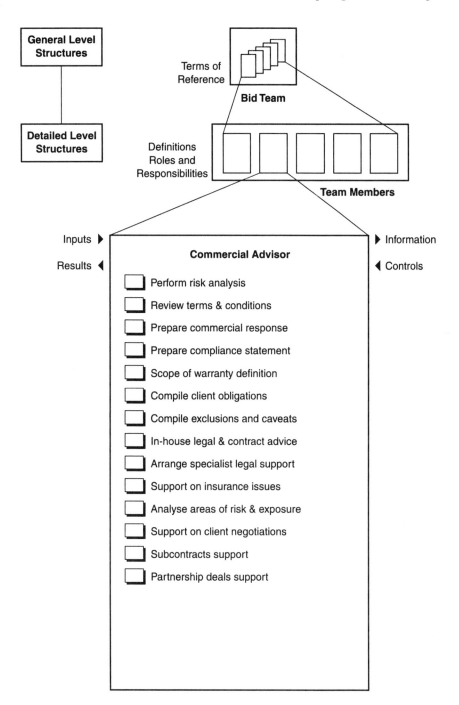

Fig. 7.5 Commercial advisor's task definition

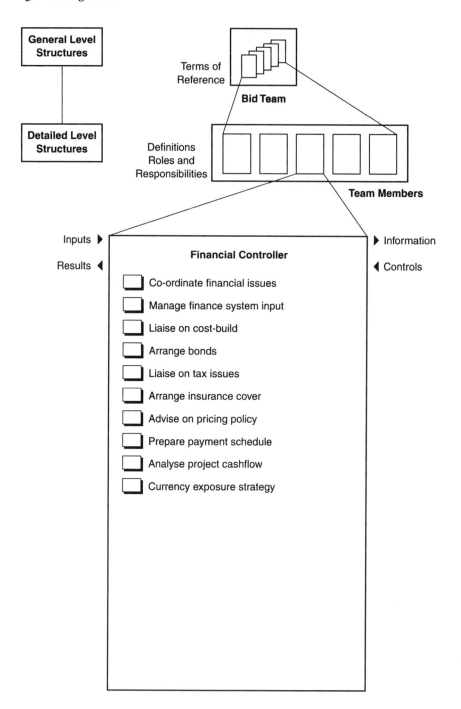

Fig. 7.6 Financial controller's task definition

engineer, or production manager, able to interpret the client's technical specification, translating it in terms of your available products or services, or into design or development parameters. The technology authority co-ordinates specialised technical resources from both within your company and other business units, or outside consultants and contractors. This could also be the bid manager on smaller bids or a specialist from another department within your business unit. Some typical tasks are contained in Fig. 7.7.

An important consideration here is to select someone who is not technologically blinkered, believing only in the product for its own sake. You need someone who recognises that the application of systems and scientific methods is only superior when it brings benefits to the client, someone who takes a pragmatic view on meeting the client's needs and delivering those benefits.

Project manager

Wherever possible include in the team the project manager designated to control the assignment when the bid is successful. Their involvement during the bidding phase will ensure the project performs to expectations of delivery, budget and profitability when you win the contract. They will also have the experience to identify any unrealistic or high-risk areas inherent in carrying it out. Sometimes the project manager is also the project engineer, project planner or even the bid manager. Tasks associated with this function are listed in Fig. 7.8.

Because of their experience you may also find they can provide support with the cost estimates for the bid. They can work with the bid and business managers to decide the final bid price based upon the products, services or resources required, grading of personnel and numbers, charge out rates and other cost factors. As they may have direct knowledge of similar working projects they can often give valuable support in ordering the costs and splitting profit and overheads. Similarly, they can provide valuable advice and liaison on currency, tax, insurance and internal accounting policy and procedures. The project manager usually liaises closely with the finance manager or management accountant on bid and project finances, invoicing, receipts and payment terms.

Proposal manager

Proposal preparation and production can be major tasks in their own right. All your efforts in building relations, preparing strategy and positioning yourself to win the bid can come to naught if the proposal is

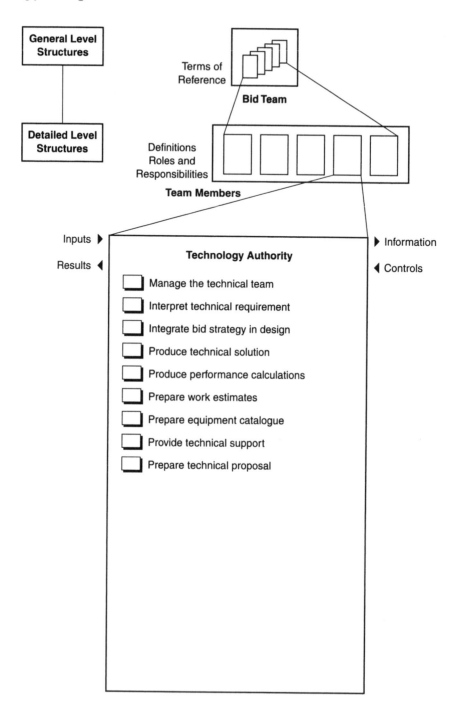

Fig. 7.7 Technology authority's task definition

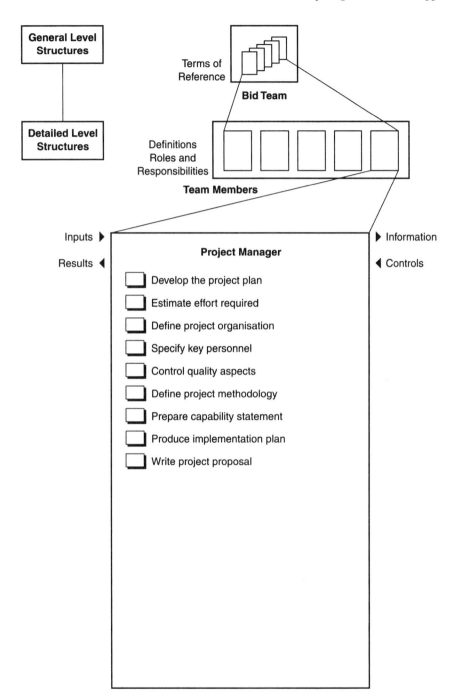

Fig. 7.8 Project manager's task definition

inadequate. So it is worthwhile ensuring that you have someone dedicated to the task. The proposal manager may also have responsibility for the document control system. They will typically have to prepare the bid and all supporting documents, producing standard documents and text to the correct issue and format. During the bid they will co-ordinate the authors' written material to the agreed structure and layout under direction from the bid manager. For smaller bids these tasks again may be assigned to the bid manager.

Other responsibilities will include the preparation of document layout, diagrams, graphics, covers and binders, printing, copying and assembly of documents to the client's requirements. They will prepare and maintain standard guidance notes for authors giving details of abbreviations and spelling in advance. Preliminary editing of received text and proof-reading is carried out as material is received. On completion of the proposal they will arrange packaging and delivery of the required number of copies to the client.

Other team members

Depending upon the scope and size of the bid, the team may incorporate other functions and tasks. These may include procurement, treasury, insurance, taxation, human resources, training and technical specialists. To keep the bid team to a manageable size the bid manager should normally assign responsibility for these additional persons to an existing team member.

Senior management role

The role of senior management is to support the bid team, allocate and assign resources as needed and undertake the review and authorisation of the bid. The senior management view is based upon what is best for the business and the bid review process is critical here. Ensure that senior managers are committed to the bid and keep them informed of purpose and progress. Use them to support the bid itself, by presenting the offer or selling your company to the client in other ways.

Getting an understanding of the commitment in money, time and resource is the critical purpose of the senior management review. For the purposes of gaining concurrence to the bid, it is advisable to obtain senior management authorisation at two stages. First, authority to prepare the bid itself, particularly if the bid cost or the risk is likely to be high. Secondly, authority to submit the bid to the client, bearing in mind the contractual commitments you are undertaking when responding to an invitation to tender. Senior management authorisation is usually part of your company bid procedures and these would state where and at what financial level you need approval.

Organising the bid team resource

By knowing the necessary tasks and who are the best people to carry them out you are better positioned to take the next step in preparing to bid. The subsequent and more difficult stages are getting commitment from those people and ensuring that they are there when needed. Undertaking a detailed study of the invitation will identify all the necessary tasks and point you towards the people you will need in the team to carry them out.

Many bids will require specialised support at certain critical stages and you should know from where you can get this support when needed. Typically, you will request resources on a bid from the managers responsible for the departments concerned. This enables more effective scheduling of people's time during periods of high demand. In the above example, for instance, the business manager will request the services of a bid manager and the bid manager requests services from the bid team. Functional leaders within the bid team may request services from other specialised support areas. Using a standard request for services simplifies organising premium resources.

Choosing the right people for the bid team is important and deciding what services you need in order to be able to complete your bid is a necessary part of that process. The matrix in Fig. 7.9 provides you with some broad selection criteria that you can use to make an initial assessment. Once you have your team members identified, you can go on to decide when and how you will organise their efforts.

THE ASSIGNMENT TEAM

You have seen that the bid requires two teams to be assembled, the bid team who will prepare the proposal and the assignment team who will carry it out. Some personnel will be common to both teams. The assignment team can be considered in two parts, those people directly in the employ of your company appointed to the project, and the external companies, advisors, contractors or collaborators whom you have selected to work with.

Selection Categories	Bid Team Resources										
	Financial services	Planning & research	Treasury	Taxation	Insurance	Procurement	Human resources	Legal	Travel service	Other
Project type										
Value										
Legal										
Commercial										
Strategic										
Technical										
Management										
Resourcing										
Location										
Other										

Fig. 7.9 Part of a typical bid team selection matrix
(Enter the selection criteria relevant to your company into each cell of the matrix)

The internal team

Most works or service assignments commit people to working with the client for the duration of the contract. Even supply contracts sometimes have dedicated personnel who will liaise on quality, order processing and delivery. In many projects the quality of the people you provide is equal to or of greater importance than the actual product or service. In these bids the client may well ask for specific information on the people who will be involved, making the calibre of these people a factor in awarding the contract. This would be particularly relevant in, say, a professional consultancy assignment where the experience and expertise of the individual are all that the client is buying. In these assignments the bid manager will need to assemble accurate and up to date curricula vitae on personnel they wish to use.

The client's invitation will usually inform you of whether you need to guarantee specific personnel for the assignment team. When selecting assignment personnel, you should ensure that they are available and suitable for the project. Some bids, such as those for World Bank projects, ask for employment and experience histories in a standard format and it may help if you adopt a similar model for all projects. Use this format as the basis of the information you need to be able to assess and select candidates after finding out what their availability is. Once you have included someone in the bid, keep them informed of progress and ask them to alert you quickly to any changes in their own circumstances that could affect their inclusion.

Support services agreement

The bid manager requires commitment from the internal team, their senior management and support services. The services carried out by the business units comprising the internal team may be *ad hoc* but are frequently essential to the success of the bid. Too often, verbal agreements made before the bid invitation arrives are forgotten or disregarded when the time comes to release the people concerned. Other, higher priority projects come along and snap up the people you had earmarked. So it is useful to get written commitment and issue regular reminders as the bid progresses.

You cannot put into place a contract between parts of the same company, so the bid manager must clearly define the obligations and project responsibilities of the business units and gain their commitment. Put in place support services agreements or memoranda of understanding, clearly stating the basis upon which they will provide their support. This will normally include the areas shown in Fig. 7.10 and should be authorised at an appropriate level within your own department and the targeted business unit.

The external team

You will frequently need to consider collaborators for your bids. You may find the cost of bidding is too high or the risks too great for you to tender alone. You may need resources or technical skills that are not available in your organisation. Furthermore, you may need to improve your chances of winning by taking on board a partner your client likes or who can provide local content that your bid needs. This is the stage where you must consider, if you have not already done so, details about the selection of suppliers, partners and subcontractors.

Consider carefully what is involved in making that selection. You may need to go through a sometimes lengthy, formal process. In many bids you can gain an advantage by using local suppliers, even if you do not need them on technical grounds. You may need to provide additional technical expertise to comply with the client's requirements, and selection of the right company can strengthen your position and enhance your chances of success.

As buyers become increasingly sophisticated they too are recognising that they cannot always meet their needs from one source. Handling multiple contracts, some large others small, can be time consuming and inefficient. The buyer frequently faces a dilemma, to commit the management effort in administering many individual contracts or to seek a single supplier, consortium or prime contractor who will take on that responsibility for them. Another factor in the equation is the buyer's need to obtain competitive bids from a wide range of suppliers to ensure they are getting the best choice. To bid collaboratively therefore requires careful analysis not just of your own situation but of the positive or negative effects on your client.

Assess your client's reaction

The first thing to consider before embarking on a collaboration of any kind is how your client will react to such an arrangement. They may have reasons for not wishing to entertain team ventures. Consortia can conjure up the image of the group manipulating the opportunity to deny

Synopsis of the project
☐ Project overview
☐ Reimbursement arrangements
☐ Tax situation
☐ Confidentiality
☐ Insurance and indemnities
☐ Duration of the agreement

Responsibilities
☐ Lead in client negotiations
☐ Support to the bid
☐ Definition of responsibilities
☐ Your unit responsibility
☐ Other unit responsibility
☐ Control of personnel

Work arrangements
☐ Analysis of work required
☐ Availability of resources
☐ Activity schedule

Scope of Services
☐ Pre-contractual services
☐ Post-contractual services

Request for services procedures
☐ Formal enquiry from you
☐ Response by business unit

Cost basis
☐ Schedule of rates
☐ Overhead recovery basis

Fig. 7.10 Typical support services agreement

the client a wider choice in supplier selection. Such perceptions are less entrenched these days with more openness and fairness in competition being recognised. Conversely some clients will encourage team participation in the bid and the contract. The UK government, in some sectors, openly encourages bids from consortia as they believe they will obtain a better result for the money.

It is wise to attempt to find out not only your client's response to a team bid but also their reaction to the individual team members. If your client has had a bad experience with one of your potential collaborators it may adversely affect their assessment of the whole bid. If they suggest that they favour the products of a certain supplier over another, then ignore that supplier at your peril. Keeping close to your client during these stages is essential, you must listen not only to what they are openly telling you, but read between the lines to interpret what they are not revealing.

Selecting a subcontractor

There are some basic appraisals you need to make before going ahead with any supplier. It is important that you get it right now, before the bid is won, as mistakes afterwards will be very costly. Changing once the contract is in place may not be possible without much effort and expense. For your regular suppliers you will probably have a vendor rating system in place, which checks their quality of supply, pricing policy, delivery lines, operational efficiency and administration. Thus you should be generally aware of how good your current providers are.

If you need a new subcontractor you have to be assured that they have the resources to carry out the tasks that you want them to perform, that they will stay around to perform them, that they are willing to do it and that you can afford them. Concentrate in the following areas.

Technical ability

Can they actually do what you want them to do? Look at their production set-up, methods and processes. See if they are following established methodologies, compliant with recognised quality systems. Carry out a site evaluation to see how they perform and visit their other clients to check that they do a good job. This could incorporate a quality assessment.

Establish what their current work load is. If it is high, this could indicate a healthy position with a full order book, or it could show that they are understaffed. It will be valuable if you can check their order book and confirm their other commitments over the contract period. See if they have enough staff to carry out the additional tasks you will be imposing, without cutting any corners or reducing the quality of their efforts. Do not immediately discount them if they appear to be working under capacity. This can also be to your advantage. A hungry supplier can often give you a very competitive price for the work, but you have to be certain of their financial stability before making any commitment.

Financial status

You need a stable supplier to carry out the work during the contract and possibly to provide ongoing support once the contract has been completed. You will probably need to have a credit check done on them and there are many companies who can provide you with such a report. You can check their reports, accounts and their order book to see if they are profitable, but you will need also to see if they have had any recent downturns that could affect their long-term prospects.

Make sure that they have enough capital to fund the project and will not go into liquidation before they can deliver. Again, do not be immediately put off if their prospects appear uncertain. The contract that you are trying to win may be all they need to turn the business around and you may therefore get a good price for the work. You will need to take full precautions by protecting any advance payments that you make to them or by staging payments over the project. Remember that on any bid it is always worthwhile having a second source lined up which you can turn to in an emergency.

Do they want it?

Do they really want the job and do they fully understand what it is you are asking them to do? Some aspects of this question will have been answered by going through the exercises above. You will probably need to fully document and specify what it is you want and evaluate the responses from any number of potential suppliers, through selective or competitive tendering. Avoid or clarify any ambiguities so that everyone is clear. If they want to do the work, they will price it accordingly and provide you with a competent and clear response. Avoid the handwritten or verbal offer, if they cannot be bothered to have their response typed they probably either do not want it or are too busy to deal with it.

See if there is any synergy between your two companies. Do you see things the same way? Do you share common goals? Although not essential, it will be easier for you to work with someone you can get along with and who shares the same corporate ethos and policy.

Using an agent

Agents can fulfil an important function in your bid by providing you with representation in areas where you have no direct presence. You will find a good agent invaluable for overseas bids in countries where you are trying to develop an opening without committing large resources in establishing corporate propinquity. Choosing the right agent can be difficult and time consuming, but getting a good one is usually critical, so give yourself the freedom to consider the options carefully.

Agents work on a variety of bases, either as your distributor or importer, on a sales commission or on a fee basis. Their degree of commitment and involvement in the bid, has to be defined in your agency agreement. Your agency agreement will be contractually binding, so you should approach it as you would any other contract that places commitment upon your company. Make sure that you include details of the services to be provided or represented, the basis of the fees to be paid and the areas to be covered. Set a date when the agreement commences. Include a description of their rights and level of authority while acting for you and define precisely who will be responsible for selling your bid to the client and what methods they will use. To prevent misunderstanding, especially with agents whose native language is different from yours, pay particular attention to the term of the agreement, the precise definition of the nature of the services to be provided and the circumstances under which either party can end the agreement. Different countries often have differing legislation covering agents. For example, in Europe there is legislation protecting the rights of agents, such as the Commercial Agents Directive in the UK, which you must bear in mind during your discussions. You must also be careful not to contravene any rules on restrictive trading practices and competition laws whilst giving exclusive rights.

As with any partner, when selecting your agent make sure that they can do what you expect them to do, and in an effective and efficient way. Run through the same checks as you would for a subcontractor. Assure yourself that they empathise with what the client is trying to achieve and can deal with any problems that they might raise. Have a meeting with them and double-check their facilities in person. If you need assistance in making contact with suitable agents, try the services of the local government representatives, your commercial attaché or chambers of commerce. Always make sure however, that the agent is acceptable to the client.

Consortia bids

The costs of bidding for complex projects, particularly in the government sector, have risen inexorably over recent years. This has led to groups of suppliers coming together to bid in consortia to spread their costs. This has long been an option for large-scale programmes in the public sector but is becoming more widespread for smaller projects, often in the private sector.

There is no doubt that this approach can achieve dividends when the partners have a natural synergy, have a common commitment to the project and where they clearly define the relationship. There is inherent danger, however. Complex government bids, say in the defence or information technology sectors, may take many months or years to reach a conclusion. Recent evidence is that this is inevitable when market testing is a prerequisite. During this period individual corporate directions and fortunes may change or costs may rise too high leading to the withdrawal of a consortium member. This may well leave the other members stranded, requiring them to find another partner at a late stage or to abandon their bid. The repercussions are severe. The remaining members may have incurred very high bid costs that they now have no chance of recouping. They may have also declined to bid for other opportunities and lost potential gains elsewhere.

The risks in such a relationship can be high, so you should look closely at all the angles and weigh up all the possibilities before making a commitment. Make sure you go in with your eyes open. There are some clear commercial decisions you will need to make before going ahead. Always assess the risk involved and the potential profitability of the contract. Decide the liabilities of each party and make sure that all contractual obligations are clearly stated. Where the risks are high, you should consider formalising the contract between the consortium members. In this you should state the terms under which you will be bidding, the extent to which each partner is liable and who will carry the risks. You may also define at this stage the distribution of revenue from the project. You will normally base this upon the contribution that each partner makes to the bid and the risks that they are carrying. Small companies may be carrying a higher risk than their larger partners although contributing less to the bid costs.

Critical to a successful consortium bid is the working relationship between the parties. If you have to ask why a company is approaching you to work with them on a bid then look carefully at the motives. If there is no clear explanation of the need for the relationship, then go on with caution. It may be in the interest of one of your competitors to team up with you to prevent another stronger competitor grabbing you first. While you may make this relationship work during the bid, there is the danger that at some critical stage after the award of the contract old competitive instincts will emerge and cause a breakdown in the relationship.

When considering a consortium, arrange discussions with all potential partners. Take the opportunity to get to know the others and assess what each partner can provide. It is important to decide who you can work with and who you cannot. Aim to get as much information as you can early on, without giving away any of your strategy. It is always possible that a company you are discussing your bid with will also be approached by one of your competitors. If you have revealed too much of your game plan, you could be seriously disadvantaged if they join forces.

For the consortium to work it is necessary for you to be more open and frank in your dealings with your partners than you would otherwise be. Defining the contact relations and working practices within a code of conduct for the bid may serve you in developing and enhancing the relationship. Within the code you can define the principals involved and their roles and responsibilities. You can also define the information and work flows during the bid, including who manages and controls what. It is a good idea to include a senior management reporting structure. Keeping senior management informed is critical. If the relationship does begin to turn sour then senior management can step in, bringing a degree of objectivity that may be lacking in the principals because they are too closely involved.

The risks in a partnership

When you are considering establishing a collaborative bid, you will have two choices of approach. As the leading team member or the instigator of the collaboration, you can act in the capacity of prime contractor, with your collaborators being suppliers to you for products and services. This gives you full control to allocate tasks and subcontracts as necessary, to meet the needs of the opportunity. Alternatively you can work in partnership with one or more of your potential collaborators, sharing the control and the risk. Each approach has its advantages and disadvantages, so you should carefully weigh up whether you become the prime contractor or subcontract to someone else.

As prime contractor you carry much of the risk, and consequently reap more of the benefits. One risk is that you may find yourself inadvertently entrapped by a subcontractor. They can exert considerable influence upon you once you have embarked upon the bid. For example, you may find it difficult to do anything about an unexpected rise in price once you have committed to using a particular supplier in your bid, or the subcontractor may decide to rescind and withdraw from the bid leaving you high and dry.

Generally, you should consider being the prime contractor when you are supplying the greater part of the products and services being tendered and where there is a good supply of the other products or services you need to complete your offer. This gives you more choice in selecting subcontractors.

Selecting who will be the prime contractor in a consortium relationship may sometimes be obvious but more often it is less clear-cut. As partners you must decide upon the best approach for the good of the bid and for carrying out the contract. Consideration of your respective roles will give clear pointers that you must gauge against your client's expectations. If, for example, one partner is contributing the lion's share of the services being tendered, while another has an excellent record of success in project management, then you must consider which factor serves the client's interest best. Which will they be happier with? Which will give them most confidence in the ability of the consortium to deliver? The chief point of contact with the client will always be the prime contractor so you must weigh up the alternatives carefully to make the best choice.

As a subcontractor your commitments are often much less and so are the rewards. You may also recover all or part of your bid costs from the prime contractor. This is safer from a business viewpoint but you may gain more from a partnership arrangement.

Finally, consider what each partner gets out of the arrangement. The funding in a consortium will usually be met by the partners on an equitable basis determined by their contribution to the project. Each will usually meet their own costs but you may decide that a degree of subsidisation is necessary. The cost to each participant is likely to be substantially higher than bidding on your own. There is an increase in communication between the companies, more travel, complicated co-ordination and consequently more management time needed. The risk in partnerships is the same as for all bidding but incorporates another level of business uncertainty: the behaviour of your partners. So, even when successful in bidding you may find that the rewards from the contract are not what you anticipated.

SUMMARY

The organisational aspects of your bid are as important as the strategic ones.

- *Bidding usually requires a team to work together. Agreeing mutual objectives, providing clear guidance and encouragement and dealing quickly with any problems that arise will help that team function at maximum efficiency.*

- *The core bid team should have persons who can manage the bid process, who know the client well, have technical expertise and can apply financial and commercial experience. The size of the team will depend on the complexity and value of the bid.*

- *Involve the assignment team fully in the bid. These are those internal people, partners and subcontractors who will be responsible for carrying out the contract if you are successful. Bringing them into the bid can prevent problems with the programme implementation later on.*

- *Make sure that your chosen partners are acceptable to the client. It is important that you identify the right people before you bid as changing once the contract is in place could be difficult. Carry out a basic supplier appraisal and vendor rating.*

- *Consortia bidding becomes more prevalent as the cost and risk in bidding increases. Look closely at every angle of the relationship before making a commitment and formalise the agreement so each party knows its role and responsibility.*

8

DEVELOPING A WINNING STRATEGY

No successful bidder enters any bidding opportunity without having a plan for winning it in place. It is a sure-fire recipe for failure to invest your considerable effort and time in a prospect without having a good idea of what you must do to win. You need to be continually testing and evaluating different solutions to the problems and opportunities that each bid presents. In well-structured bids this commences very early in the bid cycle, usually during your assessment of the prospect.

The processes of assessment and strategic thinking are closely linked; the relative importance of the opportunity to your company directly affects the depth of detail to which you need to plan. When you first begin to assess the opportunity and apply your value judgements and subjective criteria, you will be developing and propounding a strategy on how to win it. It is difficult not to do otherwise. Simply by thinking about whether you want to win, you will be considering how best to do it. But thinking about it is different to carrying it out. For most bids you will need a sound basis for bidding that covers all aspects of the opportunity. A good bid strategy gives you the best way of doing it and provides alternatives for when circumstances change.

This chapter concentrates on the successful development of a winning bid strategy. It looks first at the basis of strategic thinking, outlining some basic steps and a framework around which you can build. It then goes on to identify the various strategic business options that are open to you and how these options dictate the way you should focus your offer. Finally, it outlines how to plan your strategy, giving guidance on methods and techniques that can prove effective.

BASIC STEPS IN BUILDING STRATEGY

A good bid strategy reflects a good business plan. Your business plan will usually have two sections, consisting of the quantifiable elements and the intangible ones. Quantifiable elements are easier to deal with so when developing your business strategy it is best to start with these. You should begin by setting yourself specific, measurable objectives. These will usually begin with financial targets. The common ratios you will probably consider will include: profit, return on capital employed, earnings per share, price-earnings ratio, and growth. You may then go on to develop objectives for your corporate ethos covering: employees' responsibility, earnings, working conditions and job satisfaction. You will also possibly set out your intentions on your company management style, structure and organisation, the type and number of clients, the suppliers you wish to deal with and the role your company plays in society.

Your bid strategy is the embodiment of your corporate business strategy for a single opportunity. The diagram in Fig. 8.1 shows how it must reflect your plans on growth, product development, competition, and client penetration. It must be wholly contained by these corporate structures; a bid plan that steps outside these boundaries cannot be

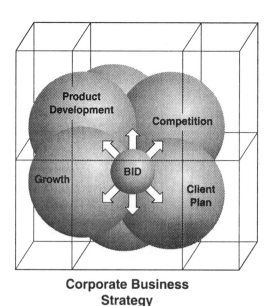

Corporate Business Strategy

Fig. 8.1 The bid strategy
(*An integral part of the corporate plan*)

judged to be successful even if you win, as it will contravene the basic underlying business rationale. That is not to say that any of these business structures are or should be immutable. Far from it. Businesses must be alert to change. A viable opportunity may cause you to rethink your corporate goals; thus the corporate strategy expands to accommodate the bid strategy.

Your first step then, when considering your corporate plans, is to put together an effective and efficient strategy that meets basic criteria; it should be realistic, it must meet the objectives of your company and it must satisfy the requirements of the client. At its root, the strategy must have the objective of winning new business for your company. You will also need to consider some winning tactics and how they can be incorporated into the bid plan to produce a structured winning strategy.

Client strategy

There are three basic steps to follow before arriving at your corporate client strategy. First divide your clients according to their expectations. Then establish precisely what their expectations are. Finally, adjust those expectations to match what you can provide.

Section the market

Look at the total market and decide which sections of it to target. Successful companies do not try to be all things to all people. If you consider the market for overseas travel for example, there are clear distinctions between holidaymakers and business travellers. Although both perhaps are travelling by air, their expectations are vastly different. One group may prefer low-cost, all-inclusive holidays, the other favours flexible flight times and convenience. So, the package tour operators and scheduled airlines services have developed services to cater for their differing needs. By segmenting the market according to what your clients expect, you will know you are selling to people that want to buy products or services of the type you sell. Focusing on this section of the market will help you to produce a highly competitive core product range. The questions you should be seeking to answer in your strategy are obvious financial ones such as: how do the size and value of a sale and the chances of repeat business vary across the client base; and what is the cost of providing the service to different types of client? When you have these answers, you can segment clients by their value to your business and by the cost of selling to them.

Establish expectations

Earlier, you considered value engineering to achieve the client's consolidated value in your bid; establish first what the client expects from the products or services they want to buy, then estimate the value they place upon the particular benefits brought by those products or services. You can then work out how much you will spend on servicing their needs and calculate the profit on the end sale.

In the previous example about air travel, the business user expected convenience, flexibility, comfort and service, and the holidaymaker weekend flights, knowledgeable tour guides and value for money. The business traveller may well have paid more in order to arrive rested and able to start work immediately. So, more leg-room and rapid baggage retrieval may be factors they value. The holidaymaker wants a trouble-free holiday. They may therefore value better brochure information to help them select their destination, and assistance before departing and on arrival to deal with any problems.

There is a strong temptation to assume that you already know what the client wants. Guessing is not part of developing an effective strategy. You must ensure that you are certain of what your client is expecting from your company and from the products they intend to buy.

Adjust to match

Adjusting your client's expectation is about influencing them towards buying your solutions to their needs so that you can bring their expectations in line with your products. Once you have segmented your clients and know what they want, your strategy needs to build on these precepts to ensure that you can meet their expectations and that your company is distinguished from your competitors.

In the same way, the airline needs to convince the business traveller that they can provide the extra facilities to help them to arrive more relaxed and effective at their destination. They offer enhancements such as an in-flight sleep-suit, seat-back video, shower and breakfast on arrival so that they can get the most from their trip. Similarly, the tour operator's detailed and accurate brochure, free illustrative video before departure, and courier services at the airport, may be just what the holidaymaker needs to ensure a stress-free and enjoyable holiday.

Product and service strategy

Although there is often a distinction drawn between products and services, there are also many similarities. The real difference lies in the intangible nature of a service. The client is frequently buying skills, experience or values that cannot be readily reproduced in the physical way that a product can. Products can be measured and evaluated against some benchmark or criteria, whereas services are more difficult to quantify and qualify. Nevertheless, the trend in bidding is leaning more towards services. Consider outsourcing, for example. Many companies, either out of choice or from the need to contain costs, are concentrating on their core business activities and contracting out peripheral services to third party providers. In many respects this is forcing services to be more like products. Although there is still the intangibility of the service, the outsourcing companies attempt to build substance into it through agreed service levels. These provide measurement criteria for service parameters such as response times, transaction throughput, cost-improvement and similar yardsticks, which hitherto went unheeded.

Your strategy will probably need to consider many diverse areas, and only by knowing your client will you get comprehensive coverage. Typically, in a bid to a manufacturer for example, you would consider the following components.

Product innovation

In specific markets such as information technology or computing, the strategy will focus on product innovation. The development of new products is critical, sometimes even before older ones have gone to market. At any given time, companies such as Intel or Sony have two or three generations of products at differing development stages. At the launch of a new product you can be certain that another one is in the final stages of completion, while design and development of yet a third will be well underway. You need to ensure that all the products are good and meet the needs of your client, and that they know it.

You also have to consider the effect of your competitor's product innovation. Could the anticipated life cycle time of your product be reduced or the product itself be superseded or made obsolete by your competitors' latest developments? If the risk is high you need to consider a strategy that takes a short life span into account. Perhaps you can offer an easy upgrade route, trade-in value or an additional bolt-on facility at some later stage. This is a strategy frequently employed by shrink-wrapped software companies. Low-cost upgrades to new releases, trading-in a competing product for their own, and continual new versions with product enhancements, are tactics designed to extend the life cycle of their product or to poach clients from their competitors.

Total quality

More clients are aware of the benefits that quality systems bring, so they will be expecting continual and rapid monitoring and improvement in your products and in your company operations. Your strategy should consider this carefully and put into effect the necessary quality systems your client expects. Integrating total quality management into your bid process will prove to them that you can meet all their needs such as performance, delivery, reliability, aesthetics, cost-effectiveness and competitiveness. You should aim to show that the links in your quality chain start with your suppliers and extend into every aspect of your organisation.

Improved product support

Support issues feature more prominently now in both product and service delivery. Your strategy has to make sure that you can prove that you stand behind your products. You should be aiming at displaying a reputation for excellence. Try to establish whether your client is considering any changes that could have an effect upon the support you provide. Find out if there are any legal or regulatory mandates forthcoming that will have implications on your product function. Any introduction or change to product standards may also affect your strategy. This is becoming more important, especially in public sector bidding, where the use of any existing recognised standards is mandatory.

In some areas, where the investment in the product is high, support attains even greater importance. Take major system software development as an example. Such systems often form the mainstay of the company's administrative function: stock and inventory control, payroll, general ledgers, and so on. Or they support the core functions, such as a pensions database or claims process for a life insurance company. The investment in these systems is not just in the initial purchase price and the ongoing maintenance, but also in the hidden costs of data, training and user familiarity. Support for the system often extends past the life cycle of the product and therefore, as so-called legacy systems, they have to be passed on and integrated with new products.

Rapid response time

You should be aiming here to show more rapid supply and delivery times than your competitors. But again, go beyond being simply competitive and aim at a continual improvement and reduction in lead times.

You should look now at ways to enhance or exploit your distribution channels. You should perhaps be reviewing your design methods and processes to take advantage of the introduction of new technology, and to allow you to get new or enhanced products to your client faster. Successful companies are those who achieve major improvements in performance by re-engineering their design processes. They are breaking away from the traditional ways of doing things, revising the way they have been done, and looking to technology, new systems and people, to provide them with the rapid acceleration and improvements their clients are demanding.

Integrated portfolio

Although specialists in certain areas will always be needed, and will continue to achieve successes by fulfilling needs in niche areas, generally clients are expecting their suppliers to fill more and more of their needs. The one-stop shopping trend that was fashionable in the 1980s has not disappeared. Clients now expect to see a comprehensive portfolio of products that work together and complement each other. As well as seeing benefits from meeting all their needs from a single source, clients now also expect products to serve many purposes. This is a throw back to the cost-effective use of resources that the recession has highlighted. Your portfolio must be broad and each element should be multi-dimensional. So make sure you remain focused and good at what you do.

Pricing

Your pricing strategy is often the most important aspect of your bid. Chapter 9 looks in detail at the various alternatives that are open to you.

Staffing and structure

Effective use of quality personnel reflects on how clients will view your bid and customer-support proposal. Your target should be to use the highest quality people. Make sure you can emphasise your approach to achieve continual upgrading of skills within a well-structured organisation.

The need for skilled people runs right through the product life cycle, beginning with the design and development stages, through to manufacture and launch, onto sales and bid processes, application and support. Consider in your strategy the skills and resources of your own people, any external consultants you may use, your suppliers and your management.

Sourcing

Clients will want to know that any investment they make in your products or services is protected. They will be seeking assurances that you are around for the long term and that they can anticipate a stable client–supplier relationship.

This also means that you have to satisfy yourself of the stability of your own suppliers. Too heavy a reliance upon a single source can make you vulnerable and susceptible to the failure of that supplier. Always look to provide a second or third source where possible. This will also reassure your client that you are not going to be brought down by circumstances outside your direct control.

Framework for developing strategy

Incorporating all the components of your corporate business strategy into your bid strategy will ensure that if you win the bid, it will be on your terms and fit in with your objectives. It does not necessarily give you the winning formulae. To get that you need to assemble and act upon information in certain key areas. Start by constructing a framework upon which your bid strategy can grow. The following areas will typically form the basis of your planning. See if you can provide answers in each of them, using the framework as a guide.

Market parameters

You should focus on the particular market in which you operate. You need to be clear that your bid fits with the stated market objectives of your company. Take stock of your company business objectives in each market sector and for each product in the range.

- *Define the markets served by each of your products.*

With a wide range of products in your company portfolio, pick out the key market sectors upon which you should be focusing.

- *What are the key market sectors?*

How can you measure these market sectors? Describe each of the key market sectors and answer the following questions: What are the buying habits of each? What are the statistics for each in terms of size, numbers, volumes of purchases, and frequency?

- *Key market sector description.*

  Buying habits _____

  Size _____

  Number _____

  Volumes of purchase _____

  Frequency of purchase _____

If you want to win good business consistently, you will probably decide to leave aside small or low-value products, product add-ons and service items, unless they support the main purposes of your bid. Bids for these in their own right are probably not going to justify the expense and effort you put in. However, they are valuable in enhancing your position with the client. Similarly, you will probably decide to leave aside the smaller client with the lower spend. Your bid efforts are better expended on projects where the returns justify it. Concentrate on the core of your business.

- *What is your core business?*

_____

Competitive parameters

Competition is a very important area and building a competitive strategy is discussed in depth, later in this chapter. However, it will serve you to consider, at this basic stage, some parameters you will need to quantify later. Consider those markets where your company does not have a competitive product edge. Is your product offering the same as the competition? What advertising approach have they adopted in these areas? What selling techniques and methods have your company employed? Is this more effective than the competition? How do you know and how do you measure it?

- *Are your products the same as your competitors'?*

- *What are your competitors' promotion methods?*

- *What are your promotion methods?*

- *What is the relative effectiveness of each?*

- *How did you measure it?*

Redundant market parameters

Finally, in this outline of a basic strategic framework, you should take a broad look at your market to see if you are wasting your time in bidding. You may find that the prospect does not fit in with your company's development plans and so you may need a strategy to exploit a declining market. First find out if there any markets in which your company should not be active. Are there any markets that do not feature in your future expansion plans? Should your company be considering a way of profiting from these areas, running the market sector down and getting out of that market?

Do not write off bids in a redundant market immediately. It is rare for a company suddenly to terminate a product or service. There is usually a slow rundown that must be managed so that existing and new clients, and business opportunities, are not jeopardised. Your bid could form part of this withdrawal strategy.

Assessing client needs

It will be useful to highlight here some key values that your client will expect. In a bid situation the demand for your company's products is more likely to come from business clients than domestic users. Individuals do, of course, frequently invite tenders for domestic work such as building, interior decorating and landscaping. Similar, if less detailed, strategic analyses will be valuable in these situations, but the motives will be different. When bidding for business contracts, you know that your clients will also be competing in their own market sectors for customers.

If you can provide your clients with a competitive edge in their own operations you are more likely to stimulate demand for your products. It is therefore important for you to sell this idea to your client at the highest level. You need to get the message across clearly that using your company products will give them a market edge. Besides gaining this market edge, your clients will be searching for ways to make extra profit. You will stimulate greater demand by showing how using your products will help them to achieve it. For example, you should consider ways in which you can reduce their operating costs, by showing potential savings in material costs and reductions in labour costs.

Your clients will also be hoping to see ways to make their operations easier. You need to get the message through that your company products will ease their operating environment; make things run more smoothly, and get things done faster. This is the warm feeling that you try to induce, encouraging a sense of goodwill and general interest in your company and your portfolio.

To ensure that you fully understand the needs of your clients you should conduct the following exercise for each new potential opportunity:

- *Describe the benefits that each of your company products provides.*

- *Put a figure to the profit and value they will each add to the client's business.*

- *Estimate accurately the savings that they will make by using your products.*

- *Have you considered everything?*

- *Evaluate your existing product range.*

- *Categorise products into each market sector.*

- *Ensure the products you try to sell the client are appropriate to their needs.*

STRATEGIC OPTIONS

Now that you have considered the basic parameters in your bid strategy you can look at some specific options that are open to you. Bid strategy should reflect business strategy but be tailored to the specific and individual needs of the client. The best options are those that closely couple what you are trying to achieve as a business with what you are attempting to provide the client. You may have a business strategy which dictates that you follow the market or you may aim for market leadership. You could be consolidating a weak domestic position or looking to expand into new international markets. Or you may be set on organic growth or enlargement through coalescence. Your bid should endorse whichever business strategy you adopt. Look at some of the following elective approaches.

Growth or stagnation

Most bid strategies will invariably focus on growth through developing your business, increasing your profits and bringing in new clients. It seems unlikely that you would deliberately set out a strategy for stagnation, or non-growth, although this often arises because of a poorly thought-out or carried-through growth strategy. There may however, be occasions when you wish to consolidate your position and consequently your bid strategy is focused on maintaining your current commercial status. In these circumstances your bids can be tactical instruments, designed to win new business in the face of other losses. These bids may be characterised by low profit margins, highly competitive stratagems and innovative promotion campaigns. You may also adopt variations on this approach to prevent or postpone events with high associated risk, or to mitigate its effects when or before it occurs. In the main though, your bid should always be based upon a strategy for growth. Anything less is unlikely to meet your commercial aspirations.

Growth can also be achieved through acquisition or merger, and bids are frequently used as vehicles for these. There are the hostile or welcomed take-over bids in which shares in the target company are purchased, but these tend to be based around the attractiveness or vulnerability of the business as a whole. However, specific projects may influence this and are often used as a means to allow two companies to work in a closer allegiance than would otherwise be possible in a traditional supplier–client relationship. If you are seeking to grow through this method, either because you need to diversify or because you cannot meet your objectives through organic development, you will be aided by having high capitalisation, and the ability to move quickly.

Bid strategy for an industry leader

No matter how important market leadership is in your company, you are still likely to encounter competitors who also aspire to it within their own bid and business strategies. If you understand these aspirations it will help you in your competitive analyses or conversely support you in achieving market leadership, if this is your intention. Leadership is a great asset in your bid, probably more so than almost any other single factor. The main attributes being that you dictate on price and quality, and set the standards that others follow. You therefore do not have to compete so hard on price, unless the bid demands it, as you can offer a unique angle that your competitors cannot.

It will do you no good at all if you attempt to become a leader in a declining market because unless you aim to maximise your share at the reduced demand, you will only succeed in postponing your inevitable demise. Similarly, leadership in a field where there are many competing and ill-differentiated products, is likely to founder. So, you must be aware of the market environment; will it sustain a leader, is it in need of something different, will it bear the additional price of innovation? Try to match your bid strategy closely to the perceived market environment.

A common failing in bids by industry leaders is that they rest on their laurels and become complacent. Do not make the assumption that as you have a solid grip on the market you are unassailable. You are not. There may be a hungry and lean bidder making all the right noises to the client and undermining your position of strength. If you are complacent, you may not know about it until too late, and the bid is lost. This could have a profound and far reaching effect upon your leadership. It is therefore important to be adaptable within your corporate and bid organisation so that you can react quickly to any threats. A stagnant strategy is symptomatic of this complacency, so you should make sure that your strategy evolves. Once you have established leadership, you should aim to retain it by looking for continual improvements in your bids and by keeping the opposition guessing.

Effectiveness for the market leader is often even more important than efficiency. As a market leader you have to deliver what you say you will deliver, which gets the results that your client expects. They will have very clearly defined ideas about what you will be proposing, based upon your prestige as holder of the lead position. Your efficiency or competence is taken for granted. If you fail to live up to their expectations, not only could you lose the bid but your reputation could suffer. Not only must your effectiveness permeate the proposal, but it must be evident in your corporate capabilities; you must be seen to do as a business what you aspire to do in the bid.

An international strategy

Although international bidding has already been covered in detail in Chapter 5, it is valuable to reiterate some basic precepts in the development of an international strategy. First you must ensure that there is a match with your corporate business plan in the region you are bidding in. The business plan should focus on existing or latent volume markets, while not neglecting your domestic market. Bidding on an international front usually requires a larger amount of money to undertake it effectively so focus your attack where the competition does not want to compete. This will make best use of your expenditure and enhance your chances of winning.

You can often strengthen your position in the global arena by building a network of alliances, always ensuring that you ally yourself with someone who counts. It is a waste of time forging partnerships with someone who has no influence on the client or who cannot otherwise support your bid.

Mass is another consideration, as you need to be of sufficient size to make an impact on the international market. You can achieve this through partnerships, by organic growth or by acquisition although this can be a risky game plan. However, you will need to generate the capability to retaliate against your competition and this generally means being big enough to inflict damage on them. If the opportunity represents a strategic initiative for your company then you must separate the cost–price relationship in your bid. You must be able to withstand potential losses in one area to make money somewhere else and this requires strength in depth.

Competing internationally can be more difficult for the smaller company operating alone. This is why alliances are so important. Your bid can often provide the impetus you need to establish yourself internationally while minimising your costs. Even large businesses often find it difficult to get established abroad. Enterprises that are successful in domestic markets frequently fail to replicate that success on the international scene. There are many examples of companies that have tried and failed. You can maximise your chances of success by making sure you have a sound strategy, and by using your bid as the instrument to gain leverage.

Diversification strategy

Your bid may be attempting to put into effect a strategy of diversification. There are several variants on this. You may have selected horizontal diversification in which you intend to offer a wider range of services. This is usually favoured when you have a detailed knowledge and understanding of the market. You can use this strategy to introduce greater specialisation within that market. Be cautious, however, if you are unclear or uncertain of the market. Through adopting this approach you are invariably moving deeper into an existing area and therefore you must be very sure of your ground and know that it is still competitive.

With vertical diversification, you will usually be looking at some integration of existing products or at producing your own facilities or products where these were previously supplied by someone else for assembly by you. This has the advantage of allowing you to specialise further, strengthening your position with the client and gaining better control over your costs. Against this approach, there is the risk of compounding a poor position. You may find, for example, that there is no technical similarity between making your own complete products and assembling parts produced by someone else, or that other similarities in the administration of the manufacturing or assembly do not materialise. This could weaken rather then strengthen your hold on the market.

You may try concentric diversification, where you create or introduce commonality between products. This allows you to build new products that share characteristics which are common to the rest of your product portfolio. You can usually gain economies of scale from adapting a modular approach. You could attempt a partial lock-in to a unique operational property, forcing clients into buying only products that have the same attributes. One could argue that the widely-available computer graphic user-interfaces allow concentric diversification by ensuring that all software has the same key control functions. The down side is that any market change impinging on the core elements will ripple through all your products making them susceptible to your competitor's innovation. If the core should become redundant, your portfolio will be wiped out.

Product strategies

Your bid strategy should take into consideration what you are trying to achieve with your products and services. Product development and design strategies are often complex and it is difficult to do justice to them in this book. At the very least you should focus on the products that make up the biggest area of demand because they will probably give you the greatest potential for developing new markets for new products or to expand demand with new users. However bids tend, in part at least, to allow you to choose from which products you want the client to select, so within the bid you can try to steer your client towards certain items. This will increase your share if you are successful and is often more effective than just concentrating on the primary demand areas.

Endeavour to put across the breadth of your product line. Use a diversification strategy to fill gaps. Alternatively try to simplify your portfolio if it seems broad but unsubstantial. You can also try in your bid to set up some form of product overlap. This is the controversial *Classic Cola* approach, where you supply products that compete with each other, but from which you benefit whatever the client selects. Supermarkets employ the tactic by pitching their own-label goods against market leaders. They cannot lose, but they stand to gain more from selling their own products. This technique is most effective if you are the potential subcontractor to two or more bidders as, if any of them win you will be awarded a share of the contract. The bidders themselves cannot usually use this product strategy unless the client allows alternate solutions in the bid, when you can offer them choices which may share certain products.

All bids should consider a degree of product tailoring where possible. Try to design the product to suit the specific needs of the client. Unless the opportunity is extremely large, thereby justifying a true one-off design, you will need to segment the market and produce variants that meet different needs. For example, you could produce different grades of product or modifications to existing ones. Some products or services entirely suit the custom-made approach; architecture, bespoke training, design and software development all spring to mind.

Consider, finally, your bid-product pricing strategy. You can sell outright or lease the product. For services, you have little choice, but there are several alternative leasing arrangements for you to choose from. Other factors to think about will include discounts, warranties, and guarantees. You then need to decide how to present your offer. The client may specify a complete price breakdown or leave it to you to present it in the best format. You have many options here. You can submit an itemised list, bundle products and services into a single figure or separate them according to type or delivery date. You could also keep part of your costs hidden from the client. You may decide, for example, to include ongoing maintenance within the outright sale price. However, always consider pricing your offer according to its value to the client. This reaffirms the need to meet their consolidated value expectations and should, perhaps, be the philosophy underlining your whole pricing policy. Your final decision relies upon you knowing the client's needs and reactions, but price must also be considered in relation to the other components of your strategy.

Market strategies

Your market strategy will be influenced first and foremost by whether you are targeting specific sectors as aiming at a selection of industries can often give you a niche and helps to avoid competition. Of course choosing a niche means that the size of the market is reduced so the alternative is to adopt an industry-wide policy and attempt to sell across the board. Your decision will be affected by the type of products or services you are selling and whether such markets exist for them. Bids are often very effective in gaining you a bridgehead in a new sector from which you can develop and which otherwise would have been very difficult to penetrate.

Once you have decided upon the industry sector you should refine your focus onto your client base. You should avoid the smaller clients unless there is a sufficient margin or strong tactical motivation to justify it. Your efforts are likely to be better rewarded by concentrating on your key accounts and larger clients. The effort in bidding is often high, and with low-value opportunities, your profits could be swallowed up in bid costs. Conversely, you may choose to enter or create the market specifically for small- and medium-sized enterprises. This may bring particular benefits if you provide extra services tailored to their needs.

With your client focus clear, look next at how your clients use the products or services you sell. If the product is already widely used, you could be facing market satiation making penetration of that market increasingly difficult. You really have three choices. First you can aim to increase your share of the existing market. Secondly, you can try to find new users for your existing products. Thirdly, you could substitute a different product and invent new applications through technological refinements. The path you take will be influenced by some key factors: the capacity of the market for expansion, whether saturation has already been reached, the possibility of market contraction, and the relative volatility or stability of the market.

STRATEGIC PLANNING

Your examination of the basic elements in developing a strategy will give you ideas as to which approaches will best suit both your own business and the opportunity you are considering. The next stage is to plan your strategy by building upon these initial thoughts. Perhaps the most important aspect of this process is that you gain insights into your own commercial position first, because only by knowing what your own capabilities and restrictions are, can you develop a plan for winning the bid. So give some thought to the following facets of your business before going on to look at the actual planning process itself. You will need to gather information in various areas of your operations so that you can make a sound strategic decision.

Your company services and products

It is important to know your company portfolio. Surprisingly, many people do not have a full understanding of the range and variety of products or services that their company can offer the client. An analysis of the portfolio is beneficial; do you think the range is too wide, or too narrow? You may find it useful to do a comparison against your competitors' product ranges. Another point of consideration is how many products you can provide in-house and how many you need to source externally; do you make or buy-in? If you make, you will be in a stronger position if you bid your own products. If you buy-in and the products are universally available then it is quite likely that your competitors will have access to the same or similar products. In these situations you should make sure that you have good intelligence on your main suppliers and supply lines. You should also look for areas of vulnerability, reliance and dependence that could have a significant impact upon your bid. If you do find any deficiencies you may be affected by price or cost fluctuations in your supply line at some later stage so put in place some contingency measures. You may find that part of your portfolio is irrelevant to your current need which means you should focus on your company's key services or products and incorporate them within your bid.

Research and development (R&D) factors

There are strong links between product management and your research and development plans. If yours is a 'me too' approach with a tendency to imitate the market leader, then your spending in this area will be lower, perhaps giving you the opportunity to attack on price. Conversely, if you are an innovative company that aims to lead the market you will probably spend much more in R&D, which will increase your cost-base. Your bid strategy will have to emphasise the benefits that your development plans bring to the client. As an innovator, you will also have the advantage of a broader commercial strategy through the licensing of your ideas and developments. The importance of these research and development factors will also depend on whether you do it in-house, or rely upon external sources.

Financial position

Your financial position will have an effect not only on your pricing policy but on your bid finance plan. New ventures are usually decided by either a product or market strategy with your financial position having a critical function. You have several choices. You can concentrate on improving cash flow, on gaining new equity, on loans or on leases. Much will depend upon your equity valuation, your price earnings ratio, income levels, capital gearing, amortisation policy and so on. This is information you will need to collect. Look to see if you are likely to be subjected to profitability fluctuations and try to identify any particular weaknesses.

Personnel and productivity

Your personnel position will be influenced by the products and services you provide, your market position and the physical assets that you own. You should know how many people you have now and estimate how many you will need to devote to the project. You will also need to consider the range of skills required, the age distribution, the remuneration packages, work location factors and nationality of the employees that you are proposing. In today's climate of cost control, it is more and more important that you look into your company's present and future employment structure so that you know whether you will have enough personnel to complete the bid and carry out the project. You will also need to ask whether it is likely that key people may disappear, and you may need to consider a contingency plan for protection should it happen.

There are many other factors that will affect your company productivity and impinge on your bid. For example, try to assess how efficient your people are and look for ways for improvement if necessary. Look at the location and design of the facilities that you will be using. Perhaps you need to select ones that are geographically closer to your client, or maybe some redesign is necessary to make them more attractive to them. Finally, identify where your centres of specialisation are; find the processes where you excel and look for the people with the skills you need to include in your offer.

Marketing and distribution

The marketing and distribution strategy you choose should accommodate your sales planning, distribution network, the promotion of your bid, advertising and marketing plans. The success of many bids is influenced by the general image that you present to your customers at large. You must therefore use your advertising and image creation to strengthen your bid. You may have to focus on your after-sales service, prompt delivery and the effectiveness of your sales force. If any of these are important factors to your client you will have to ensure that they are addressed.

Management

Consider whether your company organisation is compatible with your client's structure. Suppliers and clients who are similarly structured tend to work better together. Smaller businesses tend to prefer a friendlier approach while larger companies are more used to working with other monolithic organisations. You may have to find ways in your bid to present a suitable management structure to your client. If they prefer a more intimate management style, make sure that your assignment team is structured to reflect this, even if the rest of your organisation is hierarchical and intractable. Work out ways in which you can bring the decision-makers in both companies closer together; all clients want to feel that they are important enough to justify top-level management time.

Of course, it is not just the structure of management that is important. Another management element that justifies attention is the skills that you have available and how these are likely to change as the project develops. This includes financial management skills, control and co-ordination of the project and quality planning. You will also have to address the way in which you handle information so that you can deal with invoicing and orders, enquiries, contractual changes and so on.

Industry position

The final element in getting to know about your own company is to recognise your place within your own industry. This is clearly dictated by the size of your organisation. The larger and more influential you are, then the greater your bargaining power with your client and suppliers is likely to be. Conversely, a smaller company may have more flexibility, both in management and within its staff which means that people are sometimes more loyal and therefore more willing to put themselves out for the client. Clearly, much depends upon your reputation for dealing fairly with your staff, clients and suppliers.

Designing strategic structures

By now, your strategy will be starting to take shape. You will have a general idea of what your approach is likely to be, and a good understanding of your own commercial position. You now need to condense these ideas into a solid plan. There are several methods you can use to decide your bid strategy; some are dependent on personnel, and some are process oriented, reliant upon the way you organise your business and the skills of the people available to you. The following methods are worth trying.

The entrepreneurial method

Perhaps the essence of a good bid manager is their openness to ideas and innovation. Creativity leads to winning bids. The entrepreneurial method is very subjective and requires inspiration, but the genesis of inspiration is having a detailed knowledge of the market and the client. Why do you feel happier going with one solution and not another? Hunches, and a good feeling about a particular approach, are often difficult to express and impossible to quantify. Some people have more of a flair for this than others and they are useful members of your team.

Being innovative in your bid strategy does not rely upon luck, it comes from having an in-depth understanding.

The stimulation method

Deciding bid strategy upon inspiration is well and good, but you cannot always rely upon it to give you a winning approach. Sometimes it is necessary to stimulate thought processes to generate ideas. Decide how best to stimulate creative thought in your bid team. Brainstorming is a well tried and tested method, as are lateral thinking exercises. Apply some structure to these sessions to help you focus. Plan it in advance, agreeing your objectives and using someone from outside the bid team to act as facilitator. Try to encourage a flow of ideas which you can assess and explore in depth. But always ensure that you have the best information available. Trying to stimulate ideas when you have insufficient knowledge of the client, the competition or the market will prove very difficult. It is sometimes a good idea to bring your suppliers into the loop as you do for value assessment and engineering, as they may bring a different slant to your thinking. You can also hold separate sessions with your client thereby developing a strategy that you know will meet their approval.

The appraisal method

This is probably the mainstay of bid strategy planning. In modern competitive situations so much is known about the competing suppliers and their products that drawing out any inspirational approaches is difficult. Inspirational ideas may also attract a higher risk factor. The appraisal method steers a middle course. In deciding your strategy by this method you look closely at the opportunity. Decide what projects you are interested in; refer to the prospect assessment criteria and the results from your earlier analyses. Look in detail again at why you selected this prospect to bid.

There are two sides to this method, an internal appraisal that assesses your own capabilities and an external appraisal that puts it into the context of the bid.

- *Conduct an internal appraisal*
  What are the strengths and weaknesses of your company?
  Base your strategy on strength, not weakness
  Focus on how to exploit these strengths
  Can you correct any weaknesses?
  Look for synergy between you and your client

- *Conduct an external appraisal*
  Who are your important competitors?
  What are their likely actions, both at home and internationally?
  What is their effect upon the market?
  How strong are they in people, research and market position?

  Appraise the political situation
  What is the local, national, and international climate?
  Are changes likely and what effect will they have upon business?

  Assess the economic situation
  Is the economy stagnant, receding, or growing?
  Could your financial rewards be affected by any changes?

  Appraise social developments
  What are the social trends?
  Are attitudes to work likely to affect your bid?
  Could social legislation have an effect?

  Conduct a technological appraisal
  What new products are likely?
  Are any new services planned?
  Could obsolescence affect your bid?

Consolidating your bid strategy

A good bid strategy combines business and competitive strategies into a cohesive winning plan. You get no reward for coming second in a bid, for trying very hard, or for submitting the most stunning tender document; your aim is to win. This section consolidates some of the above ideas and summarises it into a bid strategy and tactics. These in turn are influenced by the client, whether the bid is formal or informal, the evaluation criteria they intend to use, level of the competition, and the strength or otherwise of your company.

The client plan

Plan how you will develop your relationship with the client. Seek to make the best use of every opportunity throughout the bid cycle to get yourself into the position of the preferred supplier. Consider the effect your bid may have upon sensitive parties within the client organisation. For example, outsourcing telecommunication services may be co-ordinated by the telecommunications manager whose job could be the first to go when the contract is awarded. Be sensitive to the internal and political issues surrounding the bid, you may well need to reassure, cajole or elicit support from different factions within the client organisation.

External support scheme

The award of a major contract is of interest not only to the contracting parties but to a wide audience outside. You may require support from some of these in critical situations later. Start an early dialogue and warm people up; you do not want to be trying desperately to enlist support when the contract is virtually lost. To get the best out of external people, make them aware of how valuable they are to you. They should feel that they have been involved in the development process and that you have taken them into your confidence. Typical support areas will include local and government politicians, particularly if your success may influence employment or business prospects in their constituencies. Trade union support will also come into this category for the same reason. Getting backing from the local administration is invaluable when bidding overseas; political support becomes critical and must be included in your bid strategy. Finally, although not strictly speaking external, in this category you may include other parts of your company and senior managers indirectly interested in the success of the bid.

Technical design

It seems obvious that your technical solution must align closely to the client's requirement. However, many bids are submitted which have a poor match. Your technical strategy should attempt to be compliant in all those areas that you know from your value assessment to be very important to the client. You must distinguish between the important and less relevant technicalities; it is pointless majoring on an aspect that you perceive to be a winner, only to discover that the client considered it irrelevant. Your efforts and that of the team will go to waste. Some tender documents will inform you which requirements are mandatory and which are desirable. Without this you must assess the requirement yourself and be very certain that you know which are which.

You must exploit areas of high client value and simultaneously play to those areas where you consider the strengths of your solution to lie. Your bid document should emphasise these strengths and the benefits they bring in the areas which are of the most concern to your client. Bring these out as themes to run throughout the document.

Technical alternatives

In some bids you may feel that you have a solution that although not compliant with the specification, meets the client need. Some clients such as aid agencies, may not allow alternate solutions to be presented. Others, particularly in the private sector, may encourage it to get a broader perspective of the solution. If your technical design centres on an alternative, you must consider the full implications before preparing and submitting your bid. The important consideration here is to try to ensure that you alone benefit from the time and additional resources that you have put into it. You should further ensure that your alternative proposal does not undermine a compliant main proposal and does not imply that the client was wrong in their original thinking.

There may be significant advantages to an alternate approach, to you and to the client. But there are also disadvantages. At the practical level your bid costs could be higher if undertaking multiple designs and it will certainly take longer to complete. If you are responding against a technical specification you may not have all the information necessary. The client may not have provided enough detail and force you to make invalid assumptions. Your intention in the alternative approach must clearly be to gain or retain a competitive edge. In telling the client you will probably alert the other bidders and you could lose that advantage. You cannot guarantee confidentiality of any innovative ideas. The client may like your ideas so much that they ask all suppliers to rebid against your alternative specification.

You will need to be careful about how you price the alternative. The client may ask for prices in standard formats under the tendering rules. Although technically acceptable and suitably priced, your bid may be disallowed, losing in favour of the lowest evaluated conforming bid.

Commercial strategy

Again, the important point is to identify those areas very important to the client. You should be aware of the contract terms and conditions they favour and plan solutions to any that may be onerous or difficult to comply with.

Preferably, do not get embroiled in a *forms battle* by responding with your standard terms and conditions against the client's requirements; you may lose unless you are prepared to compromise. Your plan should alert your commercial team to the fact that non-standard terms and conditions are likely to apply and you should begin developing your response accordingly. Contractual terms are all about risk and risk management and your strategy needs to consider these areas carefully.

Once you have developed your commercial strategy make sure that you raise any areas of potential conflict with the client before entering the tender stage. Discuss any non-compliant options and make them aware of the rationale behind your thinking. Try to find some alternative terms that may be mutually acceptable. Above all make sure that they are fully aware of any potential areas of non-compliance and elicit their likely response. Feed this back into the commercial plan and reassess the risks.

Pricing approach

Deciding the most effective pricing policy is covered in some detail in the next chapter. In some bids it will be the lowest price that wins and, no matter how successfully you argue the case for superior technology and the highest standards of quality and reliability, you will not win unless you are the cheapest.

Purchasers these days are more sophisticated and the winner is more frequently selected by a combination of initial price, costs over the lifetime of the project, technical compliance, quality, reliability and track record. However, if you are way out on price then you are going to find it very difficult to catch up in the other areas.

If your company operates in a regulated sector such as telecommunications, energy or water, you could be restrained in the domestic market. You must clearly comply with the pricing policy specified by your industry regulatory body.

When planning your bid, use all the information sources available to decide what price will win. You may not need to be the lowest but you need to be close to it. You could argue that the price tendered should be the highest that the client is prepared to pay. If so, you will need extensive research to be sure of what that amount is. If initial estimates show that you cannot get close to that figure then you will have to review your policy and your bid decision. You could find yourself wasting money and effort on a fruitless bid.

There is sometimes a tendency to calculate the bid price on a cost-plus basis. This is not normally recommended in bidding situations. Always start with what you consider to be the winning figure and work out your cost-build from there. Remember that cutting costs is often more effective in adding profit than increasing margins.

Standard list prices are not necessarily going to be sufficient to win you the contract. There will be occasions where you will need to challenge them and find another, usually lower, figure. You must however be in full possession of the data to support your argument otherwise you will not convince the financial authorities concerned.

The same can be said of your standard margins and overhead recovery. Frequently, prices are marked up twice, with overheads being recovered at various points within the business. Know what the workforce costs are, know what the overheads are, challenge any price that does not fit within the bounds of reason.

For bids to international lending agencies, the guidelines generally say that no bidder can alter the substance or price of their offer. This is almost the reverse of commercial behaviour in the private sector. In both public and private sector procurement ways are often sought to get past this restriction. You must know whether you can enter post-tender negotiation with the client and plan in advance what you can give away in terms of price. This must form an essential component of your pricing strategy.

Finally on pricing, consider your strategy relating to budgetary quotations. These have the advantage of providing a target for both you and the client to aim at during tendering, and you will know whether their budget for the project is realistic. It also enables you to exert influence on their budgetary controls. The disadvantages are that once stated, the client will not welcome any significant divergence from the budgetary quotation. Where regulated services are concerned the licence regulations must be carefully considered.

Financing method

Consider all the options available against which the client can offset the financing of the whole project. Orthodox financing alternatives such as supplier credit are common where the contract provides for some of the consideration in cash and the balance deferred against receiving bills of exchange from the client. To protect against default by the client you should take out cover with a credit insurer. Buyer credit is also an orthodox financing method that may be considered and although this takes considerably longer to establish there is no residual risk to the supplier.

Keep up to date on the ways in which financing can be arranged to make a package more attractive to the client as these are constantly changing. Look also at unorthodox finance arrangements where appropriate; 'soft' loans linked with credit, counter-trade, project financing and equity participation. Ask your financial experts for assistance and guidance.

Dealing with competition

Within your bid information system you will have extensive knowledge of your major threats. Use this to plan a campaign for dealing with them at the local, national and international level.

For each bid you will need to find out who the competition is or is likely to be. You can discover this by asking the client outright, by attending the bidders' conference, if there is one, or from the client's published list of bidders. Your own account manager may know who has had recent contact with the client and who are the incumbent suppliers. Use your network of contacts to the best advantage. By careful analysis of the opportunity you can come up with a shortlist of suppliers who could meet the requirement.

Once you have a clear idea of who is bidding you can refer to your competitor profiles detailing the strengths, weaknesses and threat that each pose and the resultant opportunity that this presents. Use this to counter any significant advantages that they may have over your solution. You will need to tailor and refine this approximation to construct a complete picture of the competition's proposals and pricing structures.

Your own company debriefing reports, bid closure reports and market analysis reports often provide a better indication of where the competition succeeded or failed against you. Use these carefully and make sure you are comparing like with like. You must also assess the significance of the opportunity with the competitor; how badly do they want it? Are there any strategic implications to their business? What is their recent record of success?

Bid tactics

Tactics will sometimes be necessary to bolster your strategy. Making the right tactical decision can often be difficult. Some common situations that cause concern are:

● *Should you ask for an extension to the submission date?*

Time is always tight during the bid cycle. Activities seem to expand to fill the time available and you will sometimes find you need longer to complete the bid to your satisfaction. Do you ask for an extension?

First consider the client's position; they may have deliberately imposed tight timescales to test suppliers' ability to respond under pressure. They may have a deadline to meet, or need to spend within the current fiscal period. Conversely, it may indicate a weak client who does not really understand their own requirements or what is involved. The client may well have other contracts to let; this one may be part of a larger project and therefore be bound by time limitations. Of course, they may have been co-operating closely with one company and be using time to eliminate other potential suppliers.

Your decision must consider all the possibilities. If the only reason for you requesting an extension is to put the finishing touches to your proposal, then avoid it. If there are valid reasons then you must ask yourself whether it will be considered weakness on your part and jeopardise your chances of winning.

● *Can you make a tactical withdrawal from the bid?*

The need to withdraw a bid can arise for many reasons. Perhaps the most culpable one is when an incomplete or inaccurate assessment of the opportunity leads to a bid that subsequently proves to be extremely unfavourable to you, and you have to withdraw to save making a loss. You may also encounter circumstances where your client is unable or unwilling to make a decision. You could reach the stage where the cost of maintaining a state of readiness is prohibitive; revalidating sub-contractors' prices, keeping the assignment team ready, high negotiation or travel costs may all become too much and you have to decide whether to retreat from the contest. Sometimes, merely the threat of this is enough to overcome the client's inertia and they quickly reach a decision. Other times, your withdrawal may be seen as rejecting the client and future opportunities could be threatened. Be wary of using the threat idly; make sure you have solid and sound reasons for doing so. Do not allow frustration, or stalling tactics in negotiations, to overcome your business acumen. Your client may call your bluff and you could have lost out on a bid you may have been about to win.

In English contract law, withdrawing your bid is permitted at any stage prior to the offer being accepted. However, the implications and impact this may have upon your existing and future relations with the client will have to be carefully considered.

- *What about submitting a non-compliant offer?*

Whether or not to submit a non-compliant or qualified offer is quite a common dilemma. You must consider the area of non-compliance and the associated risk. Will failure to comply result in the bid being rejected? If so, then do not bid. Could you negotiate this point with the client during post-tender negotiation? What is the risk if you cannot reach a compromise position?

Only by fully understanding the client and their objectives can you reach a reasonable decision. Unless the area of non-compliance results in an onerous contract for you, consider making a compliant offer; your risk analysis will tell you how much emphasis and price adjustment you will need to make to compensate.

Remember, people often say that everything is negotiable. Submitting a non-compliant bid may rule out your offer on a point around which you and the client would have been prepared to negotiate and reach a compromise. However, if post-tender negotiation is not allowed then you must seriously consider not bidding.

- *Should you use overpricing as a bid tactic?*

You could occasionally be put in the position of being forced to bid against sound commercial judgement. As discussed earlier, there may be genuine strategic reasons for going ahead, although you do not want to win the contract. You may be cementing a new relationship with your client, maintaining your position on their bidders' list, or showing continuing interest in them without jeopardising future opportunities. In these situations you may be faced with deliberately having to exclude your offer from being accepted. Here, you are faced with the choice of a non-compliant offer or one that will be ruled out on price. Neither approach is entirely satisfactory; non-compliant offers can still be accepted, while high pricing may rule you out but gain you a reputation for being expensive. If you adopt overpricing, ensure that it is sufficient to cover your risk if your offer is accepted.

COMPETITIVE STRATEGY

Why do you need a competitive strategy? You could argue that your bid only needs to meet the expectations of the client and should be judged on its own merits. Such an argument could be considered naive, but is often posited. Bids are generally competitive. To ignore your competition is to neglect a major influence on your success or failure. Too many companies do not have a systematic approach to analysing the competitive threats in their bids. Consequently, a major opportunity to influence the result in your favour is lost. Quite often you will build up an intuitive feel about what your competitors are doing, especially if you bid against them regularly. However, a systematic analysis will help you get a better understanding and win more frequently.

Although you always strive in a bid to cross the consolidated value threshold that makes your proposal the one the client selects, your competitors are trying equally hard to do the same. The client selects the bid that meets, or betters, its consolidated value expectation. When more than one bid achieves this, the client will consider other differentials to make the decision. This could be brand name, previous experience, appearance, or another esoteric reason outside the main factors of price, technical compliance, quality and performance.

The ideal bid, and the ideal outcome from successful bid management, is a single tender, a bid without competition. This as you know, is becoming more difficult to achieve and you should expect competition in all your bids. Therefore winning the bid means not only satisfying all the client's value expectation, but convincing them to select you over your competition. In some bids, you will face tough challenges, in others it will be easier. Consistent winning requires you to manipulate the opportunities in your favour, selecting those bids where the rewards are high but the competition is weakest. To do this you need a thorough understanding of your competition and a strategy for your bid to counter the threats they bring.

Business strategy and competitive forces

In considering your business strategy, you will have identified which of the many options open to you are appropriate for the target market and for your bid. You cannot separate business strategy from bid and competitive strategies. The business strategy sets the direction to be followed, and the bid and competitive strategies are the tactical achievement of the business plan.

It is likely that much of your analysis relies upon gut feeling and instinct, supplemented by an in-depth knowledge of those competitors you encounter regularly. In many ways, bid strategy is far more difficult to figure out. You can analyse trends more readily, look at how they have approached bids in the past and extrapolate a position for them with your opportunity. Providing you have enough data, you can get a good idea of their general philosophy. Of course they may decide to buck the trend, change tack or try another method. A good indication is if they have been repeatedly unsuccessful in one approach, or had limited recent success by adopting an alternative strategy to their previous one. That is why, in a one-off opportunity, trying to second-guess can be very difficult. Gut reaction plays an important part, but so does knowledge and the application of a structural analysis of the threat they offer.

A good starting point is to look at the competitive forces at play in the bid, as illustrated in Fig. 8.2. There is of course the pressure exerted by the client. After all, they have the effective power to select your competitors for any bid, through pre-qualification, selective tendering or preference. They also exert pressure through their procurement policy and buying power. Powerful clients, buying in large quantities or regularly, put pressure on suppliers forcing some of them out of the competition. Then there is the power that your suppliers may have, especially if they are suppliers to your competitors as well. This gives them power to dictate price and supply lines that again could influence the numbers of competitors or their bid pricing policy.

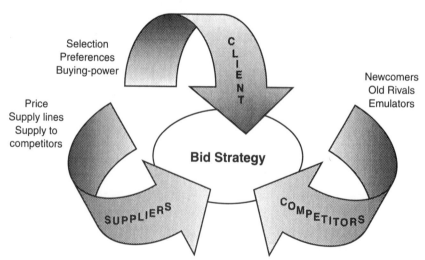

Fig 8.2 Competitive forces

Finally, there are the direct forces that your competitors bring to bear. Traditionally in a free market, competitors fall into the categories of newcomer, me-too, or old rivals. The threats represented by these vary depending on what they are trying to achieve. The newcomer wants to enter the market and overcome all the obstacles to entry that exist displacing the incumbent supplier and so building up market share and gaining additional investment capital with which to move on. Typically the newcomer prices aggressively, even bidding a loss-leader if the client is strategically positioned for them to take advantage. They need to overcome the resistance to change that the client may feel; there may be an incumbent supplier, or one whose record in this market is strong, which the client may favour. The newcomer has to differentiate themselves from these and prove that they offer an advantage that the others lack and that will justify a change and the costs associated with it. With no performance record, experience, market share or existing client base this can be difficult. Your competitive response to the newcomer is dictated by how easy or how difficult it is to enter the market and what obstacles are in the way. If it is an easy market with few barriers to entry, then the newcomer will expect a rigorous defence from the market leaders.

Emulation, or me-too competition, appears inevitable these days. Advanced technology in all areas of industry allows an alternative to an innovative product to be on the market very quickly. A quick look at your supermarket shelves with own-brand labels or the plethora of personal computer clones available, suggests the extent of the problem. It is more difficult than ever for a supplier to retain an innovative edge for any significant period. The reason for the client inviting competitive tenders is just because of that fact; there are likely to be many different products or services available to meet their needs and the competitive element helps them choose. Dealing with the me-too threat is not easy. The client perceives the function of each product as similar. In many instances every player in the market follows the me-too trend, so that differentiation on product function alone becomes impossible. In that sense, it is easier to deal with the me-too competitor where the technology is comparable. You will be familiar with the technical strengths and weaknesses, design and performance criteria and reliability, and can counter these readily, looking for differentiators elsewhere. More difficult to handle is the me-too threat that competes on a functional level but from a different technological platform. Take for example, the energy industry, where the function is to supply heat, light and power. This can be achieved by electricity, oil or gas, three very different energy technologies. Or look at the competition between labour-intensive tasks and innovative-technology that replaces the labour. You can dig a trench by hand to lay a pipeline, or send a drilling mole underground to achieve the same thing. Competing against dissimilar products requires a different approach.

Competing against old rivals can lead to complacency. You know each other well, understanding the product, the price, the performance, the marketing strategy, the distribution channels, the sales technique and the success and failure rate. Your task is to win this bid by beating the competition and complacency leads inevitably to failure.

These bids become more like a game of chess, with tactics coming into play and a set of established 'rules' that you play by. Each player attempts to gain the upper-hand by employing price cuts, marketing ploys or product variations. Look at the telecommunications sector where prices are adjusted regularly, each undercutting the other, offering a premium service, or changing the charging structure. Each change is designed to win new business that will be retained. Similar tactics have been used in the broadsheet paper wars where price slashing is the weapon being used to win new readers. The danger with this strategy is that the market becomes unbalanced; one or more suppliers could suffer to the extent that they are forced out of business, reducing the choice to the client. Aggressive marketing on the other hand often stimulates a general demand that benefits all suppliers. However won, the product has to convince them to stay and therefore has to be a quality one. You may find yourself adopting similar tactics in your bid. Cutting prices is one approach but without a quality product you will find it hard to retain those clients. You must also be careful that you are not undermining the market and profitability for future opportunities.

Much depends upon the relative strengths and number of bidders; if there are many bidders the rivalries among them will be high so that rules are abandoned and one-off tactics out of line with previous policy are tried. You will find it difficult to predict the strategy in such cases. Similarly, if the bidders are balanced in strength, tactics will be employed to tip the scales towards one or the other. Where the number of bidders is few, or one supplier is clearly the market leader, the relative strength of the bidders becomes easier to see and tactics designed to shift the balance have less effect.

Techniques for analysing competitors

What do you need from an analysis of your competition? You should be aiming to build a profile of each competing bidder that tells you the nature of their bid, the chances of it being successful, their probable responses to your threat and the range of tactics they might use to support it. With your profiles established you can then decide which threats you should take seriously, whether you should attempt to ignore, counter or mitigate them, and decide how to go about it.

Competitor profile

Start by using your information sources to compile a competitor profile for each bidder. Analysis of relative strengths, weaknesses, opportunities and threats (SWOT analysis) has long been an established technique for building the profiles. It also serves as a self-assessment to promote a better understanding of your own position in the bid. Performing a SWOT on each bidder and on your own company can highlight the main areas where you need to focus your bid.

The diagram in Fig. 8.3 shows a typical analysis. The purpose of the analysis is to stimulate thinking in each aspect of competition. Explore these four main categories to identify areas of concern. Some typical sub-categories are shown and these should prompt questions that need answers. Areas you would typically include in your profile will be: price, technical capability, experience, history, quality and timescales, although there may be many others which are also more appropriate for your business.

Another technique is to chart your position compared with your leading competitors. Take the same main profile areas and plot the advantages and disadvantages in each area as illustrated in Fig. 8.4. This serves to spotlight where your advantages and disadvantages lie compared to your main rivals. Again, you would normally break down each section into its related component parts, depending on how detailed you wanted the analysis to be.

These techniques will provide a general idea of your competitive position, but you need to put them into the bid context to try to foresee the response your opponents are likely to make. You can achieve this by incorporating into the competitive analysis the value assessment you conducted earlier when you identified the important areas for your client.

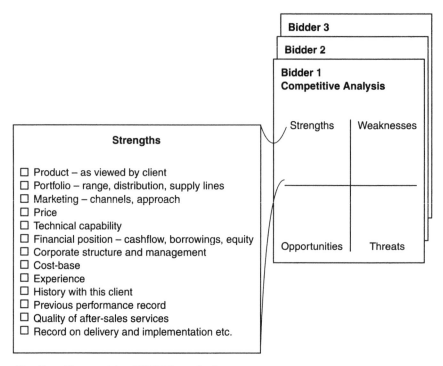

Fig. 8.3 Competitive SWOT analysis

Bid response chart

The profile gives you the fundamental information necessary to understand your competitors. In itself it serves no purpose. You have to interpret the profile to extrapolate the likely response that each bidder is going to give. This is where your skills of judgement, intuition and management will be tested. Each bidder will respond to the opportunity in one of three ways. They will either make a passive, attacking or defensive response. You should chart the likely response using the guidelines in Fig. 8.5. This chart looks at the three areas that may provoke a response; moves made by you, moves made by the client, and outside events. For each of these changes you will need to assess how vulnerable your competitor is to it, what avenues are open to them to retaliate, and what effect their retaliation would have on you.

Passive response

The passive response is the easiest for you to tackle as your competitor adopts the same strategy and tactics that they have used in the past.

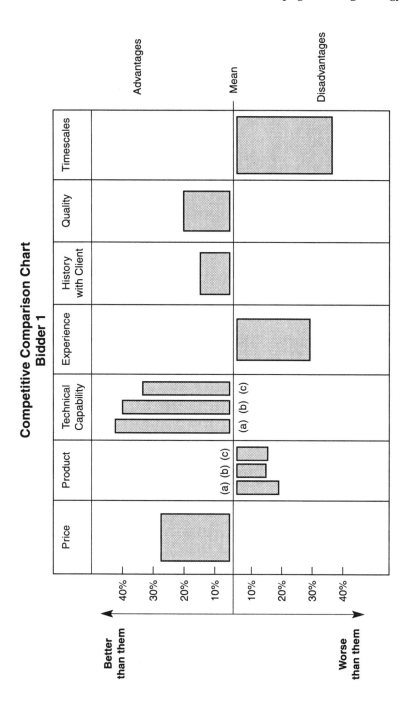

Fig. 8.4 Example of competitive comparison chart

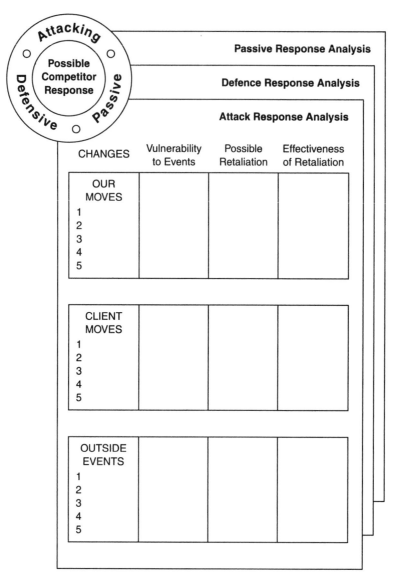

Fig. 8.5 Competitive analysis response

There are no changes or alterations, so you will have a clear idea of the threat and will develop a counter to it. The passive response can be a very strong one. If the supplier has a proven record with their approach, why alter it? Of course, it can also be a signal of complacency. One defeat could be sufficient to cut the ground away from this supplier and start a winning trend with you. If they have not been successful in this passive approach, then they are unlikely to repeat it and you should look at the other options open to them.

Dealing with the strong passive response requires you to be very active. Typically, you will have bid against them in the past and lost. You now need to review those past bids and find the weakness in their strategy. Look at each aspect of the requirement and their response to it. Time has passed and you can probably get much more information now than you could at the time. Could you have countered it then and failed to? With the benefit of this experience you need to assess the situation and decide whether you can do it now.

Attacking response

An attacking response is the result of change. The more likely a shift in strategy, the greater the chance of an aggressive response. Be aware of signals coming from the marketplace, rumours of reorganisation, new products, pricing policy, new marketing campaigns. These should all suggest that your competitor is poised to attack the market and win the bid through adopting an aggressive posture. You have to ask if they are content with their current strategy (passive response) and if they have been as successful as they should have been with it. Have they had any recent major failures, bids they should have won but didn't? If they are unhappy, what moves can they make? How strong can these moves be and what can they expect to gain from making them? The attacking response is one most likely to cause you problems.

Defensive response

Your competition is most likely to take a defensive attitude to the bid when they know they are under threat and are unable to attack. Again, you have to seek answers to questions such as how susceptible they are to change? Are they vulnerable to political alternations or other world events? Perhaps they are being stretched beyond their capacity. What is their record of achievement? Do they have projects that are overrunning on schedule or budget? Are they facing litigation? Have they had to withdraw from any bids, and why? You should also look at whether any likely moves by the client could force them into a corner. What methods do they have to retaliate? The possibilities are many, but how they will react to change is an important consideration.

Develop your plan of attack

Even with the competitor profile and their bid response chart, you are not adequately prepared to win the bid. You now need to translate this information into an attack plan for your own bid and incorporate it into your bid strategy. Usually you will achieve greater success by attacking where your competitors are weakest. For example, try to find the area where they are least comfortable, where they have prepared least or where they have displayed least enthusiasm. Finally, look at the areas where their costs are highest.

Should you keep your strategy secret or should you reveal it? This is an interesting point that will clearly depend on the circumstances, but it is certainly worth your while discussing it. You have to assume that your competitors are aware of you and the threat you represent in the same way that you are of them. Your plan will be to fight them on issues that are critical to the client and where you stand the best chance of winning. Ideally, select an area where they cannot mount an effective response because the difficulty or costs to them are prohibitive and remember, they will have the same objective. If you reveal your plan overtly, either through advertising, promotion and talking to the client (conversations which usually manage to get to the ears of other bidders) or surreptitiously, you may allow them to create a defense against it. On the other hand, you will be taking the fight to them, forcing them to put effort into bolstering areas where you are strong and they are not. This is made even more effective if you can create internal conflict in their ranks and force them to focus on areas outside their normal strengths. Established companies are vulnerable to this type of attack from newcomers. You will never confuse them completely, but you could create sufficient conflict of interest to give yourself the advantage.

Conversely, if your strategy is weak or susceptible to attack, or if it relies upon innovation that could be copied by a me-too bidder, then you will want to keep it secure. By doing so, you prevent competitive retaliation but lose out on influencing the areas where you will fight. You clearly need to know the relative strengths of each stratagem and this is the art of bid management.

THE NEED FOR BID INFORMATION

There is much information available to businesses these days from many different sources. You could argue there is sometimes too much, which has the effect of overloading the gathering and assessment process so that the information is never used to the best advantage. Applying a structured assessment technique will filter the flow of data, allowing you to select that which is most useful and relevant to the bid in hand. Make certain that the information you gather is recent; working from old information is often worse than having none at all as it could mislead you. Get your data from a reliable source; try to get confirmation from elsewhere to check its veracity.

To perform analyses effectively you need a great deal of reliable and up-to-date information. Focusing on what your competitors will be doing will assist you in positioning your bid effectively. It will improve your offer and counter the threats your competitors will represent. Possibly, there will be a database of competitive information already existing in your company. The chances are that this is gleaned mostly from secondary sources, report and accounts, brochures, newspapers and on-line databases. You should use this information to complement your knowledge of your competitors obtained from the business and client managers. If the threat is unknown, you may have to consider obtaining an external market report. Always check what information you have already.

The most valuable information comes when you are bidding and finding out firsthand information on your competitors. This is really useful material that is valuable to all other bids your company will be making. Make sure that you update your database with anything you find out. You should include information on who won the bid and the approach they used.

Building a bid information system

Go about building a bid information system in a structured way. You are unlikely to have all the information you need at the outset, so will need to build it over time by gathering the correct data and keeping it updated. The bid process is very time sensitive, you have a deadline to meet and cannot therefore expend too much time getting information which you should already have. You must start early. Similarly, the extent to which you will formalise the system will depend on the size of your company and the organisation and structure of your bid process. Adapt the following outline to meet your own needs. Begin by looking at what your bid information system needs to achieve. It should have four main objectives: to provide a definition of the range of opportunities to be considered, to assist the analysis of prospects when identified, to help select those opportunities on which to focus, and provide you with assistance to win them. Fig. 8.6 shows a typical structure, work-flow and classification. To keep the information topical, classify each subject into information that is either permanent or transitory; that is, information which is relatively stable over the bid or which is very likely to change. The transitory data will be reviewed and updated more frequently as changes occur so make sure that your system can cope.

To identify the information you need, first set up a source directory. This will list where your information is normally located and the type of information you think you will need. For example, you should list relevant publications in each subject area, the people you need to speak to on specific details, the internal and external reports that you need access to, and the databases you need to search. This could be a master directory, which you can then subdivide if necessary to tailor it to the needs of the current bid. The information from each source is then filtered and categorised, rejecting anything that is out of date or irrelevant. Then compile it into the various bid categories such as opportunities, client information, competitor data, environmental and geographical data, status and situation reports. Include those categories that you think you will need. Try to rate each piece of information on how important it is to your bid. Check its validity, concentrating on the most important items before feeding it into your strategic analysis process. Your analysis will influence your business, competitive and bid strategies. Instigate regular reviews of data to check sources for changes, topicality of transitory information and to feed back any developments.

Typical categories

Areas in which you will need information may include: background data, country reports, legal position, economics, environmental data, client data, supplier data and competitors. The earlier data in Table 3 (see page 42) gave a checklist that you can use to establish your source directory. Primary data is that which relates directly to the bid and comes from a verifiable source. Secondary data is usually background material to support the primary data.

When bidding overseas you will find location data useful. This is usually secondary information which may cover country information, legal aspects, economics and environmental data. You will need to maintain quite extensive information on your clients, both existing and

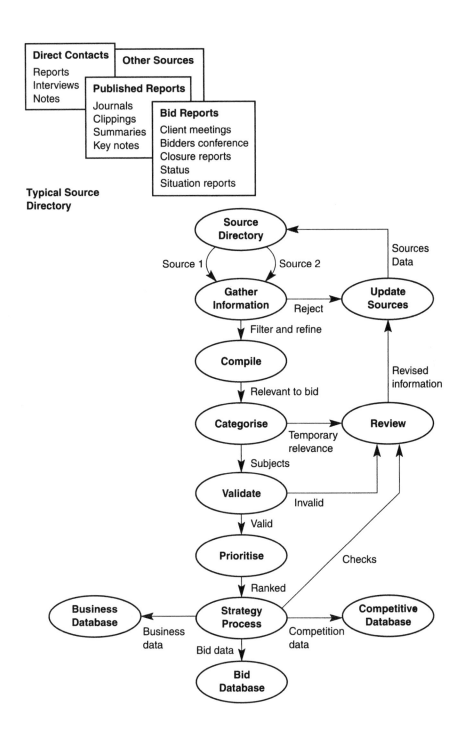

Direct Contacts
Reports
Interviews
Notes

Other Sources

Published Reports
Journals
Clippings
Summaries
Key notes

Bid Reports
Client meetings
Bidders conference
Closure reports
Status
Situation reports

**Typical Source
Directory**

Source
Directory

Source 1   Source 2

Sources
Data

Gather
Information   Reject   Update
Sources

Filter and refine

Compile

Relevant to bid

Revised
information

Categorise   Review

Temporary
relevance

Subjects

Validate   Invalid

Valid

Prioritise   Checks

Ranked

Business
Database   Strategy
Process   Competitive
Database

Business
data   Competition
data

Bid data

Bid
Database

Fig. 8.6 Building a bid-information system

potential. Find out about their businesses, financial data and the people involved in key positions.

Keep separate information on your suppliers, both existing and potential. You will need to include any other organisations that you may want to co-operate with in the future. Competitor information is clearly a prerequisite and you should try to get as much as you can. Concentrate on their products, strengths and weaknesses, market position and success record.

Finally, it is valuable to maintain files on opportunities and potential projects that fit with your business strategy. Keep a watch on these even if you are not bidding for them, as they may provide valuable insights into the way a particular client or competitor performs.

Information sources

The best information will come from your direct sources. This is likely to come from contacts with the client, interviews with knowledgeable companies and individuals, and account manager and business manager reports. Of course, this can often be the most subjective form of information, so you should always ensure that you validate this data from an alternative, independent source.

Some publications may also provide relevant information. National newspapers and journals may give information on opportunities or key developments. There are often special reports published on geographical areas and industrial sectors which frequently give constructive advice and facts. You can also read reports from the leading banks, financial houses, consultancies and business services, and although sometimes quite lengthy, the summaries and digests are often useful background material. It is also rewarding to read your client's trade paper; this can give clues to market trends and developments, and can point the way towards what they are expecting from you. For example, you may see what approach your client's leading rivals are taking and from it divine the direction in which you expect them to go. In the same vein, your own trade journals and papers can provide information on what your rivals are doing along with details of their recent successes or failures. All this background data, once consolidated and assimilated, is valuable in helping you to reach your strategic decisions.

Of course, you should also get as much information as possible on the financial status of your client and of the economic climate in which they are operating. Use their own financial reports as a starter and build a comprehensive financial profile, by assembling relevant reports from finance houses and credit agents where necessary.

When it comes to knowing where to find the information you need, you can do worse than to start at your public library. Most cities and large towns have a good main reference library open to the public where you can find directories of companies and organisations for virtually every part of the world. There are also many general business directories, as well as some on specific industry sectors. For most developed countries you can find the key details of any large company, including the names of recent key executives, turnover and other financial and operational information.

Within your company you will probably have several information sources: the marketing department, publicity, strategy department, legal office, sales manager, product manager and so on, will all probably have files used for their own functions. There may also be a company-wide library. Try to become familiar with them all and the type of data that each can provide. Take a few minutes to list some of the best ones and enter them into your source directory.

SUMMARY

Your bid strategy is an integral part of your corporate plan.

- *A good bid strategy should reflect your business plan. It must incorporate your plans for the client, dealing with the competition and developing and growing your business.*

- *Your client strategy should first establish what they are expecting from your bid then go on to influence them towards your solutions.*

- *Focus your product and service strategy on innovation, total quality and continuous improvement. Demonstrate quick delivery, quality of personnel and security of supply. Show that you can provide an integrated product portfolio at an affordable price.*

- *Construct a framework upon which your strategy can build to help you evolve a winning formula. Build in all the key market and competitive parameters then assess the needs of your client against them.*

- *An effective bid strategy couples what you are trying to achieve as a business with what you are attempting to provide to the client. Corporate factors such as growth, market leadership, international presence, diversification, product and market forces will determine how you tackle each bid.*

- *Methods to help create and plan a strategy include: taking an entrepreneurial approach using flair and initiative, stimulating ideas and suggestions within the team, and applying formal internal and external appraisals of the information you have gathered.*

- *Competition is the biggest threat to you winning new business. Find out your competitors' strengths and weaknesses and select a strategy which exploits them. Build a competitor profile and use your assessment of their likely responses to develop your plan of attack.*

9

PRICING YOUR OFFER

Of the many factors that decide the success or failure of your bid, perhaps pricing makes the largest single contribution. It is also arguably the most difficult single aspect of the bid. Within a traditional sales environment you will often have the opportunity to test the market price you set for your products or services. You can carry out market research and analysis to assess the competitiveness of your pricing policy. You will judge the profitability of specific products and make pricing decisions accordingly. Bidding in the competitive marketplace does not always allow you the flexibility to test the market; more often than not your bid will be a one-off project. You will have nothing exactly comparable to test against. So pricing in the bid environment takes on a more significant role. You will have one chance to get it right and if you fail to take that chance you may have lost the bid.

The price of your bid differs from its cost. Your price should include a margin for profit on costs and direct and indirect overheads. If your price does not cover all the costs involved in the bid you will incur losses. Making losses is not often a business objective, so a profit making bid is what you would usually favour. Where you expect a bid to incur losses for strategic purposes, you should consider carefully your approach and thoroughly review your bid strategy. Ask yourself if this is the only alternative or are there other ways. You might want to think about a more flexible financing package or reductions in cost. Consider also what your competition is offering as market forces are critical in bidding.

Usually, you will expect to gain profit from your bids and will have evaluated their profitability during the assessment leading to your bid decisions. You should expect to know the income and the direct costs of the project and therefore its contribution to your company overheads.

In this chapter the complexities of bid pricing are explored. Bid pricing has four stages. First of all a pricing policy must be established within your company and, secondly, by applying the specific attributes of the opportunity to this policy, you translate it into a pricing strategy for the bid. This strategy takes into consideration the expectations of your client and the likely responses from your competitors. With the strategic decisions made, the third stage where the costs are built up to ensure the project is profitable and can be sustained, begins. Finally, in constructing the financing plan you specify when and how the client will pay you.

PRICING POLICY

Unless you are bidding for marginal business or as a loss-leader to gain future opportunities, you will want your bid not only to win but also to be profitable. This means that your pricing policy and the strategy and tactics that you will employ to carry out that policy for your bid should reflect the level of profitability that you are trying to achieve.

Profitability is sometimes misunderstood. Retailers do not achieve profit on the sale of any one item. They mark up the direct costs of the product to provide a gross profit, but then have to consider their running costs or overheads. Only by achieving sufficient volume of sales to cover these costs will they break even and sales above this limit decide the profitability of their business. To be profitable in bidding you will also have to consider the overheads associated with running your business and therefore seek to recover these from your successful bids. However, bidding can incur high direct costs too; costs that you would not incur if you did not bid. Those bids you win also have to recover the direct costs of unsuccessful bids. This is why careful selection of bid opportunities is so important. A poor record of success caused by poor selection of prospects may make it impossible for your business to become profitable even when successful in several bids.

On the other hand, bid opportunities tend to be of higher value than sales made through regular selling channels. This is one reason why your client may have decided to invite tenders. So the normal rules of pricing for profit require some modification. Winning a single large profitable contract can take a business from below the break-even point to well above it, whereas the sale of a single product is unlikely to do that unless the product is itself of very high value.

Business policy

The first consideration in profitable bid pricing is to your business policy on price which is part of business planning and of your marketing strategy. In large organisations this may be a stated and documented policy, while for smaller companies it may be an accepted work practice. In whatever form your business pricing policy exists you should have a good understanding of how it will impinge upon your bid pricing. Your business goal, or mission statement, will encapsulate the way in which your organisation functions. It will shape the structure of your organisation and reflect the areas in which you are strong and those in which you have some limitations. It will help you in identifying new opportunities by establishing a framework for the short, medium and long terms. By strategically planning your business policy you will put in place plans, policies and procedures to support your bid activity and to manage and control it effectively.

The first aspect of your pricing policy that you will need to consider is the general level at which you are pitching for business. Your business may have at the centre of its policy the aim of being the lowest priced and best value on the market. Your bid pricing will therefore attempt to undercut your competitors thereby enabling you to gain extra market share in the short term. To operate successfully, a low-price policy needs to have costs that are minimised, well under control and at levels that can be sustained.

However, you may favour a high-quality, top-end of the market approach where price is high and quality, workmanship and reliability are paramount. You will present a discriminating image to your clients and your bid pricing will reflect this superior quality. You will achieve greatest success where you are operating in a market of high demand and low supply or you have near exclusive control of the market for your product or service. Clearly you must have a product or service that supports the superior image you are presenting and be in full control of access to it. You could aim to become a price leader and effectively set the standard for pricing, which your competitors will follow.

Alternatively, you may adopt a mid-range policy providing a convenient alternative between the lowest and highest price. Your bid price will then sit between these limits. With this, you will be aiming to maintain your current market position by pricing at the mean of the market level.

Business objectives

As part of your pricing policy, you will also pay regard to the strategic objectives of your business and what you are trying to achieve. For example, you may be attempting to develop your domestic market share or seeking to expand internationally on one or several fronts. Possibly you are aiming at the introduction of new technology and innovative ideas, or maybe focusing on traditional skills and attention to detail. Your objectives therefore could include improving your cost-base and productivity or looking for additional deployment of existing people. These are factors in your strategic business objectives that will affect your bid price.

Your intention in managing and winning the bid will be to ensure that you also meet your business aims. Bids can be vital in helping you to achieve that. An example is a company wishing to expand into a new geographical region. There are three ways they can go. They can expand organically, by establishing a company infrastructure or joint-venture in the country, setting up offices, employing staff and beginning to trade. They can expand by acquisition, buying into an existing company and seeking to develop it to meet their aims, or they can proceed on a project basis, using a successful contract as a vehicle to gain a foothold in the target market. Organic and acquisitive expansion frequently requires considerable equity and capital commitment, joint-ventures less so. Expansion by winning new contracts does not commit the business to a large speculative financial outlay other than that of the bid costs. If the bid is successful the company will meet the costs of its expansion through the returns on the contract. So bid management can play a major role in allowing a company to achieve its corporate business policy and strategy.

Pricing strategy

While considering your company's business policy on price in preparation for your bid, you will either encounter, or come to develop, a set of objectives that you and your organisation wish to achieve. Document these when developing your bid price so you do not overlook them during the bid. These pricing objectives will also give you guidance on which particular route you should be going down and where alternatives exist. You should expect to set objectives such as:

- Add value to products or services to improve their perceived worth
- Increase short-term profitability over the next financial year
- Use improved profits to fund organic growth
- Increase share of the market
- Attain industry leadership and dictate price
- Attack competitors' entrenched positions

- Make it difficult for newcomers to enter the market
- Expand into new markets by acquisition.

Finally, consider what are your own strategic objectives.

BID PRICE STRATEGY

The pricing for your bid will depend upon your interpretation of your business policy and pricing strategy and will be modified by the critical components of the opportunity. You must structure the bid price to take advantage of your strengths and unique selling proposition which are the factors that distinguish your bid from those of your competitors. You will need to assess the marketing position before deciding your approach so find out who is competing and how strong they are. You will need to weigh up the client's budget and price expectations, deliberate upon your own organisation, its cost-base and profit targets, before deciding your bid price strategy.

Price objectives

The outcome of your analysis will be a set of price objectives around which your strategy will develop. Your objectives may well look like the following examples:

- To win the bid by matching or bettering the prices of all competitors.
- Apply a promotional discount in your key market or geographical areas to gain a foothold and steal a march on competition
- Focus on reducing your client's costs
- Offer a formulaic link between bid price and cost-reduction
- Use open-accounting to enhance your position with the client

Now list your own price objectives for the bid.

In practice you will use a combination of approaches, strategies and tactics from the many alternatives that are available. Use the following system to allow you to select a framework for your particular bid.

Pricing strategy framework

When it comes to deciding what price strategy is appropriate for your bid, there are two main criteria, the offer price and the profitability.

Getting the right balance is essential. Although high profit is probably what every bidder aspires to, your client will be hoping for the lowest price. The two are sometimes mutually exclusive; if your price is too low, you may not reach the break-even point and if it is too high, you may not win the bid. Achieving the best position, which suits both of you, is often a case of assessing the relative strengths of buyer and seller and reaching a compromise.

Fig. 9.1 shows how different factors will influence the position you finally take. Some examples of these varying strategies are explained below:

The low-price method

As many bids are chosen on price alone, a low price approach may be one that you will adopt frequently. In these bids, the cases for superior technology, quality standards and reliability take a back seat to the bottom line. You still need to comply with the specification in these areas but your bid will not win unless it is the lowest price. If you know you have an advantageous cost-base when compared to your competitors this framework will yield excellent results while retaining reasonable profit levels.

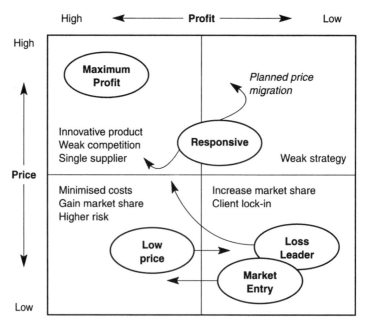

Fig. 9.1 Framework for price strategies

This approach will win bids at lower profitability than higher pricing strategies but will enable you to increase your share of the market. Use this framework to construct your price when you are sure that your costs are minimised. Any missing cost lines may greatly affect the viability and ultimate profitability of the project.

Maximising your profit

In order to maximise your profit, you must first establish that your client is prepared to pay a high price and that the competition is weak or unable to comply with the client's requirement. Under this framework you will price high where, for example, you have innovative technology or an exclusive licence, or when you possess some unique aspect that none of your competitors have and which your client needs. Make sure that the margins are healthy and you cover all costs and contingencies. It is unlikely that your competition will be able to mount a serious challenge in the short term leaving you to take maximum profit from the opportunity.

This is also true in a single action tender, one in which you are the only invited bidder. Again you could consider maximising your profits, but be realistic, you might scare off your client or jeopardise future business by appearing mercenary. Remember that you may be looking to the client for more sales or to act as a reference for other opportunities. Manage their expectations. Antagonising your client or making them feel that they have been forced into paying too much will always harm your relationship.

Gaining market entry

To gain market entry quickly or to build market share in an existing market you may decide to price on the low side. But, although your profit margins are not going to be high, you will still want reasonable returns. The intention with this strategy is to gain entry into a competitive marketplace, discourage competition with aggressive pricing and aim to build up market share over time. This means using your bid as leverage to get you established. The likelihood is that you will not be looking to increase your price in the short term because of the risk of affecting your new market position, so you will want to aim to increase overall profitability by building up your client base and increasing your number of sales. Consequently, you must be sure that you are making a reasonable profit and have included all costs.

Loss-leader bids

Bidding as a loss-leader has inherent risk but can be valuable in many situations. In this scenario you price the bid low to establish future market share, either with the client or in the region or commercial sector that the client operates in. Using this strategy you will be able to increase your client base by attracting the interest of other associated businesses. You can also hope to get your foot in the door or lock-in your client to your product or service line so that you can sell more profitable products or services at a later stage.

As you are bidding at a loss, you will have to be able to withstand the costs involved in the bid. Your ambition should be to increase profits and prices later on. You will need to put an upper limit on your costs in terms of money and time, and be prepared to cut your losses if the strategy does not prove successful. Exercise caution with this approach as it is often difficult to raise prices later when your client's price expectations have been lowered. This is particularly risky where your competition is strong and plentiful. The client may have easy access to a second source in the event that your prices rise too high.

Responsive framework

It is inadvisable, in most bids, to fix your price strategy without giving thought to other relevant factors. Your final price position is bound to be influenced by your competitors and by the client and market conditions meaning that you will be adjusting your price according to a complex relationship between a number of considerations. You will probably favour this approach where your competition is strong, especially if they are attempting to gain market entry and their pricing is low. In the same way, where the client requirements or budget have been ill-defined, you will price the bid so you can respond to any changes that are likely to occur.

The winning price

It is the job of company chief executives to ask bid managers if they have the winning price and any bid manager who gets the right answer every time, is a valuable asset to any company and very much sought after. Finding the winning price is a conundrum that perplexes many bidders and yet without a close approximation you stand to lose, or, if you win, to reduce your profit. Your clients today are likely to be sophisticated purchasers. Selection of the winning bid takes account of a combination of factors such as initial price, costs over the lifetime of the project, technical compliance, quality, reliability and track record. However, if you are way out on price then you are going to find it very difficult to catch up in the other areas. It is this multiplicity of variables that makes pricing so critical.

Whichever framework you base your bid price upon, you have to set, and aim to reach the target of the winning price. If you have ever requested an estimate from a builder, you will understand the situation. You will often receive quotes that vary wildly; the highest price might be twice or three times the lowest. How does this come about? Why is there such a wide variance in performing the same task? The problem lies in bidding without being fully conversant with all the facts and all your expectations. If your builder asks for information, or you supply it in your specification, you will see a narrower price variation. For example, you can give them your budget for the job and say who else is competing. You can describe what funding arrangements are in place, such as with an insurance claim and then, providing they use this information, you would see a much closer range of estimates.

The principal element of deciding your price strategy is to consider the winning price. By getting to know the client you can probably estimate the figure that they have in mind. But, no matter what relationship you have established with the client, if they do not have sufficient money to buy your solution then you will not win the bid. Consider some of the following methods for arriving at what you consider to be the winning price. There are advantages and disadvantages in each.

Cost-plus method

In this pricing method, you decide the bid price based on costs plus a suitable margin. The major influence on this approach is not the client, market or competitive forces, but your own base costs. You will build your costs up considering all possible cost items. It is likely that you will not always be able to predict costs with a high enough degree of accuracy so you will be forced to work on the best estimates. In a complex multi-discipline bid, you will invariably overestimate or underestimate costs which means you will need to include a contingency element within the cost build to allow for potential variances.

Because of the uncertainty and inflexibility in this approach, you probably should not use this method of pricing in bidding situations. If you have the advantage of a low cost-base then you will have the edge on competitors who do not. However, always begin your costing with your estimate of the winning figure and decide your cost-build from that basis. Remember that cutting costs is a more effective way of improving profit than increasing margins.

Standard price method

Many organisations price bids according to their standard product lists. This is a solid and easy method that gives you the reassurance of knowing that all necessary contributions and profit have been included. Being unambiguous, your client knows where they stand and what they must pay. There will be occasions however, when standard list prices are not necessarily going to win you the contract. Your client may want additional volume discounts or you could be competing against a known undercutting competitor. This is when you need to challenge the basis of a list price and look for an alternative. You must, however, be in full possession of the data to support your argument otherwise you will not convince your product pricing authorities.

This is also true of your standard margins and overhead recovery. It is frequent for prices to be marked-up twice (or more) and overheads recovered at various points within the business. Know what the workforce costs are, know what the overheads are, challenge any price that does not fit within the bounds of what is reasonable.

Budgetary method

Budgetary prices are those you give your client where you cannot be sure of the final bid price. This is another area that requires some thought and planning. They might ask you to submit a budgetary price or estimate during the pre-tender phases of your bid. It has the advantage of giving you and the client a target to aim at during tendering and will mean that you will know that their budget for the project is realistic. It also enables you to exert influence on their budgetary controls. The disadvantages are that once stated the client will not receive well any significant divergence from the budgetary quotation. Furthermore, where regulated services are concerned, the licence regulations must be carefully considered.

Bargaining method

You may decide to bid a low price and increase the margin through negotiation with the client. This is worth thinking about but first make sure, by getting to know your client well, that you have a good chance of negotiating a better deal. If you cut the bid price and are unsuccessful in your negotiations it may significantly impinge on the viability of the project.

For bids to international lending agencies, the guidelines, in general, state that no bidder can alter the substance or price in their offer. This is almost the reverse of commercial behaviour in the private sector. In both public and private sector procurement, buyers seek ways to get past this restriction. You must know whether you can enter post-tender negotiation with the client and plan in advance what you can give away in terms of price. This must form an essential component of your pricing strategy.

Revenue and capital pricing

A revenue package may be much more attractive than a capital investment programme, even if the client has funds allocated for the purchase. Look to see if you can amortise the capital amount so that regular payments come from the client's revenue account. If they can pay for your bid through income earned while using the products or services, they can perhaps benefit from improved cash flow. There is a higher risk to you of their defaulting but you could, perhaps, offset this by retaining ownership over the period.

The decision on whether to structure a financing package based upon capital or revenue spending may not be yours as the client may have firm views. Nevertheless, you will probably need to give it some consideration within your pricing strategy. You should be aware of current trends and conduct an analysis of recent spending patterns within your client's market sector.

What might your client consider to be revenue items: running costs, general maintenance, support, training, staffing and other costs of ownership? These are likely to figure, ever higher, on your client's list of priorities as the economic position grows stronger. In a recession, capital expenditure will tend to dominate all purchasing decisions. Keeping a tight grip on the purse strings is a fundamental of cost containment. Capital spending is therefore likely to be reduced. However, because of this, your client could spend more on maintenance, support and other cost-of-ownership issues. You should explore each possibility very carefully, as closing down in one area may open another opportunity elsewhere.

Marginal pricing

The final pricing method to consider is that for marginal business. Although a low-price strategy, it differs from those described above, because it involves you in reducing your profit margins to a level below that which you would normally expect to achieve. Marginal pricing is useful when business is quiet. You cut prices and profit margins to win the bid and a new order. You would consider this when you have excess capacity that you need to utilise or that you would be paying for anyhow. Be careful how you operate this pricing approach however. Try to establish a plan that reflects your trading conditions. Begin by setting yourself a target for marginal business and do not go above it. It is advisable to set a percentage limit of your total gross profit, so you can make sure you are not jeopardising your business by losing potential added profit.

Although marginal pricing is often used, you should be careful to avoid using this approach too frequently when bidding. It is true that any new orders or contracts that add even low profit levels do still contribute towards the total profitability of your company. However, the danger is that if sales are below break-even level or your cuts are too high, you will never reach profitability and your business will fail. Try to see it from the client's point of view: although they may welcome a low price, they will also want you around to deliver. If they feel that you cannot sustain business at this marginal level, they may be reticent about awarding you the contract in the first place. A final word of warning though: once you have set a precedence for low prices, you may find it difficult to raise them later without losing credibility and sales.

BID COSTING

Costs play an important part in pricing your bid but should not alone influence what the final bid price will be. You have seen from the pricing strategies that bid pricing based solely upon costs may not be the most effective way of winning profitable business. Prices should, however, reflect the cost base that supports them to prevent low profitability or even losses occurring on the bid. As a bid manager you will be getting cost information yourself and from many other sources both in and outside your organisation. On a major bid this could involve you in much effort. Costs can be critical to your success. It is worthwhile reviewing each item with your cost accountant or finance department so that you have a good understanding of the relationship between your costs and profit.

Budgeting costs

As you will not yet have incurred most of the costs associated with your bid, you need an accurate budget based upon the available information.

There are two parts to the bid cost budget. First there is the estimated cost of preparing your bid, which can often be quite high. Then, there are the cost estimates for carrying out the works or services that make up the contract and are covered in the actual bid price. Moreover, you may decide to recover the bidding costs from the price tendered. Knowing that your costs are accurate is a great benefit in bidding and having at your fingertips a full breakdown of those costs can be of immense value when negotiating a final price with your client.

Fig. 9.2 shows a checklist of some typical cost items for bid preparation and bid pricing budgets. Use this as a guide when developing your own. You have to bear in mind that any costs omitted from your analysis will increase the pay-back period. This is the phase of a successful contract when you will recover what you have spent and reach break-even. If you have omitted a sufficiently costly item or one that reccurs regularly, you could find that you never break-even, and the project operates at a loss.

Budgeting techniques

There are several ways of approaching the costs of your bid. Some of these have been touched on earlier, but it is an area which is so critical to making a bid successful that it is worth repeating. First, you can obtain estimates based on established criteria and quotations from potential subcontractors using your assessment of the client's requirements. If your bid is dependent upon a few critical suppliers then this may give you all the information you need.

Another approach is to decide what price you need to achieve in order to win the contract and then to seek estimates and costs based upon meeting that target. This gives you greater flexibility where you have known and fixed costs and means that you can adjust the margins to achieve the winning price.

However, your organisation may have standard costs, in which case you will base your bid costs upon historical assumptions and data. Typically, this would be the situation for a manufacturing business. For preliminary price estimates you may have a standard cost listing for your organisation. This sets out standard man-hour rates, agreed rates for other personnel or outside agencies and other standard costs. You can

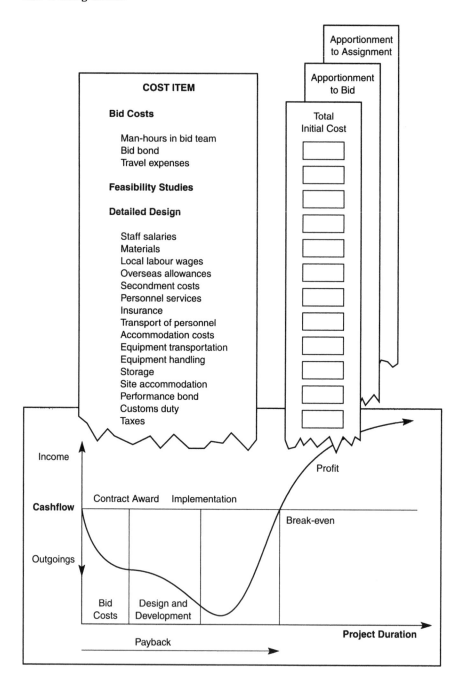

Fig. 9.2 Cost breakdown and payback

use this at the outset of the bid to gain an appreciation of the value of the opportunity, man-hours available in the budget and approval to go on.

Each approach has its advantages and you must decide which is most appropriate for your bid. For example, where the client weighs technical capability high, the cost-plus basis may be appropriate. Where price is critical and competition is fierce you may select the best price approach. But whichever method you use, you should ensure that it is accurate.

When you need to have the final bid price before the submission of the bid, always prepare a detailed cost build. During the bid preparation, it is easy to overlook cost elements that arise during project execution. This can turn a profitable project into a loss-making exercise so make sure you take all items into account during the cost build.

Estimating operating expenses

Budgeting for expenses is too often a finger-in-the-wind exercise in many bids. There will be times when you are uncertain of your expenses and so will need to estimate them. Try to base your estimates upon some certainties. If you have to incur travel and hotel expenses you can find out the exact fare and the room rates, even if you are unclear of the precise number of journeys. This allows you to produce an estimated budget based upon length of stay, approximate number of tickets, class of travel, size of hired vehicle and so on.

Besides travel, many other expenses will be a function of the number of people involved in the project. Personnel insurance, stationery, computers, telephones and office furniture may be necessary. If these are not part of the corporate overhead then you will need to include these costs within the operating budget for your bid.

Some operating expenses will directly relate to the length of the contract. You may have to rent office accommodation or use a warehouse. Interest may be payable on monies borrowed. Work out utility expenses like gas, water and electricity on a daily basis. Thus you can prepare a reasonable estimate of these costs based upon the known length of the contract or upon your project plan.

Cost analysis

In forecasting your anticipated spending, your budget will be a projection consisting of known facts based upon historical data and assumptions, which will be your best guesses about the future. Strive for accuracy all the same and do not base a forecast upon an assumption derived from a projection. Any uncertainties in the equation will be multiplied as they work through the costing and you may find yourself well off-target. Always base your projections upon known facts, maintaining a logical link between data and assumptions.

How detailed your budget has to be depends on the degree of leeway you have on your price. If you have a large degree of tolerance then you can probably take simple historical data and add a percentage increase in line with a standard price index. If you need to minimise costs, then you may need to conduct a detailed analysis of all cost items to the nearest penny. Bear in mind that although accuracy is important you only have limited time available to prepare and if you go into too much unnecessary detail you may well find it difficult to meet the deadline and your efforts will be wasted. You should consider a degree of detail that suits the bid. Normally this will be a detailed analysis where costs are high and saving can be critical, and a less formal one when the savings you can make are not so significant.

When doing your analysis your task is to fit the costs within the boundaries imposed by the winning price while still making the requisite profit. This means you should be continually assessing the costs as they build up and testing them for cost-effectiveness, cost-reduction, redundancy and overlap, to see where savings can be made. Do this as you go along and with every cost item. If you get towards bid submission and find you need to shave your costs, you will be hard-pressed to do so effectively unless you have carefully dissected every cost item along the way. Your analysis of the costs breaks down into several areas as set out below.

Direct costs

Your direct costs are those you do not incur if you are unsuccessful in your bid. These are the production costs for any equipment you will be manufacturing or supplying and costs associated with the sale such as freight and forwarding, packaging, and insurance. The budget for these will relate directly to the schedule of services or products contained within your bid and you should be able to accurately calculate them.

You should also include tax as a direct cost where it relates specifically to the goods or services being supplied. The interest you pay on funds advanced to build or develop the tendered solution, for supplier credit financing or for bid and performance bonds, will also be a direct cost. Check for any other items that may fall into this category, such as any licences you may need to purchase, insurance premiums for transportation or carrying out the project, and so on.

Work-force costs

The total cost of labour, both in preparing the bid and delivering the solution, is often difficult to calculate accurately. Labour costs occur throughout your organisation. Some staff salaries may be charged to a profit-centre and these are the people who provide the business with revenue. The costs of these people are met generally from their operating budget which is based upon achieving sales. In other words, your bid needs to recover their costs. Other staff salaries may be charged to a cost-centre. These people generally provide common corporate services which reduce the total costs of the business. Their costs would not normally be recoverable from a single sale. You have to decide which labour costs have to be recovered in your bid and which are part of the corporate overhead.

Work-force costs are often the single largest expense over which you have some control. It is also the area in which you have the greatest scope for achieving a winning price by reduction or modification, and it therefore deserves a great deal of attention. Setting the head-count too high in your bid can result in inefficiencies that may take you over the client's budget, too low and it may affect your ability to deliver on time.

Work-force costs will include standard elements such as those listed in Fig. 9.3; check that none are overlooked or overstated. Gross salary should include basic pay, performance related bonuses, commission and overseas allowances, if appropriate. Remember to include the employer's pension and National Insurance contributions and any other benefits provided such as car, telephone, mortgage, health insurance and other subsidies. If your contract from a successful bid extends over a long period, you could include some mechanisms for increasing these costs over the project duration. Estimate cost of living increases from the Retail Price Index and include any gross salary changes due to promotions or length of service. Also take into account the introduction of any changes to direct and indirect taxation and include any bonuses based upon performance during the contract or on its completion.

Transfer charging

Large organisations are often decentralised into autonomous or semi-autonomous operating divisions or units. Each division has a degree of latitude with respect to its pricing policy and has responsibility for contributing profit into corporate coffers. Problems can arise where

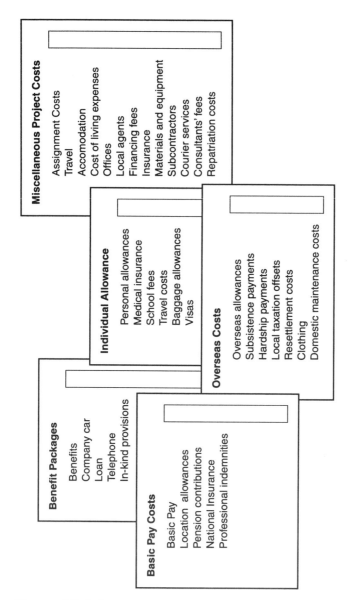

Fig. 9.3 Work-force costs

independence is not total and one division provides products or services to another. A transfer charge is usually set to account for the revenue of the supplying division and the costs of the consuming division. The basis of the transfer cost can often create conflict within the organisation as each division has its own revenue targets to meet.

You must know the basis of the transfer charge. The transfer may be at full cost or cost-plus in which case you may get a better deal from another supplier. The supplying division may gain nothing from the transfer or could be worse off. Transfer costs may be set at the market rate, in which case you should try to negotiate a reduction based upon lower sales, marketing and shipping costs to the supplying division. This basis will be restrictive for you if you are not able to seek supply on the open market. Transfer costs may be negotiable in which case you can again ask the supplying division to compete against other suppliers for the lowest price. This is a more flexible approach that may be advantageous to the supplying division if they have excess capacity that they wish to fill, for example.

How do you decide? You may have no choice, you may be forced to buy internally and accept the price proffered. If the market is competitive it does not matter to the supplier if they sell to part of their own company or another. You should try to buy internally where the cost to you is below that which you can buy on the open market.

The conflict with transfer costs is inherent in many organisations that strive for independence. It can only be resolved by having a full understanding of the competitive marketplace, the fixed-cost base, the variable costs involved, the production capacity and order book of the supplying division. In a bid, you will not have time to deal with these issues. However, good communication on transfer costs between each division and senior management will help your company develop a transfer strategy that fits the bill.

Perhaps the most common problem in calculating transfer workforce costs in large organisations is multiple-accounting of overheads. The difficulty lies in other departments which supply you with cost estimates or charge-out rates for their people that already include a contribution to overheads. If you then unknowingly add your own contribution, the rate for the job can soar. On principle you should challenge every cost you receive and understand how they have been derived. Only then can you be sure that the cost is accurate.

FINANCING PLAN

Arriving at the winning price through careful policy-making, strategic planning and cost control will often be sufficient to win the bid. Frequently, however, you need to take it one step further. This final stage is the financing plan, containing the analysis of how the client will pay you. These payment arrangements are a critical aspect of the bid finances, particularly if the client has specified terms that you find unacceptable. If this is the case, an alternative or compromise must be sought and this will require some creative thinking. Use your finance and project planning managers to the full to help you develop a suitable solution.

The options here are many and the decisions are critical. For example, your client may look more favourably on a bid that extends credit over the term of the contract, with relaxed payments terms. Or they may prefer a bid that offers a discount for full payment on delivery. Though you may have the lowest price, if the client is looking for credit that you cannot offer, you may not win.

The bid financing strategy, therefore, will often dictate the success or failure of the bid. It is a complex subject so you should consider all the alternatives. The final word on your finance planning rests with the client, so look for ways that they could offset the financing of the whole project. You should have looked at all the options, but none of them will be effective unless they appeal to your client. Before making your decision, review what they are seeking, both in terms of the price they wish to pay and how they want to pay for it.

As they will most probably be seeking the best deal possible, your bid should offer a cost-effective solution that meets their needs, and at a price that is within their available budget. What will convince them that your proposal can meet those objectives? Much depends on the way in which they assess the bid. The client may prefer a bid that is superficially the lowest and therefore you should take every opportunity to reduce the apparent costs, no matter how transparent it might be. Review again the options open to you: such as reducing staff costs, lowering operating costs, and decreasing fixed direct costs. At this stage you will have already investigated ways to offset non-core activities through outsourcing, managed facilities and contracting out.

See if the client would appreciate a discounted cash flow. You should always consider the possibility of packaging the price to take advantage of a positive cash flow to make the deal more competitive. You can weight, in terms of price, the services or products you will provide first, or include a separate item for set-up costs paid pro rata on progress.

Using financing to add value

Financing can be a powerful weapon in your bid arsenal. There are two basic routes: conventional financing favoured by the banks, and other, more unorthodox methods, which carry higher commensurate risk. Orthodox financing alternatives include supplier credit where the contract should provide for a small proportion of the consideration to be paid in cash. The outstanding balance is then deferred until bills of exchange are transferred. This will require you to make arrangements with a credit insurer against default by the customer. Buyer credit is also an orthodox financing method that may be considered and although this takes much longer to establish there is no residual risk to the supplier.

These customary methods are internationally accepted and regulated. Keep up to date on these ways to arrange financing as methods and regulations are constantly changing. In addition, these financing methods variously offer you protection against non-payment. You can usually include short-term credit insurance from banks or credit brokers.

Beside the standard approaches you should look into other ways to make a package more attractive to the client. Unorthodox finance arrangements may be more appropriate, but usually carry a risk relative to the degree of non-conformity. You will more often find these methods used in developing countries or those with less well-established economies. For example, look into the possibility of providing a soft-loan linked with credit. You could perhaps look for some counter-trade component; getting paid in kind instead of by cash for example. Equity participation may be another option where you take a share in your client's company instead of being paid.

Usually, however, your financing package should consist of several components. You may find it worthwhile to investigate a few of the following methods to see which is best for your bid and for your client. There are advantages and disadvantages to each, so you should be selective, making sure they fit your needs. You could perhaps consider breaking your price down into its component parts allowing the client to select those parts of the offer that they require now, with variations and additions purchased at a later stage. Conversely, a turnkey system at a single price may provide the customer with significant advantages. Look at both options from the client's perspective.

Export financing

Using the main lending banks, export houses or the Government export credit guarantee department to help finance your bid can often help you appear more competitive to the client. You arrange a loan in advance for the value of the contract and when you are successful, full or partial funds are provided to you by the bank. With the amount available in full, you can extend credit to your client that may give you the edge and the client need never know the source of the credit which you are effectively providing. By taking advantage of the lender's insurance and guarantee schemes, your risk of payment default by the client is reduced.

Factoring

Factoring is another method to enhance cash flow, allowing you to offer credit advantages to your client in your bid. You receive full or partial payment by the factoring agent when you raise a sales invoice. With funds available quickly, you can buy supplies in bulk or take a larger order than your cash flow would otherwise allow. Again the factoring agent will normally include insurance and guarantees that protect your funds, whether the client pays you or not. Most of the larger banks offer a domestic or international factoring service.

Foreign exchange rate

Consider the currency in which payment is being made and consult with your bank or your treasury departments to establish the degree of risk involved. You will need to consider how to pay any bid and performance bonds, as well as taking payment from the client if you are awarded the contract. You should seek professional advice on these exchange rate and taxation issues.

Other financing advantages can arise because of these fluctuations in foreign exchange rates. Using a *forward exchange transaction* when submitting your bid, you can fix a rate of exchange for payments made by your client at some later stage. This eliminates the risk of negative currency fluctuations. The down-side is that you also miss out on any positive fluctuations from which you would otherwise benefit. Furthermore, you may be forced to commit to the exchange without knowing for certain whether you will win the contract. To get around these disadvantages you could consider taking a *currency option* to buy or sell an amount of foreign currency at some future date. With this you also fix the exchange rate, but being an option you do not have to make the transaction.

You may be tempted in your bid, to raise your prices to cover any possible losses on currency exchanges. This is a fatally-flawed tactic; you are adding a contingency for a risk that can be better mitigated by taking out one of the above protection schemes. If for any reason you are unable to reduce the risk by these approaches, you could offset some of it by retaining the funds in a local currency bank account. Use this account to pay local charges, agent's fees, consultants and subcontractor operating costs, in local currency, and if necessary repatriating funds later at a more advantageous rate.

Letters of credit

Letters of credit are used by supplier and client, each to their advantage. You can ask the client to provide you with a letter of credit that ensures you get payment when your goods or services are delivered in return for giving them better credit terms. The client may offer you a letter of credit in which they stipulate the precise terms of delivery; you only getting paid when all the conditions have been met. This is usually something you can negotiate.

It is vitally important when dealing with letters of credit that you keep all your records and documentation in order and deliver it on time. Because of errors, most letters of credit are not paid first time. The issuing bank will check all the paperwork and if they find an error they will not pay. Fresh authorisation will then be needed from your client and you will have to involve yourself in additional effort and costs as well as losing your payment guarantee.

Retention of money

If the client has specified mandatory terms of payment in the tender documents your scope for financial creativity is reduced. Here your only real room for manoeuvre may be on money retained by the client. This is usually in the form of a performance bond, where a percentage of the total price is retained by them pending acceptance testing or compliance with other performance criteria. If you are confident of meeting all the delivery qualifications, you could offer a higher performance bond, enhancing your client's cash flow. It is also a useful area for negotiation.

Counter-trade

Counter-trade is simply the taking of goods or services as part or full payment for the products or services you are providing. This is quite common in international bids to the less developed nations where hard currency is often a problem. Your client may ask you to accept some proportion of locally manufactured goods in lieu of cash payment. You must think carefully before making any commitments as it is possible that you will have to arrange for the importation of these goods and then their resale. This may be acceptable if you are offered goods that you can use yourself, or if you are knowledgeable in the resale market for them but if you are a computer manufacturer, for example, bidding to supply latest technology processors then taking a consignment of leather tool-wallets or protective overalls in part-exchange may be difficult to justify. Clearly there is a place for this type of financing arrangement but it will be more suitable in certain markets than in others. If it makes the financing package more acceptable to the client and if you feel that you can benefit from the goods, then consider it by all means. However, if the bid has strategic connotations, then you may see this as overriding any commercial detriments that the counter-trade might bring.

In well-developed markets, this practice is rapidly disappearing. But you may still be asked to take some other material goods as part payment. An airline may offer you discounted fares or a car manufacturer discounts on buying your company vehicles. These are often worth contemplating. Always remember though, to consult with your tax advisers in case there should be any particular aspect of taxation law that you will need to bring into the equation.

Soft loans

A soft loan is another device employed by larger companies to ease the purchase of their products by the client. The funds for financing the project are lent by the supplier of the goods, generally on very favourable terms. The repayment period of the loan is often deferred and the interest rates charged can sometimes be quite low. Governments are also frequent lenders of soft loans. In these cases, the loan is made in support of their export drives, a condition of lending being that the goods are purchased from one of their national companies. Again, these types of arrangements are far more common in under-developed countries where there is a paucity of hard currency. If you are faced with making such a loan, you will have to think carefully about the risk involved. The amounts can be large, and there is an inherent risk that you may not recover all the funds that you have lent. Soft loans are often the only way in which projects in poorer countries can go ahead. If you are bidding against a supplier who is prepared to make such loans available while you are not, you should look at your strategy and assess what your chances of winning the bid are likely to be.

Equity sharing

Another aspect of your financing plan is the sharing of equity in your client's company. Effectively, you will be taking a slice of their business in return for supplying the goods or service. The key to success here is not to look on this equity share as payment, but as the makings of a partnership arrangement. This makes more sense when there is synergy between your operations. If you supply electricity-generating equipment, taking a share in the company with the natural resources, such as coal, oil, gas or water, needed to generate power may make strategic sense. Too many companies try to diversify by taking stakes in businesses that have only weak links into their core activity. This can only serve to dilute the effectiveness of both companies. Reflect on this if there is no clear relationship between you.

Leasing agreements

Leasing agreements are another means of financing the bid that may be appropriate to the products or services you are supplying. In leasing, you convey the product of service to your client for a specified period, usually on payment of a rent. Typically leases are considered in the supply of company vehicles, computer systems, machine tools and other traditionally high capital-spend areas, for reducing the overall capital cost to the client. Before suggesting a leasing agreement you should seek advice on the tax position for your company and the client as different products have different tax treatments in different countries.

Rental leases

The most common form of leasing is where the client pays a rent for the products supplied for a fixed period. The rental payments generally do not cover the value of the products supplied, but a residual value is worked out beforehand. You retain the product at the end of the leasing period and gain additional profit from its resale. There is limited financial gain to the client but they gain a technological advantage through upgrades. Also, there may be considerable tax advantages to the client as they can offset the rental as an allowable business expense. Ownership of the product remains with you as the supplier. Consider this approach for high value equipment with low depreciation and high residual value.

Finance leases

These differ from rentals as the client gains immediate ownership of the product, phasing payment over the period of the lease. These generally cost more than rentals. Consider carefully your strategy on termination before the completion of the lease. The client is not getting technological benefits from this agreement but they have the advantage that the products appear on the balance sheet. Interest payments can be offset against tax and the products are depreciated as a capital asset.

SUMMARY

Price is probably the most critical single factor in any bid.

- *Your pricing policy is determined by the profit you are seeking. In order to price low you should have a minimised cost-base. High pricing should reflect superior quality or market dominance. Mid-range pricing offers a convenient alternative and will mantain your market position.*

- *The objectives of an effective bid-pricing strategy are to add value thereby improving perceived worth, increased profitability, fund growth, increase market share, support market leadership, attack competitors and deter newcomers.*

- *Unless you are below or close to your client's winning price you cannot win.*

- *Cost-plus methods of pricing can be risky and lead to overpricing. Budgetary pricing gives the client a target but implies uncertainty. Bargaining methods are valid when you know the client will negotiate. Marginal pricing is useful when business is slow, but can set a precedence for low prices that may be difficult to alter.*

- *Bid costing requires accurate budget forecasts. Budget for the cost of preparing the bid and for carrying out the contract. Having accurate cost breakdowns help you when negotiating a final price with the client.*

- *Prepare a financing plan that gives favourable terms to your client while offering you a degree of protection.*

10

BID PLANNING AND MANAGEMENT

Good planning and bid management is the key to converting your strategy on price, competitors and client into a winning proposal. This is when taking advantage of your early preparation, team work and strategic planning, becomes critical. With the anticipated arrival of the invitation to bid, the most frenetic stage of the bid cycle begins, and without good planning, control and management, the bid will run unchecked and haphazardly.

This chapter covers bid planning, management and control and describes the processes and procedures that will maintain a reasonable level of supervision through the bid cycle. A fundamental bid plan is examined, with an analysis of what it needs to achieve and how it does it. A good bid plan consolidates all your thinking and sets out how to win the contract. It should focus the bid by providing guidance and instruction to the bid team throughout the bid cycle. Of course, just stating what must be done is rarely sufficient, so controls are needed to ensure that the plan works. From time to time you will need adjustments to adapt to changes and to keep bid production on schedule and within your budget. Bid controls ensure these occur when they are supposed to. In addition, you need to establish the essential management interfaces necessary to maintain the direction and focus of the bid.

BASICS OF BID PLANNING

An effective bid plan should not just issue instructions, it should be an essential part of controlling and co-ordinating activity and it should also serve to illuminate your purposes. Having a structure to the bid helps you to clarify your bid objectives systematically, to make strategic decisions and check progress. Through making it a dynamic tool and not a static document, you gain an instrument for updating, reviewing and quickly reacting to change. This is essential during a bid as corrections are made and strategy develops.

In making the decision to go ahead with the bid you will have developed an outline bid strategy. Preparation of the bid plan enforces a review of your strategy, enabling you to refine it using the information you have gathered meanwhile. At this stage you should look at having outline solutions in each important area. The consolidation of these independent factors into a cohesive winning plan is the essence of bid management. Furthermore, you can use the bid plan as a tool to issue guidelines to the bid team and authors, and you can include within it advice on how to prepare the proposal to take account of the strategic emphasis.

Components of the basic plan

What should be included? A basic bid plan should encapsulate your strategy on the client, the price, the competition and the other factors in your analysis and assessment of the opportunity. The plan needs to take each of these areas and list what must be done to win.

As a dynamic tool, it will need to include the status of the various bid elements. For example, it should state what stage your client has reached in their buying programme, which competitors are bidding and where you are in your bid cycle. It should detail the methods you will use for promoting your offer to the client. It is useful to use the plan not only to identify the gaps and deficiencies in your own strategy, but also, and more importantly, how you intend to overcome those inadequacies.

For controls and resource planning it needs to include details of who is involved in your bid and assignment teams. It should also include a time plan for the bid, giving the critical path and listing priorities, and so that everyone knows what they have to do, assign responsibilities to all the actions in it. Finally, at the basic level the plan should specify how and when you will review progress. With these elements in place, your bid plan will help to consolidate your strategy and provide guidance to the bid team. The illustration in Fig. 10.1 shows how these components come together.

Although at first sight this may appear daunting, your plan need not be a cumbersome or lengthy document. Simple bids may only need simple plans. More complex and valuable opportunities stand to benefit more from effective planning. Many bid managers argue that because of

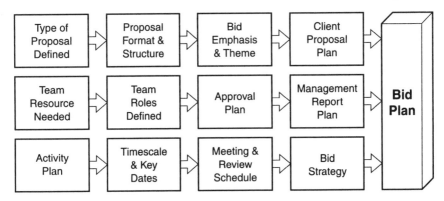

Fig. 10.1 Basic bid plan

the tight constraints the client has imposed, they do not have time to prepare a plan. But perhaps by spending a bit longer in planning the bid, they would in fact make more effective use of the time available. If you find yourself struggling to come up with a plan, you could be wasting your bid effort or trying to fashion something out of nothing. If you do not have the information needed or even know what is missing, then that is a sure indication that you have not properly assessed the opportunity. The solution is to review your original assessment and see whether you have considered all the relevant information or if you have overlooked something important. If you cannot fill the gaps you should look hard at whether you should be bidding at all.

Bid management plan and procedures

As a guide, the following outlines the structure and content of a typical bid plan for a valuable opportunity. When you are thinking about your bid plan, you will decide whether all or some of this information is needed.

Bid overview

The bid plan will be circulated to the bid team, the assignment team, senior management, subcontractors and others with an indirect interest. It is a good idea to give them a concise overview of the opportunity so that they are fully informed of the scope of the bid. In this overview, briefly outline the opportunity. They would expect to see summary information that will add to their understanding of the prospect, the client, the estimated value of the project, and the other bidders. To aid document control, you should also include local sector reference, bid and file numbers.

Bid strategy

Everyone in the team needs to know how you intend to win the bid, and your plan is the ideal way of disseminating details of your strategy. This should be a synopsis of your complete analysis of the opportunity and your strategy for winning the business. You probably will not need to include all the strategic information amassed during the preliminary stages of the bid but you should provide a concise recapitulation of the approach and the objectives you expect to meet.

It is valuable to analyse your own chances of success. This will state your company strengths and weaknesses, emphasising how the bid will play to the strengths and eliminate potential weaknesses. The tasks needed to achieve this should be included in your bid timetable. If your strategy is complex, split it into its component features – client, competition, pricing, products and so on. As not everyone on the team will be involved in every aspect, this will let them focus on the areas they are responsible for.

Bid and project timetables

The activity during the bid is often intense, involving all or parts of the team for most of the time. Your plan should state all the timescales for preparing and reviewing the tender activities through to submission to make most effective use of these people's time. Although usually agreed during negotiations with the client, you should also include the provisional assignment timings; key dates such as contract award, delivery schedules and implementation milestones will help in the project plan. It is always a good idea to include the project plan in your proposal as these details will help the project manager to make the project realistic. Include an assessment of the main bid and assignment tasks to be completed with the names of whoever is responsible for them. Other dates such as the bid review meetings, sign-offs and authorisation schedules are valuable for getting everyone together at the right time. A useful pointer is to be consistent in the scheduling of reviews; for example on a lengthy bid, schedule it for the same time each week or fortnight, so that people know when they have to prepare for it.

Commercial review

To help the commercial team, use all the client knowledge you have accumulated to prepare an analysis of the terms and conditions under which the contract will be let. Highlight any potential problem areas and stress those terms which the client is sensitive about. If you already have a solution to these or wish to prepare one, suggest the approach that you think the bid should take in its response. It is far better to deal with anticipated difficulties earlier so you can challenge your commercial manager and then produce possible solutions acceptable to both you and the client. You can use this review to begin preparing your negotiating position.

Bid team and responsibilities

Everyone needs to know what they and the other team members will be doing. Refer to Chapter 7 on team building to make sure that you gain mutual agreement on these tasks and that the team sets the goals and objectives together. Within your plan, detail the individual bid and assignment team members as well as support personnel, deputies and contingencies. So that everyone knows, try to relate specific responsibilities to the tasks that have to be carried out. Again, it is important to agree these responsibilities with the individuals concerned before going to print and so avoid creating conflict in the team.

In a large team, a contact list is a useful addition to the bid plan. You can include names, addresses, telephone numbers and faxes with contacts for normal working hours and for exceptional circumstances. The list should contain the bid team members, assignment team, support personnel, external support agents and reporting lines in case you need to escalate any problems.

Response format and theme

The preparation of the proposal document itself can often be a difficult task and you should include in your plan any details that will facilitate this. If the client has specified a format for the response then you should make sure that everyone in the team complies with it; otherwise, select a structure and format to display the offer in the best possible fashion. Some clarification on style and consistency for authorship is advisable so that you finish with a document that is cohesive and readable. You may also include guidance on responding against compliance statements and other information on preparing a quality proposal.

Your proposal will be more focused and useful to the client if it has a pattern to it which shows your company in the best light and presents the benefits you offer in the right way. This theme could run throughout the proposal, emphasising some specific corporate attribute such as quality, cost-effectiveness or reliability. Complement this with specific themes for each volume or chapter which you have discovered will hit the right spot with the client reading the tender. Use your plan to guide the team on incorporating these themes within the document and on the tone they should adopt in emphasising them.

Competition profile

Your competition profile is a very important part of your bid strategy and you will want to make sure that everyone knows how to deal with it when preparing the proposal. Include in the plan details of who are the major threats, what they will be offering, their strengths and weaknesses and your plans for countering and negating their efforts. This will be a summary of the competitive analysis which you undertook earlier.

Assignment partners

Be cautious in your plan if you have not yet got agreements in place with subcontractors, suppliers or other assignment partners. If you are involved in negotiation with several you probably do not want this information to leak out. Find out who the likely subcontractors are, what agreements are in place between them, and which services or products they will be providing and why. You would normally include all cost and delivery schedules, lead times, order methods and other relevant information. Usually the project manager or procurement officer will have responsibility for subcontracts under guidance from the bid manager.

Authorisation and sign-offs

You should ensure that your plan goes to anyone involved in authorising the bid before submission. Other members of your team will normally have to prepare material to meet any sign-off deadlines. The plan should specify the authorisation procedures you are using in the bid, the managers responsible for sign-offs, the processes for signing-off on time and the timetable of events leading to obtaining signatures.

CONTROLLING THE BID

You should write your bid plan to simplify bid control. It has to include all the necessary information to complete the bid, adhering to the bid objectives and timetable. This requires specifications on meetings, management documents and control instruments.

Bid team meetings

The bid plan should contain a schedule of review meetings. Meetings can be wasteful and time consuming, but in the main they are still the most commonly used way to maintain progress, distribute information and make decisions. You are unlikely to need all the bid team members attending every meeting. For large projects it may be necessary to assign subordinate levels of reporting such as a technical team reporting to the technical manager. You would not therefore expect the whole technical team to come along unless it was absolutely necessary. Having the complete bid team at every meeting can be difficult to manage and unproductive as they could be getting on with something else.

Review meetings

Hold these bid review meetings regularly; during the preliminary phases they may be monthly or every two weeks. As you enter the tender stage you may want to increase them to at least once a week. The review meeting has several functions which you should define.

Broadly speaking you will want to develop further your understanding of the bid in areas such as the client's requirement, your technical solution, and your competitors' strategy. You will need to review progress against the bid plan and timetable, making sure that all outstanding actions are chased and completed. Finally, you should expect these reviews to approve the various contributions made by the team such as the technical proposal, the commercial proposal, project plans and quality plans, for example. If there are problems, any shortfalls in people, resources, knowledge, or capability should be quantified and actions agreed in line with the bid strategy to overcome them.

Bid launch

A good idea is to use the initial bid meeting after receipt of the invitation to tender to launch the bid phase of the project. Hold it when all the members of the bid team have read and commented on the documents received. The objectives of the bid launch meeting will be similar to a review, but in addition you should assess the client's requirement against your earlier understanding of the project and against technical and commercial compliance. Try to conduct a detailed analysis of the risk areas by identifying problems or shortfalls and specifying an action plan to mitigate the risk. Your bid plan will be nearly completed by this time, so finalise it with the bid team to ensure a comprehensive understanding of its contents by each member. Use the launch to identify all the major inputs into the bid process, who will be supplying what information and when, according to the plan. It is also a good idea to discuss and complete your bid strategy and sales plan at this meeting. Finally, when all the facts have been presented and discussed, make the decision to carry on with the bid, or to withdraw. Compare your original bid criteria against the client's invitation to confirm that you will continue with the proposal preparation and production.

Timetables

Bids invariably take place under time constraints, sometimes very severe ones. Beyond the points already discussed on the timetable and action plan for the bid, pay particular attention to the following issues.

Schedule sign-offs

Schedule the meeting to give final authority to submit the bid to the client. It always takes far longer than you expect. If several signatures are required, then try to get all signatories together at the same time. If you have to chase authorising managers around the country, proposal in tow, you are wasting valuable time so always ensure a thorough briefing is prepared and dispatched to all parties well in advance keeping them informed of any changes to schedule. Arrange the meeting in the office of the most senior signing manager; the others are then less likely to miss it.

Schedule bid production

No matter how experienced you and your team are, invariably your estimate of production lead times will be wrong. Always allow yourself time for slippage. Murphy's Law says that anything that can go wrong, will go wrong. And it is always at the last minute and with the most important item, that breakdowns occur.

Authors of the bid proposal will always need longer than first thought, but clear guidelines will help. The 80:20 rule applies; 80 per cent of the content is prepared in the first 20 per cent of the available time. You may be forced to apply rigid deadlines for receiving material, but it is better to have an imperfect proposal on time than a perfect one that misses the cut-off date.

Schedule final review

In the final or *red team* review never allow the reviewers to nitpick over style or format nor to question your strategy, unless they know you have made an obvious error. The final review team is there to check for consistency, for compliance against the requirement and for conformance to your corporate policy.

Allowing the review team to alter text line by line is fatal. Unless it is an obvious oversight and the meaning of any phrase is not as you intended, do not allow semantic or stylistic changes. Issuing clear guidelines on style and maintaining close checks on early draft material will identify any problems with particular authors. Put remedial action into place early; do not leave it until the last minute.

Procurement and subcontracts

Remember to allow time for all internal and external agreements to be put in place. Submitting the bid with a critical commercial relationship, such as a supplier or subcontractor still undecided, could lead to problems later.

Document control systems

If your company follows recognised quality management standards, such as ISO 9000, you will have a document control system in place, as this is a prerequisite of compliance. Even if you do not aspire to quality standard accreditation, the control of documents, particularly in a large and complex bid, is a necessity. Failing to keep track of essential parts of the specification, tender and response is a sign of ineffective bid management and makes your job far more difficult than it would otherwise be.

The bid file

Use a bid file system to aid your control of the bid and keep a written and accurate record of agreements, understandings and other verbal reports to help you remember the contents. Reports and results from actions should be maintained and filed; you might otherwise miss an important point during the bid preparation. When the pressure is on during a bid, things get overlooked; using an effective document control system will help in your total management of the bid.

Document control

All key documents should be controlled and recorded. It is good practice to show a date, an issue number and the electronic file name on all important documents generated by the bid team. Those sections of your company that operate according to quality standards need to do this anyway. You can undo much good work and dishearten the team if you let them labour on an obsolete version of a key document.

Preparing the bid document

Preparing your final copy represents a significant part of your bid control. Some general guidance is given here which is elaborated upon in the next chapter.

Follow instructions

Any instruction contained in the client's bid documents in terms of bid bonds, authorisation, forms of tender, notarisation and other specific areas should be followed to the letter. Do not let your bid slip away on a technicality. Wherever a specific instruction to tenderers is issued, it should be observed.

Submitting your offer

Submit your proposal in time but not too early; leaving it lying around may be risky. Bids should be kept secure until submission. Where difficulties could possibly occur, preventing arrival of your bid in time, put in place a contingency plan with two complete sets of documents travelling by different routes. This is particularly important when delivery is overseas, involves long distance travel or is to an isolated or remote location.

Bid contents

Pay particular regard to those areas you identified earlier as important to the client; be positive in what you say, emphasising the benefits. Look for ways to impress the client and show how you have understood their problem. On points of major significance to the client, explain in detail how you achieve the stated objective.

Qualifications

Unless, as discussed earlier, it is seen as strategic to qualify the offer to the client, try to keep the degree of non-compliance or qualifications to a minimum. You could possibly negotiate on some of these issues later, so hedge around them. By being non-committal you may gain a chance to discuss it round the table, which is better than being ruled out for non-compliance on a key point.

Post-tender negotiation

If you expect post-tender negotiation, consider leaving a contingency or negotiating margin. However, do not price yourself out because of it.

BID MANAGEMENT INTERFACES

Finally, this chapter examines how a typical complex, high-value bid is managed once the client's invitation to bid is received. Your bid plan should have included an activity list which schedules the key events during the preparation of the bid, based upon the contents of the client's invitation. The earlier Fig. 10.1 (see page 223) shows a typical bid plan that includes most of these key activities. For smaller bids some steps in the plan may be foreshortened or the size of the bid team reduced.

Managing a typical bid

Alert the bid team to the fact that the client's invitation is due. Use whatever methods you have, telephone, faxes, electronic mail or just call on them, but make sure you get positive acknowledgements. If any team members are going to be absent or diverted onto other projects you need to know now so that replacements can be found. Use this opportunity to stress the relevance of the bid and how you plan to approach it.

Usually, a core team will be most active at the start. This could be the business manager, bid manager and client manager, the technical manager and project planner. First, you should acknowledge the receipt of the client's invitation. Then, together you will review it, calling in whatever specialist support you need. Pay particular heed to all instructions to bidders, stated evaluation criteria, contract and commercial terms. Prepare any questions that you need to put to the client.

The bid manager should finish gathering information from the bid information system, external and departmental databases. Finalise the format of the response paying special attention to areas that need long lead-time, such as special graphics and covers. With the format in place, decide who will be writing which section and prepare guidelines to authors. Fig. 10.2 charts the process after the invitation to bid has been received and shows the main tasks the bid manager will control.

Once all the relevant factors have been assessed, the bid manager will make a recommendation to the business manager. It may be the business manager's decision on whether to bid or not, although they should take note of all advice and recommendations from the bid manager. Make the decision earlier rather than later. Much depends upon the timescales you are working within and you may wish to delay a decision to await further developments. However, generally speaking it is better to divert resources to another opportunity than keep them tied up on a no-bid

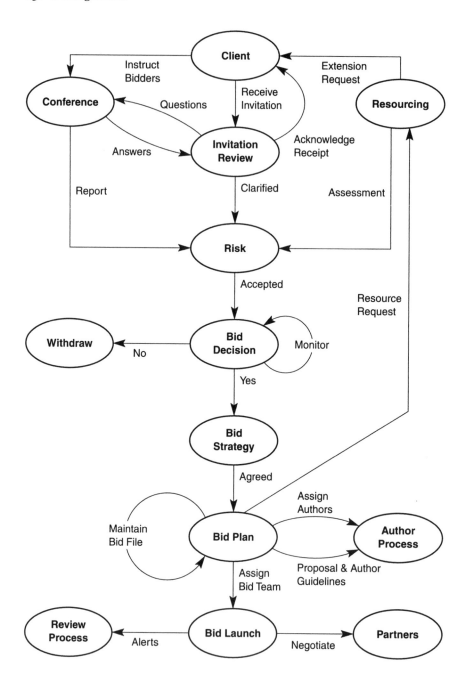

Fig. 10.2 Procedure on receipt of bid invitation

prospect. The business manager must make a supportable case for any bid made on strategic purposes against advice. Fig. 10.3 describes the activity leading to the bid/no-bid decision.

Managing the bid team

The bid team consists of persons chosen for their knowledge and expertise. Certain functions, such as proposal management, are not client-specific, but you would still include the proposal manager in the team. Choose the bid team carefully by selecting people who can contribute what you need. Do not select people just because they are available. The bid manager will manage the team and they should have the right degree of technical, commercial and sales experience to achieve the right balance. The business manager, client manager and bid manager will often form a triumvirate to decide the direction to take and this core team needs to work closely together. There can be only one person controlling the bid however and it is the bid manager who has that responsibility.

Keeping the team on track and focused is an important task for the bid manager. If it is you, start by setting team goals and objectives before summarising these in the bid plan and instructions to authors. Some general advice is to ensure that the appropriate people are involved. It is important to use specialists where necessary, although the bid manager can probably contribute some of the general text.

The proposal manager should maintain control of the documents produced, keep up the momentum by motivating the bid team and rewarding efforts. Everyone must know what they are producing and when you need it; set early dates for first drafts, (80 per cent of the document is produced in 20 per cent of the time). Use the bid plan to avoid any confusion. Send out a meeting schedule so that the bid team knows in advance when they are to meet. The proposal manager is responsible for starting work early on graphics, artwork or photographs as these will take a long time to complete.

Manage the team meetings

Meetings are necessary, but probably not always with the complete team. Keep minutes short and apposite. Issue an agenda beforehand and minutes quickly after. Also, you should maintain a running action plan so that you know what has been done and what is outstanding. Do not

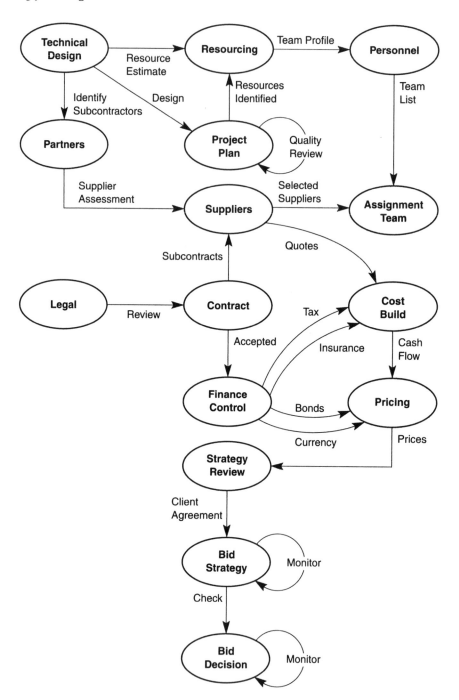

Fig. 10.3 The decision-to-bid process

pull-in key personnel if they are working on essential elements of the bid unless it is absolutely necessary.

Manage information

Information is extremely valuable. You need accurate and up to date knowledge to make decisions. Similarly, other managers in your company who are working on bids or determining strategy, for example, can make use of the information that you discover and vice versa; keeping people informed is a critical aspect of effective bid management and putting in place a reporting system is one way of informing people.

You should establish circulation lists of who needs what information and when they need it making it easier to maintain a system with minimal effort. The illustration in Fig. 10.4 gives typical examples of the type of reports that could be generated during a bid and who would benefit from receiving them.

Ensure you have access to accurate and up to date information. There are many sources of data but it must be both valid and useful. Gather and keep information systematically and make sure it is focused on the objectives of the bid. Areas in which you will need information may encompass: background data, country reports, legal position, economics, environmental data, client data, supplier data and competitors. You can get much of this information from company databases, internally and externally, as you saw earlier when developing your bid information system.

Manage the assignment team

The bid manager must keep the assignment team aware of progress, and check on any changes that will affect the project accomplishment. Regularly update the internal and external personnel on the status of the bid, the likelihood of the award of the contract and the result; win or lose.

They will need to respond quickly if the bid is successful and delay could jeopardise the profitability of the project. Stand the assignment team down if you are unsuccessful in the bid. People not directly involved in the bid but critical to the assignment will appreciate being kept informed and will be motivated to participate again.

Managing the bid upwards

During many bids it seems that the problems that occur have nothing to do with the client, the opportunity or the competition, but are generated

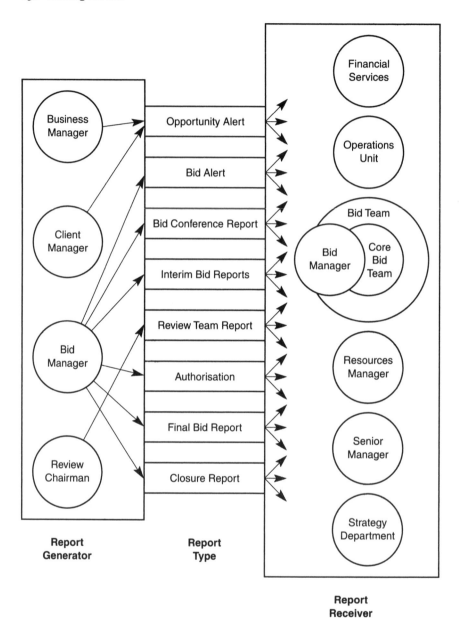

Fig. 10.4 Management report flow

internally within the company. The successful bid manager has to over-come both these internal and external hurdles. This final aspect of planning, controlling and managing your bid, is to look at the management interfaces you will encounter. You must see how others involved with the client might react to the opportunity. View them as the client manager, the business manager and senior management.

The client manager

Your client, account or sales manager should play a major part in the sales team and bid team alike. You should not consider bidding without having detailed knowledge of the client, or someone in the team who has a day-to-day relationship with them. This is usually your client manager.

It is often difficult for people not directly involved in selling to clients to understand the motivation and objectives of the client manager. These are likely to be complex and multiple, perhaps differing greatly from the business manager's or your own. The most important aspect is that the client manager usually has the responsibility of selling your services. Indeed their remuneration may be based upon achieving certain sales targets, which is a strong influencing factor on their thinking and decision making.

Problems sometimes arise if the client manager is targeted on sales and has no responsibility for the cost of bidding. Without cost containment controls, they are likely to want to bid for every opportunity, no matter how unrealistic. Their function is to sell profitable business into the client account and they will have developed an account strategy to enable them to do this most effectively. They may not be always fully aware of your bid strategy and policy beyond this account plan and consequently this strategy may override other considerations.

You must make a more objective analysis of each bid opportunity, applying the criteria and bid factors that you have already highlighted, to decide whether to bid or not. You have to substantiate the reasons for incurring bid costs for lost projects and therefore must be careful and accurate in your decision making.

The business manager

The business manager will have a different set of objectives from both the bid manager and the client manager. They will be accountable for profit and loss and will fund all the bid costs for lost opportunities. Consequently, they are more likely to be targeted on achieving a return on investment within their business sector.

Cost control is often easier to manage than increasing sales or margins. The project, when won, must be profitable because if it loses money the business manager may have real problems. Risk management is the key to understanding the role of the business manager. They must balance the risk of losing the business, incurring bid costs, or winning the contract under unfavourable terms, against the possibility of winning profitable business.

Senior management

Senior management usually views bids from two perspectives. The first view concerns risk and authority, with every risk decision being properly qualified and quantified. This authorisation takes place at two stages: first in giving you the authority to spend time, money and resources to prepare to bid and produce your proposal. Secondly, management must sign to commit your company to delivery of the contracted-for products or services at the offer price and under certain delivery terms, to the client.

Senior management's view extends further to encompass the corporate goals and objectives of your company. They may perhaps consider that they have a better understanding of what the company needs to achieve and can add this value judgement to the bid. Therefore, your senior management should be consulted early in the bid process, kept informed of progress and allowed to make their contribution at the right times.

The bid manager

The bid manager must balance the objectives of the client manager and business manager and incorporate the views of senior management. Objective decisions, based upon known facts and careful analysis of the opportunity, must be made.

At all times during the bid process, the role of the bid manager must as far as possible be seen as professional, neutral, and non-partisan. This will make the achievement of any signatures for the authority for the bid ultimately easier.

SUMMARY

Good planning and bid management converts your pricing, competitive and client strategies into a winning proposal.

- *An effective bid plan does not just issue instructions but acts as a tool to control, co-ordinate, monitor and manage the bid activity. Used correctly it will help you make the right decisions.*

- *A typical bid plan will give an overview of the opportunity, summarise the strategy, provide bid authorisation and project timetables, contain a review of the commercial issues, define roles and responsibilities of the team, state the format of the response, and give profiles of the competition.*

- *A bid often consists of many individuals carrying out many tasks. Use project planning techniques of critical path analyses, scheduling and resources control to make sure everything required during the bid is delivered on time and within budget.*

- *Managing people in a bid team requires a matrix approach. Choose people who will contribute what you need . Keep them focused and motivated. Make sure that everyone knows what is required of them.*

- *Bid management also means controlling the assignment team, external partners and subcontractors, as well as your own peers and senior managers.*

11

BID SUBMISSION

Most bids require some form of proposal to go to the client and arguments vary on the relative importance of this document in winning the business. Clearly, if you have prepared well, established a sound position with the client, developed a good strategy and dealt with the threat from your competitors your position will be strong and the significance attached to your proposal is reduced. That is not to say however, that a sparkling proposal makes up for deficiencies in substance, planning and strategy. The opposite is true; every proposal is the culmination of your efforts in assessing the opportunity, developing your position with the client and your competitors. The only way to judge the bearing of your proposal is by reference to the client and the type of opportunity. Some prospects will need to have formal, bound proposals; the client expects them and your competitors will be submitting them. Some will need a less formal approach. Other clients may view a glossy package as lacking *gravitas* and credibility, while some may like its bright, innovative and refreshing approach. As with the rest of your bid, you have to select the style of proposal that will satisfy the needs of your client. The proposal itself, although not the sole factor in dictating success, is still critical. If you do not submit an offer, or foul-up in doing so, then you cannot expect to receive the rewards.

This chapter analyses some proposal documents, looking at what they must achieve, and then examines the proposal production methods. These include getting the proposal authorised and delivered to the client.

PROPOSAL PRODUCTION

Usually you will be submitting a formal bound proposal, although this may not be always needed. For example, if the proposal is to an existing client for a change or addition to current work or for a very simple project, you may consider using a letter or a presentation instead.

You generally expect to submit formal proposals where the opportunity is new and of a high value, and where you expect competition. This encompasses situations where you are responding to a client's invitation to bid, request for information or pre-qualification, in fact any occasions when you need to present a good image of your company to the client. If you are unclear of which style of proposal best suits your client, talk to someone who knows them well, such as the client or business managers. If they are an existing client, look at how you have done it in the past; emulate that method if you were successful and consider changing it if you were not. If there is any doubt, you should submit a formal proposal.

Maximising the proposal's effect

Before rushing to the keyboard and dashing off your response it is wise to think first about what you are trying to achieve with it. You are trying to set out the terms of your offer as clearly and unambiguously as possible. You will want to convince the client that you have the solution to their stated needs, but also that you understand them well, know their position and can help them get what they want. The benefits to them of selecting you should be clearly defined. Furthermore, you have to convince them that you can do the job better than someone else could. Fig. 11.1 summarises what your proposal should be trying to provide.

Pitching to the right reader

Your proposal is likely to have a wide readership in the client organisation. In some bids, the document is segmented into its various volumes or sections with relevant parts being distributed solely to those people who will assess it. In World Bank bids, for example, you may well find the technical section being assessed separately from the commercial and financing proposals. This is designed to give a degree of objectivity to the adjudication process. With other proposals, only one or two people may be responsible for the assessment.

Usually, there will be three types of readers; executive readers, who need a full overview of the benefits and costs; specialist readers, who will pore over the fine detail in their area of expertise; and finance readers, who will be interested in what it will cost. The proposal has to appeal to all of them.

Executive readers will want to have a summary of the main points of your proposal to form a general picture of your offer, the business bene-

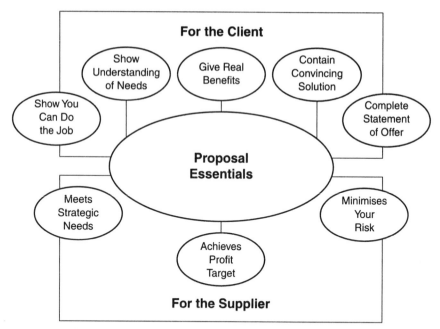

Fig. 11.1 The essence of a proposal

fits that they can expect to see and the cost implications. They may well want to focus on specific areas, browse, or find out points that are important to them. To emphasise the benefits, you must ensure that your selling points are obviously displayed.

The specialist will want to find the details that convince them that your offer meets their specification or presents solutions to their observed needs. Your response will therefore need to be fairly explicit in these areas, laying out in some depth the precise nature of your solution. The important point here, however, is that it is all too easy to lose sight of the benefits in the minutiae. Specialists need to see the benefits too, even though these are likely to be technical, or commercial in nature, rather than pure business advantages.

The financial reader needs clear price information and details of exactly what is being offered. They will want the prices laid out so that they can easily read them with all elements displayed so they can make direct comparisons to other bids. Again the problem sometimes arises of financial benefits being buried beneath rows of figures. Aim to highlight the beneficial effects of your financing package and pricing policy, through a narrative or commentary to the spreadsheets.

What happens to your proposal?

To make sure you pitch the proposal correctly it will help to know what will happen to it when it is received by the client. Imagine a formal proposal being opened by a typical client. Before opening, it will be checked by the receiving official to see that all the correct delivery requirements have been observed. In very formal bids this may include being plainly wrapped, with no identification marks and the correct number of annotated original copies supplied. Then, the bid documents will be opened and if applicable, Forms of Tender will be scrutinised.

Your proposal and the others received will then be perused by the chief members of the assessment or purchasing panel. Your covering letter will be read in full as will your executive summary. These therefore, should emphasise the main themes of your offer, the key benefits and the commitment your company is willing to make. This will obviously include price summaries with the financial benefits clearly explained.

The bid document is then separated into its various sections; different volumes will go to the finance assessor, technical department, operations, commercial and legal people. Each of these members of the assessment team will read their individual sections in detail, commenting and responding accordingly, marking and weighting each point against a compliance table.

Some parts of the document may be copied and sent to people outside the main adjudication panel. The executive summary is clearly a prime candidate for this, perhaps being sent to the chief executive or board of directors. You could anticipate and facilitate this by providing separate bound copies of the executive summary for distribution to board members. Eventually, your bid document will be logically recombined, if not physically, as the final assessment is made and a shortlist drawn up.

From this analysis you can conclude that your proposal must be very readable, well-structured and orderly. Each volume must be clearly identified and self-contained; avoid cross-referring between volumes as your reader may not have the complete copy. If necessary, repeat the important points in each volume. Set out each chapter so that your reader can easily find any specific point when checking against other proposals.

The bid document must be cohesive and coherent with good subtitles and numbering, using a clear typeface and including apposite graphics and illustrations. Try to avoid using jargon, abbreviations and acronyms unless absolutely necessary, especially in the executive summary. If you have to use them make sure they are fully explained in each volume.

Everything in your proposal has to present you and your offer in the best way possible, coming together to make something that the client wants to buy.

Emphasise client priorities

As mentioned before, the proposal represents the realisation of your bid strategy. You have built up a comprehensive knowledge of the client and it would be a pity not to use this to help you win. Your analysis will have identified all the client expectations and your proposal should explain how you will meet them. Focus on meeting their top priorities; do not major on something that is of only passing interest to them.

Remember that not all their needs are explicit; there are some which are unlikely to come out in their specification, but are equally important. The known needs are those that they have specified and made known to you through the bid invitation. Other needs are implicit within the opportunity and may be normal for this type of work. The client may also have certain needs that they choose not to make you aware of. There may be some hidden agenda or ulterior purpose behind the procurement that they deem commercially sensitive. Then there are the needs that the client themselves are not aware of, but that you know about. You may have gleaned something from your analysis of their business and their competitors. By emphasising this knowledge in your proposal you are showing your value to the client which can only enhance your chances of success.

Provide solutions

Many companies fail in their bids by forgetting the most basic rule of selling. Customers buy benefits, not features; the flame not the match. Your client is hoping to find solutions to their business problems or ways to take advantage of opportunities; they are not buying the features of your product or service, but the way these are applied to give them the business benefits to meet these challenges and opportunities. It follows that you should not be focusing on your product, but on the benefits you bring to their business.

Your proposal has to convey these benefits and describe how you will help them to improve their business operations. Once your client recognises this, they will be anxious to buy your solution. Getting this across to them is therefore critical. This is where your record and experience come to the fore, with relevant reference sites really helping to establish your position with them. Before you quote a third party reference, make sure you have their agreement as you could breach client confidentiality. Many companies will agree to act in some capacity, either as a reference site or by supplying an affidavit. The evidence of your ability to deliver what you say you will is best provided by statements from independent third parties. When quoting a reference try to select something similar to that for which you are bidding; look for likenesses in client size and type, product range used, business application, and solutions provided.

Organising the proposal

You have seen that producing the proposal document is a complex task that you must control carefully. If you have a proposal manager either in your bid team or in a separate support service, get them to work closely with you to make sure that you meet the deadline and that the document is consistent with the bid strategy. The process in Fig. 11.2 describes the activities necessary to complete the proposal.

Your bid strategy sets out the theme for the bid and the bid plan has informed the authors of how to fit the strategy within it. One task of the proposal manager is to maintain a common style and ensure that the bid authors emphasise the theme. By establishing some common guidelines defining the conventions that authors should use, the proposal manager will avoid later editing of the material. These author guidelines should include information on common abbreviations, client and project names, how to refer to your company, format standards, writing conventions and document control procedures

Proposal structure

It is advisable to put in place early a structure to your proposal so that the authors know where and how their material fits in and can therefore gain some guidance on the length, contents, themes and other variables in the document. The proposal manager will probably need to seek advice from the bid manager as the structure often requires a thorough understanding of the client's requirement. If they have set out a format in the bid invitation, this is the one you should use. Otherwise it is down to your discretion and knowledge of what the client is expecting. Fig. 11.3 shows a typical instruction format, which gives the information needed to ensure that the authors adopt a consistent structure.

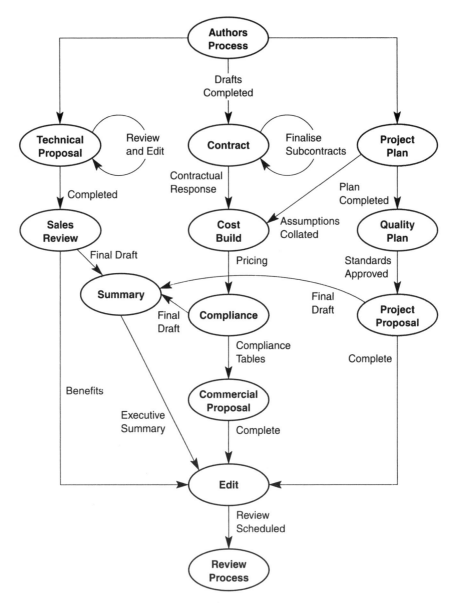

Fig. 11.2 Proposal production procedure

Using standard documents

Many proposals rely upon material borrowed from previous documents
or templates. As many of the proposals you are likely to submit will
probably be of a similar nature containing comparable products, services

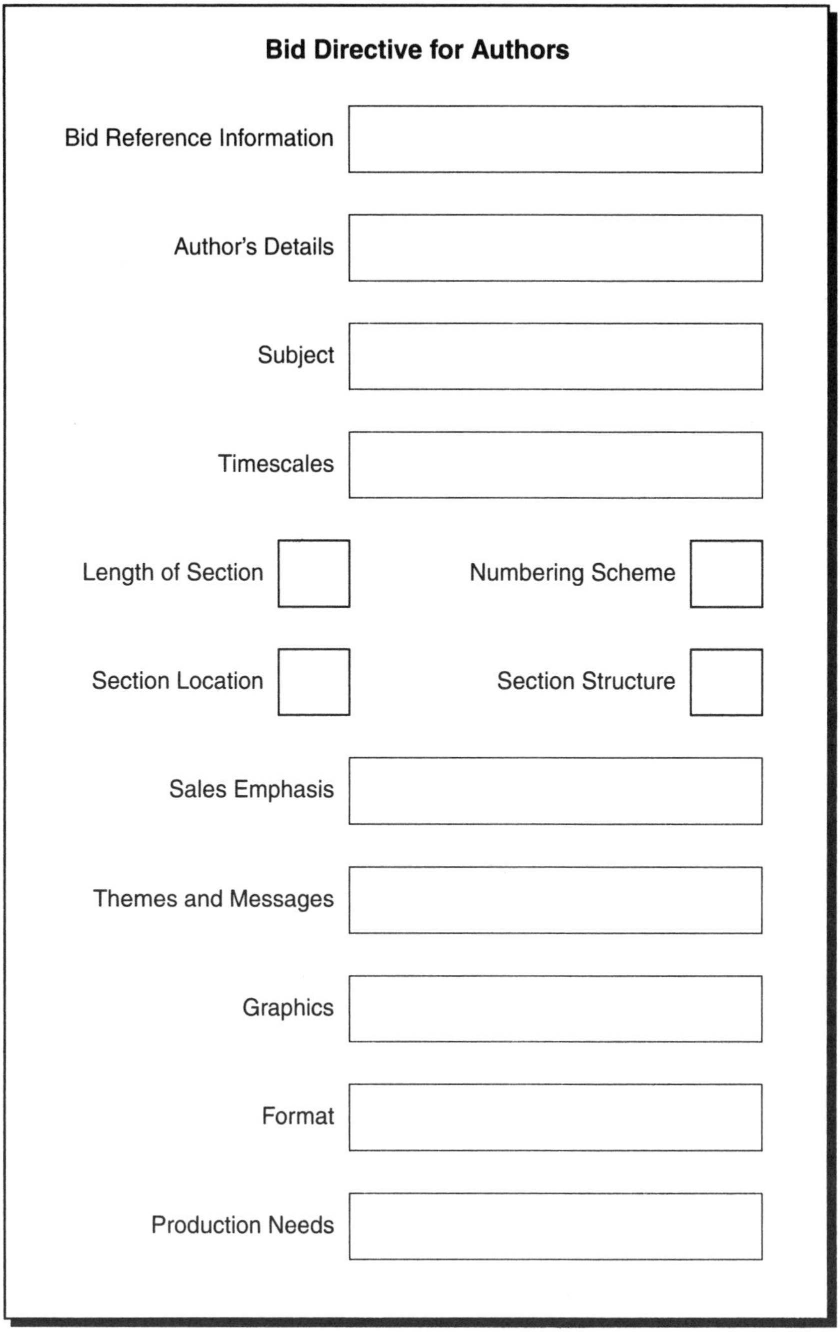

Bid Directive for Authors

Bid Reference Information

Author's Details

Subject

Timescales

Length of Section

Numbering Scheme

Section Location

Section Structure

Sales Emphasis

Themes and Messages

Graphics

Format

Production Needs

Fig. 11.3 Typical guidance for authors

and capability statements, there will inevitably be a degree of commonality. It is often much easier to revise existing documents than to rewrite them from scratch. However, always make sure that the documentation you use is relevant, effective for the purpose and up to date.

There is inherent danger in borrowing text direct from a previous bid to another client, so exercise extreme caution and check carefully if you do. Problems such as the wrong client name slipping through or irrelevant responses to the specification are common.

You will usually have some generic documentation that will go into the proposal. This will include such things as capability statements, terms and conditions of contract, confidentiality statements, resource profiles, curricula vitae for the assignment team, standard forms, company report and accounts, and product descriptions and brochures. The proposal manager should maintain the latest version of all such standard documentation within the document control system and you should use this in preference wherever possible.

Typical bid contents

Every proposal will be different and will need to meet any stated requirements within the client's invitation. There is normally a degree of latitude in interpretation and it is useful to have a contents structure in mind when doing early preparation and before receipt of any formal layout. Similarly, when the client does not impose any contents structure upon you, such as when asking for pre-qualification proposals, requests for information and so forth, you should consider what you need to include. The basic outline in Fig. 11.4 shows the contents of a typical proposal document.

The technical proposal

The technical proposal contains the basis of how you intend to carry out the assignment. Clearly, your approach will depend upon the precise nature of the work. This section will normally be read by the client's technical evaluator, so structure it appropriately making it clear enough to be understood by technocrats and non-technocrats alike. If the client has issued you with a detailed technical specification, it is advisable to respond against each point in turn. You would usually be expected to include a full technical description of your solution to back this up. This is where the benefits of your proposal must be drawn out, but be sure to stress benefits too. It is far too easy to list technical features without telling the client what it will do for them. Also, do not ignore commercial aspects, as this section may have readers outside the technical department.

Use the technical proposal to show your knowledge of the client's need and their priorities. Bring in your understanding of the competition. Take the information you gained from your analyses of your competitors and stress your strengths against their weaknesses. Always consider what your competitors are likely to be offering. Beware of over-engineering the proposed technical solution however, as this often results in over-pricing the bid.

The commercial proposal

The commercial proposal contains your response to the contract terms and conditions, and forms the basis upon which you will reach an agreement with the client. Quite often this will be in two distinct sections, a point-by-point response, in which you state your compliance with every term in the specification and a narrative section enabling you to expound upon your commercial ideas and bring out their benefits.

Again, always consider what your competitors will be offering and attempt to counter their threat. Consider carefully before submitting a qualified or non-compliant proposal. Wherever possible you should try to leave room for negotiation if you cannot comply strictly with the terms and conditions. On formal bids your offer could be rejected out-of-hand by non-compliance in a mandatory area.

The implementation proposal

The implementation proposal, variously called the project plan or the assignment, is where you will describe how you will actually do the work once you have been awarded the contract. This is therefore a critical section, covering all the tasks necessary to carry out the contract. You should include delivery of the products and services, the provision of people and support services, such as training or maintenance, and how you will meet quality standards. It is useful to include an outline project plan giving a provisional timetable, a project implementation plan that describes your methods, and a project quality plan showing how you will follow recognised quality standards.

The designated project manager will normally be of value in preparing this section and should use project control tools as appropriate. They will have the depth of experience and knowledge to ensure that what

Bid Tables of Contents				
Proposal Structure	Author		Completed Due/Status	
Covering Letter				
Forms of Tender				
Confidentiality Statements				
Executive Summary				
Commercial Proposal				
Technical Proposal				
Compliance Statements				
Compliance Tables				
Project Proposal				
Quality Plan				
Training Plan				
Reference Material				
Sales Literature				

Fig. 11.4 Contents of a typical proposal document

goes into the proposal is realistic and achievable. A tip in this proposal is to find out about your competitor's track record on keeping to schedules and attempt to beat it. Also, be wary of taking a belt-and-braces approach when a lean and responsive methodology is what the client wants. Try to make the section easy to understand and, again, do not forget to bring out all the benefits.

Preparing the financial proposal

The financial proposal is quite often the most critical section of the bid and yet it is the one which is nearly always completed last. This can be understandable sometimes, as the costing depends on the technical design and prices from subcontractors. Careful management of the bid will enable you to complete the foundation of the financial proposal early and avoid any last-minute panics. Fine tuning the spreadsheets is much easier than starting from scratch with the bid deadline looming.

The bid manager normally prepares the financial proposal with support from the project planning manager while the finance manager provides additional support and assistance in preparing the necessary information they need. When you are preparing the proposal consider the various aspects contained in the checklist in Fig. 11.5.

What should your financial proposal try to achieve? Too often it is just a price list with no value other than to inform the client of how

Financial Proposal Checklist

Category	Completed ✓
Cost-build	
Have all costs been accounted for?	☐
Can any costs be cut?	☐
Have we the best price from our subcontractors?	☐
Are contingencies included?	☐
Pricing	
What margin is required?	☐
What contribution is needed?	☐
Have we included a negotiating margin?	☐
Are we close to the winning price?	☐
Finance package	
Is orthodox finance package applicable?	☐
Discounted cash flow considered?	☐
Could we consider less orthodox approach?	☐
Does client prefer revenue or capital spend?	☐
Could we bundle/unbundle to advantage?	☐
Could client benefit from retained money?	☐
Benefits in proposal	
Emphasis on client's cost reduction?	☐
Creative financing of the project?	☐
Is price clear and unambiguous?	☐
Are all benefits thoroughly stated?	☐

Fig. 11.5 Financial proposal checklist

much your offer costs. An effective financial proposal should be much more than this. Yes, it has to inform them of the price, but it must also sell the financial benefits of your offer. You will have a very good idea of your client's own financial position and objectives from your bid information system and the analyses carried out while assessing the opportunity. The financial proposal is your chance to match their value expectations and demonstrate clear benefits to them which your competitors may not have. Chapter 9 discusses pricing and financing strategies in some detail, but it is worthwhile exploring these again and deciding how they could be best presented.

Show improved profit

Begin by reviewing how you can improve the profits of your client (assuming it is a profit-making organisation), by increasing their return on sales or by reducing their costs.

Ways in which you can improve their sales return are various. You can either show them how using your solution will help them to increase their margins or show them how it will help them to be more effective in selling. Show them that it is your offer which will improve their market share by allowing better promotion and advertising. If, for example, you are bidding to provide financial software or information technology, you could show how your products will facilitate just-in-time stock control, meaning that less of their assets will be tied up in stock, which has the benefit of using less space and improving the stock throughput. You could show the ways in which your system can identify debtors earlier, recover those debts and so improve their cash flow. Show how the automation or improved technology you are selling results in better use of their existing facilities giving higher quality products and therefore more sales. Or show how it will quicken production giving them better output, make better use of people and improve the way they work together. Prove that by buying what you are proposing they will gain better financial security and stability, thereby winning more orders themselves.

Display cost reduction

As well as improving their returns, your financial proposal should show any ways your solution can reduce their costs. And, of course, cost control is often a more effective way of improving profits than increasing sales.

Investigate their operational and manufacturing cost-base to see where your solution can effect savings. You may enhance their financial control systems for example so that improvements in invoicing and purchase order systems could reduce the number of operations needed and reduce the personnel requirement. Or perhaps you can offer more convenient systems for stock control, process control and quality assurance showing that with fewer rejects, they will gain better use of materials and reduce wastage. Similarly, you could display benefits in ecological and environmental factors by showing them how you can save them office space and warehousing or provide an improved and quicker distribution service.

Other areas to consider are the client's administrative functions: distribution, sales and marketing. Try to show how your solution results in more effective sales methods and improved sales productivity. Possibly you can save them time or reduce their transportation costs. Or by allowing them to manufacture to a higher quality standard they will have less complaints and improved customer services.

Financial empathy

Tailor the financial proposal to the financial needs of the client. Understand how they measure their financial performance and put your offer in these terms. If your client is a retailer, express the financial proposal in value of sales per area of floor space, or in stock improvements, or added margin. If the client is a manufacturer, express your price in terms of their initial purchase cost, capital costs, running costs and personnel costs. A financial proposal to a telecommunications company might express the price in cost per call unit. One to an airline could use price per passenger mile, yield, or fuel costs. An energy company may relate better to a price stated in pounds per kilojoule. Although not always practical or possible, you probably can show financial benefits more clearly when presenting them in the units that your client is most familiar with.

Once you have the benefits clear, the ways in which you present them to the client in your proposal become critical. Remember that benefits must be real, attractive and easily understood, both by the client and yourself. Take care not to submerge the benefits under too many confusing facts and figures.

REVIEW AND AUTHORISATION

The production of your bid proposal normally takes place under stress and in haste; that is the nature of bidding, there are always tasks that will expand to fill the time available. Do not therefore neglect the review and authorisation of your bid in your haste. It is just those times when you feel that you do not have time to get the bid reviewed and signed off that doing so becomes doubly important. These are the times when mistakes slip in unnoticed and you could be committing your business to unnecessary risk or simply making an error which could rule out your offer.

Many larger companies have a range of approval, authorising and review levels for proposals that depend upon the classification of the project. For example smaller projects, of a lesser value, may gain approval at middle management level, while high value or high risk projects may need executive committee approval. Fig. 11.6 shows the flow of the review process in a typical large organisation.

Review processes

You and the other key members of your bid team will regularly review progress and the shape of the bid as it begins to develop. This should be a hand on the tiller approach steering the bid direction rather than causing abrupt changes in course. You should be holding regular bid meetings when you can so that you can revisit the way the proposal is coming together.

A contextual review of the proposal usually takes place just before you assemble and complete the bid. This is sometimes known as the red team review (because of the predilection towards marking changes in red ink) and it checks for compliance against the requirement, conformance with the strategic objectives and continuity of the proposal. Syntax errors, style, format and especially strategy, are not included having been covered during earlier reviews.

For this red team review, you should try to form a review team comprising people who have not had a direct involvement in preparing the bid. They will be better able to look objectively at the proposal and, by placing themselves in the position of the client, may pick up on issues that anyone closer to the bid may have overlooked. The bid manager will usually act as chairman of the review team, offering guidance and clarification and taking note of any changes required before submission.

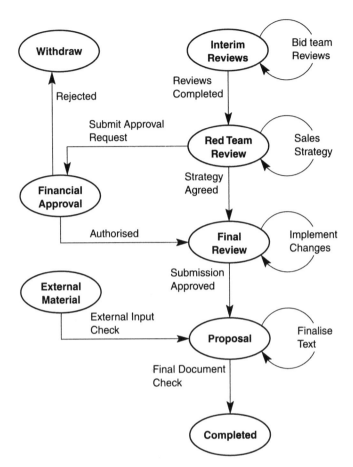

Fig. 11.6 Review process

Use the last check before you submit the bid to scrutiny for consistency of strategy and errors. Final reviews may take place in conjunction with approval meetings. But you cannot allow reviewers to change completely the emphasis or substance of your bid. You can prevent this occurring by adopting a few simple rules: always give advance warning of the proposal that includes why, when, how you are bidding and what you expect to achieve.

Authorisation to submit

When the proposal is nearing completion, you will need to seek approval to submit it, if this is necessary. Make sure first, that you know at what level, and who, is responsible for approving your offer. This is often dictated by value and risk, so make sure you have the right person lined up. Always circulate drafts (including the price) in advance giving approvers time to read and understand. When it comes to the approval meeting make a succinct presentation that emphasises the benefits to your business. Applying the same simple rules as above should mean that you do not have to chase around rewriting the bid at the last minute.

You will possibly need to go through various levels of authorisation before you can submit your bid to the client, so you must leave sufficient time for these. Invariably review and authorisation take much longer than expected, particularly for large bids.

As a general guide, you will need to seek approval for any proposal containing a financial or technical commitment from you to the client. Keep a record of proposal authorisation, so that everyone is clear about the commitment being made. The final level of authorisation usually concentrates on the financial and strategic aspects of the bid with approval normally obtained from a senior manager. So make sure at this stage that you have your final bid price agreed, and that it is very close to what you think will win it.

FINISHING THE PROPOSAL

Before the bid is submitted, you need to check that everything has been completed to your satisfaction. The red team review generally recommends areas where you can improve the bid so you will need a final review to decide how to put the red team and senior management recommendations in place before you freeze it and make no further changes.

You should then study the proposal for sales emphasis. Check that your company is presented in the best way possible with all your benefits emphasised. Make a final check on the price. Is the price right? Too high and you could lose the bid, too low and could lose money. Once you have completed all textual changes, check the proposal is complete and consistent. With the substance of the document finalised you will need authorisation, as described above, to submit the bid and to get signatures on the covering letter and financial proposal.

You can now print and copy the proposal and deliver it to your client. For some unknown reason, final preparation generally takes place on weekends or late at night. It also seems to be at the time when several bids are being prepared simultaneously and when you have a major equipment failure. Invariably something will go wrong so put in place a contingency plan. The bid manager should plan printing ahead of time and make sure the proposal manager has everything needed to complete the bid. Order in advance the binders, paper and consumables you need to complete the printing.

You should do a final check on every copy, making sure that they are complete and that any special conditions, such as annotation of all original copies, has been done. Make sure you include the covering letter. Package the document securely, referring to any conditions that the client may require, such as keeping them unmarked. Watch out that your company name is not inadvertently displayed on the packaging. It could be quite embarrassing explaining that your bid was not accepted because the franking machine in the post room automatically printed your name.

Delivery to a post office box number, as sometimes specified for overseas bids, can present difficulties to you or a courier trying to find the address. It will help if you can obtain a full delivery address beforehand or arrange for the courier to check in advance whether they can deliver to an alternative address. Bids have been known to sit uncollected in the wrong box.

Once the proposal has been completed, the proposal manager has the task of ensuring that internal copies are distributed under your document control system conditions. They should also make sure that electronic copies are filed to the correct issue and protected against copying or accidental erasure or deletion. Check to see that all backups are carried out and the bid file information is complete and handed to the bid manager.

Getting the bid to the client can also be fraught with difficulty. If it is overseas then always prepare a backup that can be sent by another route. Strikes, transport difficulties and lost luggage are commonly accepted hazards of bidding overseas. To prevent your proposal going astray you should deliver by hand or use a reputable courier company. Do not entrust bids to ordinary postal services.

Delivery of the proposal should be timely. If you miss the deadline your bid may not be accepted and bids submitted too early have been known to disappear. You should obtain a receipt for the proposal. Sometimes there will be an opening ceremony that the bid, business or client manager should attend. Try to get as much information about competitor bids as possible. Feed the information back into the bid team and your bid database.

SUMMARY

The proposal you submit to the client plays a critical part in your eventual success. If you do not submit an offer you cannot expect to win.

- *Make the most of your proposal by showing that you understand the client, know their needs and have solutions to them. Convince them that you can do it better than anyone else.*

- *Make your pitch so that it is relevant to the wide range of readers to which it will be exposed: executives, specialists and financiers. Your proposal must be readable, well-structured and orderly so that each type of reader can find what they need quickly.*

- *Emphasise those aspects of your offer that meet the most pressing needs of your client. Your client is buying the benefits that your solution offers, not the features it provides. Focus therefore on the business benefits you can bring.*

- *Organise the proposal production so that everyone involved knows what they have to produce and when. Give suitable guidance to the authors on the style and format you wish to adopt and the emphasis and benefits that you want to incorporate.*

- *A typical bid document will contain a technical proposal stating how you intend to carry out the proposed task, a commercial proposal with your response to the contract terms and conditions, an implementation proposal showing the project plan and a finance proposal stating price and financing plans. An executive summary should encapsulate the main points from each of these.*

- *Use the financial proposal to inform them of your price and to sell the financial benefits of your offer. Show how your bid provides: improved profit, reduced cost, and financial empathy. Make benefits real, attractive and easily understood.*

- *Make sure that the teams for proposal reviews and authorisation are briefed on what to expect well in advance. Tell them what they have to do, and what they cannot do.*

12

FOLLOW-UP ACTIVITIES

The period following your bid being made is very often seen as a hiatus before the contract is awarded. Many bidders feel that once the hard work of preparing the bid is completed, the onus shifts away from them towards the client, which of course it does, but not to the extent where bidders should abrogate responsibility for their bid to fate or a third party. Submitting the bid is not the conclusion of the bid process, it is the starting point for clinching the deal. The difficulty of course is that your bid is now under the control of your client, so nurturing and steering its direction takes on a new dimension. No longer are you able to change or modify your offer to meet your own corporate expectations; you now need to influence and negotiate with your client to get what you want.

There is clear value in an effective follow-up programme. Timely intervention by bidders has been known to retrieve many a lost cause, turning a bad situation into a winning one. Just as importantly, well-positioned bidders have been known to lose the contract through handling the post-tender activities poorly.

There are of course some situations when the client does not allow any communication during the adjudication stage, but more often than not you will have some opportunities, albeit infrequent ones, to exert influence. By doing nothing during this period you can miss out on chances to affect the outcome.

Not all follow-up activity is directly with the client. Your bid management function continues as well because you will have to maintain control on the bid and assignment teams. You may be called upon at any time to clarify your offer, make a presentation, negotiate with sub-contractors or arrange a site visit. This chapter looks at activity with the client, and the bid and assignment teams during this period, and at what needs to be done to move the bid from a proposal to a contract.

MANAGEMENT ACTIVITY

It will be the bid and business managers who are mainly involved in carrying out the key actions needed to follow up the bid. These include all post-tender activities with the client, the bid team and the assignment team as necessary. Others who have been involved in preparing the bid, such as the project manager, finance or commercial managers, are also likely to be active in all or some tasks, but under the control of the bid manager.

Fig. 12.1 lists some examples of post-tender management activities you should expect to carry out. The bid manager has the task of keeping people informed of progress and of the best way of planning and scheduling these follow-up activities.

Informing people

Submitting the bid does not conclude the bid activity as you can see in Fig. 12.1. However, not everyone involved in the bid needs to be kept

Post Tender Activity Check

- [ ] Bid file house-keeping
- [ ] Document control
- [ ] Check receipt of bid
- [ ] Attend opening ceremony
- [ ] Prepare client report
- [ ] Prepare and give client presentation
- [ ] Prepare and conduct site visits
- [ ] Lobby key-contacts
- [ ] Prepare negotiation plan
- [ ] Obtain negotiation authority
- [ ] Alert negotiation team
- [ ] Alert assignment team
- [ ] Negotiate contract
- [ ] Complete closure report
- [ ] Update management information

Fig. 12.1 Post-tender checklist

informed of progress. It can be burdensome to them and to you. The work of some of the team concludes once the bid has been produced and they may not be interested in it until there are some significant developments. To simplify your management role and prevent unnecessary interference, prepare a list of the key people who need to remain involved once the bid is in and who you need to keep updated on major developments. Make sure you do not omit anyone whose support you may have to call upon.

In the international business environment, the time between bid submission and negotiations with the client can be very long. This adds to your difficulty in keeping people properly informed. The negotiation team needs to stand by when it appears likely that the client will ask you to the table. You do not want key negotiators missing at this crucial time. Interviews may be needed for personnel proposed in your offer so make sure they are available. If a reference site visit is needed, plan it carefully and provide early notice to the people involved. There will, however, be other situations that do require involvement of a greater part of the team. For example, the client may ask for a rebid or an extension to the validity period of your offer requiring a revalidation of your prices and those of your subcontractors. Keep on top of the situation by carefully monitoring the progress of your bid through your established network of client contacts. When you hear of such a development, alert the people you need to help you.

Closure processes

If you win or lose a bid, always find out why. The client may be happier to give a bid debrief when you win but they will frequently give the losers details on why their bids failed. This is very valuable information that you can use on future bids. Identifying weaknesses and strengths in your bids and your competitors' will help you win more contracts in the future.

Once you know the result, close the bid. It is courteous to inform the bid team and senior management of the result and it is strongly recommended for maintaining good relations. Informing the assignment team is essential if you win, as they need to apply effort to carry out the programme of work. Use a bid closure report as a convenient way of passing on information. A bid closure report should include a range of information: the result of the bid, who was bidding, a summary of their offers, the basis of the selection, prices, why you won or lost, the plus points and the negative points in your offer as seen by the client, recommendations for improvements, and any other information that you feel will give benefit to your future bids. Just knowing you lost is not sufficient; neither is just knowing you won. You need to know why. When you have completed a bid closure report, put it to use; no value arises from just filing it away. Use the report to make changes. If the client saw deficiencies in your product set, feed that information back to product development. If your pricing was out, alert the finance department. Inform your corporate strategy department of any new approaches or deviations taken by your competitors.

Being unsuccessful in a bid can often be as valuable as winning if you use the information you receive to put right mistakes and win more business in the future.

Financial closures

As far as housekeeping is concerned, there are a few tasks to do to keep things tidy. These will obviously depend upon your internal accounting practices and systems. Typically, to maintain accurate accounting records you will need to inform the bid finance manager or management accountant of the result so that they may make the financial closure. If the bid has been unsuccessful, you would probably post the costs incurred on the bid to a bid code before closing it. This means that those costs have to be met from a cost of bidding budget rather than a project budget. Should you intend to recover your bid costs from the successful bid, you will probably raise a new project code and transfer the bid costs into that budget.

It is a good idea to arrange for a financial completion report of some kind to help your management accountants assess profitability, improve forecasting accuracy, monitor actual spend against budget, and so on.

Project handover

When your bid has been successful you will need to hand it over to the assignment team who will be carrying it out. The chances are that it is the bid team at that point who has the best understanding of the client and the project. But it is the project manager, delivery or implementation authorities who now need to know about it. You should ensure that all your hard-won information is passed on to those who now need it. This is an essential part of the quality process and keeping the client satisfied.

If you brought the project manager into the bid team you will have gone some way to achieving the continuity you need. They will comprehend the bid as they have prepared the project and quality plans and contributed to the financial forecasting for the assignment. This makes the handover much easier. You will probably have to arrange financial and budget transfers and transference of the bid documentation and contractual information. Your bid information file should now become the effective project information file. If you have maintained common control of these documents, through a document control system, this will present no problem to you.

CLIENT ACTIVITIES

The most important part of your follow-up programme is the interaction between you and your client. You have to continue to persuade the client by any means possible that it is you who should win the contract. The opportunities can be quite broad. These may range across direct contact by letter, telephone or face to face meetings, making formal or informal presentations, reference site visits to your premises or those of your other customers, post-tender and post-contract negotiations, and seeking out new opportunities for more business.

The important thing is to continue the process of persuasion until the contract is awarded and beyond, through to the completion of the project and onto the next opportunity. Your bid is not lost until the contract has been awarded to someone else.

Pre-contractual agreement

You know from previous chapters that in making your offer you are accepting the client's invitation to enter into a contract; a contract exists if your client accepts the offer in your bid. In most cases however, there are areas for further discussion, often centring on the contractual terms and conditions. The client will wish to agree these before drawing up a formal written contract. Sometimes this can cause problems. First, there is the possibility of delay in reaching agreement and starting work, especially if there is detailed discussion on the finer contractual points by the two commercial departments; time is needed to conclude discussion and formalise the agreement. Secondly, there is a possibility that new or variant terms and conditions will arise from these discussions, possibly affecting your bid strategy.

When delays are introduced in signing a contract there is a strong temptation to commence work on the project. This is often reinforced by intense pressure from the client. This is particularly true if there are completion deadlines to meet. There may be specifications and designs to be created, long lead-time materials to be ordered, people to alert and put in place. A common way of addressing this is through the client providing a letter stating their intention to give you the contract. This letter of intent has been known to cause many problems. Suppliers start work on its basis, commit time and money, only to find that a contract is not in place. Litigation in contract law frequently involves one party working in the belief that they had a contract when none existed.

Understand that a letter of intent is not a contract, and as such, it has no legal standing. Any work that you do on the basis of it, you must regard as speculative. Apart from the commercial risk, by starting work on the project, you are likely to dilute the strength of your negotiating position during post-tender negotiations.

If you are placed in this position you should try to secure from the client a form of indemnification or guarantee for the work you are doing. As an example, the client may agree to pay you for the initial work you are doing up to a specific amount, pending the formal contracts being completed. In many ways this is a separate agreement and contract, distinct from the one for which you bid, so you must consider all the commercial implications therein.

Making presentations

In your bid sales plan you will probably have considered making a presentation to your client. There are some very good reasons for wanting to do this; your offer may be complex, which you will wish to elucidate upon face to face and you may have special benefits that you want to emphasise, your proposal may not lend itself to the written word or you may be proposing computer software or design models, for example. Typically, a presentation should be sought where you feel able to enhance your bid, but be wary of undermining a good proposal by a sloppy exposition.

If you have planned for a presentation you will have built hooks into your proposal and preliminary work, to hang it on. The direct approach is often favoured, requesting the opportunity to give a presentation to them outright. Another favourite is inviting the client to visit you or a reference site, where you can lay on an exhibition for them. Whatever hooks you have used, if the client bites and asks you to present your proposal, make sure you take full advantage of the opportunity. You can assume that you are not alone and other suppliers have also been asked to appear.

Make sure that you have a fully briefed and knowledgeable presentation team, that know the offer and the client. Your client will use the opportunity to examine the key points of your offer and possibly quiz you in depth. They may ask you about a variation to the specification, picked up from a competitor's offer, or the possibility of changing some aspect of your offer. Your presentation team therefore needs to be switched on and alert to all the possibilities. Make certain you are versed in the client's culture and language; do not ruin your chances by accidentally insulting them. You must be careful not to talk yourselves out of a winning position by making a clumsy presentation that misses the important client benefits. If you do not have good presentation skills, develop them or get someone on board who does.

Reference site visits

Visits by the client to your own sites, or those where your products or services are in use, give you further chances to influence the result. Your client will be making an assessment of many factors, possibly as part of a formal evaluation. These therefore are very important events upon which selection often hinges. It makes sense then, to plan the visit and not leave it to chance. Attention to the detail will ensure a smooth and successful visit. Build any specific areas the client wants to cover into a programme for the day. Make sure that you deal with the important things at the start; concentration can begin to flag after a while and you want to ensure all your benefits are put across strongly. Divide the visit into three parts; you could start with a short introduction and presentation of your offer, visit the production or development facilities, and conclude with a summary and open forum.

Simple things will often make the difference. Brief everyone involved and other personnel that your client may meet, so that they treat them with respect. Keep to a timetable, demonstrating that you apply quality standards in all things. Provide something for them to take away; a recap of your offer or slide presentation material. By managing and controlling the event well, your offer will be reinforced.

Look for other prospects

Even when contracts are about to be let, never forget that there could be additional business to obtain from your client within the same project. For example, although they may have let the main contract go to someone else, there may be additional work or products needed, which was not included within the original specification. If your client has negotiated a low price they may have extra funds available to buy these. So it is very worthwhile assessing the situation in defeat or success, to see what else may be available. Any new business that can be added to an existing project could be very profitable.

NEGOTIATIONS

Perhaps the most important interaction comes when you and your client sit down to finalise the contract. This can take place before the bid is made, and many bids involve a degree of early negotiation as you saw in Chapter 6. You may have the chance to negotiate once you have submitted your offer and again when contracts have been awarded but before work starts.

Post-tender negotiation

Post-tender negotiation occurs after all the bids have been submitted and before the award of the contract. Often this is undertaken only with the supplier submitting the lowest acceptable offer, where the client's intention is to get an improvement in either price, delivery or content. The circumstances for these negotiations should be such that other suppliers are not placed at a disadvantage, nor to otherwise adversely affect their belief, confidence and trust in the competitive tendering system. Unfortunately, these ideals are not always realised.

Post-tender negotiation is an area of bidding that arouses controversy and questions over ethics. In many situations, particularly in the public sector, it is still frowned upon or prohibited within the rules of tendering whereas in certain industries in the private sector, such as construction, it is the norm. The argument goes that if it is ethical for a supplier to tender at the highest price that they believe the client will pay, it is equally ethical for the client to challenge and negotiate the prices tendered. As bidders you will assume the former is acceptable and assume the latter will inevitably occur.

This is not always true however and you must be very sure of the basis upon which the tenders will be evaluated. Find out whether the opportunity for post-tender negotiation exists, before making any rash assumptions in your pricing. It can relate to almost any contract but your client is only really going to consider it where the anticipated saving made outweighs the cost of negotiation. Find out if your bid qualifies. They may only negotiate when they require clarification of your offer. Or they may have a policy on price that says all orders over a certain value or extending over a certain period are negotiated. Other times it may be used are when the final bid evaluation does not give an outright winner or when there are doubts over the quality or performance.

Post-tender negotiation normally only takes place with one or two bidders, those who have come closest to meeting the exact needs of the client. This gives them the opportunity to alter their bids. It is further argued that in the interest of fairness all bidders should have the same opportunity. Providing that all the bidders understood the basis upon which the bids were to be judged and they played to the same rules, that argument does not stand up. If the client is prepared to negotiate then the supplier should be too and if their selection process chooses bidders with whom to negotiate on a fair and similar assessment, then there should be no complaints.

As a bidder about to enter post-tender negotiation you know that the stakes are high. You can feel confident that not much stands between you and the contract; much or all of the competition has been eliminated and now it is down to brass tacks. The pressure to get the sale now is strong and the pressure on the client to make the selection is similarly intense. It is more important than ever to remain cool and in command of the situation. In the rush to do the deal you could upset a carefully planned bid strategy and transform a successful project into a failure.

Bear in mind what your client expects to get from it. They could be seeking a price reduction, improvement on delivery or implementation timescales, extra items, possibly identified from other bids, at little or no additional price, or some other motive that you have to discern. Too many bidders in these situations allow eagerness for the order to override commercial aptitude.

SUMMARY

The bid is not lost until someone else has been awarded the contract.

- *Post-bid management activity includes keeping the right people informed on progress, putting into effect the bid and financial closure processes, and handing over to the assignment team when you are successful.*

- *Activities with the client are critical during this final stage. You should continue the process of persuasion until the contract is awarded, and beyond.*

- *Be wary of starting any pre-contractual work on the assignment. There may be variations or delays in the final contract that will affect your strategy. You may also dilute the strength of your negotiating stance.*

- *Client presentations and site visits should emphasise the benefits within your proposal. Make sure that everyone involved is briefed and knowledgable. Be careful of talking yourself out of a winning position by a sloppy visit or an inept presentation.*

- *Client negotiations are the most important post-bid activity. Check whether post-tender negotiation is expected and prepare well for it. Be careful not to give too much away under the pressure of trying to secure the sale. Do not allow eagerness to override commercial competence.*

13

BID MANAGEMENT WORKFLOW SYSTEMS

Bid management can really be considered as two distinct spheres of activity, conceptional activity and practical operations. The conceptional area takes cognisance of corporate policies and your strategies for the client, competition and price. It uses these to develop the tactics that you need to carry out the bid plan and produce a winning bid. Practical applications are those which manage the bid, establish systems and support structures and control the people and resources.

The conceptional side of bidding calls for initiative and creativity to generate ideas and stimulate developments. These have to be translated into a working solution through the practical applications of bid systems and processes. This chapter focuses on these practical issues and how they can be made simpler and easier to control using computer-based software applications.

HANDLING COMPLEX BID TASKS

Most bids require the performance of many tasks which have to be handled by a large number of people. The bid team, the assignment team, external partners, your suppliers and subcontractors or consortium members, need to work together to get the bid completed. They need to keep in touch with each other both throughout the duration of the bid and while carrying out the resulting assignment. Each member of the team has their own tasks but these are all inter-related and interdependent within the context of the bid. Further complications arise when team members are working on several simultaneous bids or other operational tasks which are part of their everyday routines.

Often this complex relationship between tasks, responsibilities, resources and timescales causes management problems and it is usually the bid manager who has to bring all the right elements together at the right time. The bid manager must ensure that everyone involved carries out their tasks when required and to the standard needed. Delays in carrying out tasks, or carrying them out incorrectly may not only place additional burdens and pressures on the other members of the team, but could also result in a deficient proposal.

HOW WORK FLOWS IN A BID

Many tasks associated with a bid fall naturally into distinct stages. These stages have to be interlinked so that the task gets completed. As a team member completes one stage of the task, they hand it over to the next person to allow the subsequent stage to begin. A complex bid in a large organisation usually requires complex interactions; there may be several groups of people tackling each bid task, with stages being worked on sequentially and concurrently. A simpler bid in a small organisation might require minimal co-operation from others; there may only be one person working alone on each stage of the bid. In both cases the bid task is broken down into stages and people work on each stage to get it done. As work finishes on one stage it commences on another with the effect that work flows through the organisation until the task is completed.

In most bids this *workflow* is a mixture of arbitrary and structured tasks where work either moves from person to person as the particular task dictates, or follows through an established routine. Structured workflows can be formally defined in the bid process, can evolve through trials and testing, or may simply be the obvious way to get the task done. Most bids require some form of control, which implies a structure to the workflow instead of reliance upon the individual team member to decide how to progress each task. Frequently these workflows are badly managed and would benefit from active workflow management. Other workflows call for innovation and flair, but they still usually have to deliver their results on time and to a specified format.

MANAGING THE BID WORKFLOW

Both the arbitrary and structured workflows in a bid need to be managed if it is to run smoothly. You need to make the best use of your available resources and ensure that you meet the bid deadlines. This takes on even greater significance when several bids, which are underway simultaneously, share resources and people. The objectives for bid workflow management will normally be to:

- Direct the ways that work will flow to improve bid planning.
- Use the defined workflow to track and enforce progress so that nothing is missed.
- Ensure that someone always has responsibility for work.
- Keep those responsible for work informed and reminded of what they have to do.

To achieve these objectives and allow workflow to be measured and regulated you will need a definition of the best way the work should flow, a record of the character of the work done as it flows, and a means to define who is responsible for work at any point in its flow.

The traditional method of bid management uses standard management tools such as the bid plan, bid meetings, reviews, bid directives, forms and other manual and paper-based systems. However, as in many other aspects of business, the way in which the bid management function is performed is changing. The emergence of the personal computer or computer work-station as the universal business tool, the use of work groups connecting similarly-minded people over a common communication platform, electronic mail, and other advances in technology, means that the dependence on paper-based systems is reducing. These technology trends have also promoted a change in work patterns making it easier for geographically separated teams to work together. This allows more people to work from home or on the move. Similarly, business partners can now interact more quickly and be more responsive to situations as they arise.

These enforced changes in working practices make the task of the bid manager increasingly difficult. Instead of easily monitoring the progress of groups working within the same building, they now have to manage across geographical and cultural boundaries. As each member of the bid team could be in a different location the bid manager has to rely upon computing and communication media to help.

ACTIVE WORKFLOW TOOLS

Active workflow management systems and tools have been developed to aid general business processes and are particularly suited to managing bids. These software applications generally run on the enterprise or departmental computer network and interconnect individual bid team members. Such systems provide many advantages:

- bid documents are stored on the network file-servers meaning they are readily available
- all information needed by the team is delivered when and where required and acknowledged when it has been received
- reminders are sent automatically when deadlines are approaching or past
- delays in performing any of the bid tasks are automatically escalated
- all the bid processes and tasks are co-ordinated and integrated with any external events
- the bid manager and senior managers are automatically kept informed of progress and can peruse the available information at any time.

This means that bid costs are reduced with less time spent by the bid team in tracking down documents and progress chasing. Productivity improves because the bid manager can quickly identify resource problems or bottlenecks. Efficiency increases as the status of any task is immediately available with access to a range of management statistics. These combine to alleviate the management overhead which means you can spend more time deciding how to win.

SELECTING A WORKFLOW SYSTEM

A workflow system is best suited to departmental or corporate networks, so that it can be used by everyone on the bid team. It should provide access to a database for storing the bid information system, with competitor profiles, client information and other data specified in the bid file. It will feature an electronic mail system and file transfer capability that will alert all team members to events through their mailboxes and improve communication. Electronic forms are presented for resource allocation, risk analysis, financial approvals, bid authorisation and so on, which will be completed by the appropriate member of the bid team and stored within the system. The system will initiate and provide connectivity to external applications such as financial models for bid costing and pricing.

Your workflow system must be able to route work between people and groups so that if any member of the team is not available for any period, their workload can be transferred to someone else. Monitoring and control is very important as is notification of work queues. You need to be aware of problems as quickly as possible so that you can take any urgent action. All work must be assigned to a named individual. This means that you will always know who is dealing with any particular task. Work can be reassigned to a different person but never allowed to have no-one responsible for it. Authorisation features will help to approve and complete tasks with the least delay. This will be valuable in gaining authorisation to a technical design by the design authority, or to the bid price by the finance manager. Finally, the system must manage the bid procedure, taking the range of forms, documents and data that is generated, and then instructing and informing the team of what has to happen next. By guiding the team through the process the workflow system provides a framework for the complete bid.

Types of workflow systems

There are several different categories of workflow systems available to meet the needs of different business processes. It is important that you choose one that is suitable for bid management. Production systems are those that support the core activities of the business. These could include mortgage processing for a building society or insurance claim processing for an insurance company. For less urgent tasks there are administrative systems that deal with areas such as purchasing, expenses accounting and management reporting. Finally, there are co-operative systems which are useful when many people need to work together on tasks such as proposal writing, designing new products and bid management. It is likely that you would select a co-operative system for bid management, but you may find that it can also help certain mission-critical and administrative processes, so select a system that provides you with capability in all these areas.

When selecting your workflow system you would be wise to consider what else you may want it to do. Make sure that the system you select can easily engineer and redesign specific business functions. It must easily allow for routing work around different people and provide you with the flexibility to modify the process when required. Supplying links into the corporate executive information system will enhance control at the board level. And connecting different operating divisions may reduce the duplication of jobs and processes resulting in significant cost savings.

Workflow systems come in several formats. Some vendors provide bespoke developments that are specific to one or more business processes. These tend to be expensive and rely upon expertise which you must buy in. At the other end of the spectrum there are packaged solutions which offer standard processes, such as claim processing or sales and order entry. These are usually cheaper to buy but may not fully meet your own requirement, so you will have to change your process to fit the workflow management or go through a redesign if your process changes. Finally there is the tool-kit approach which provides you with a range of building blocks to build and develop your own workflow system tailored to your own business and bid processes. This has the advantage that you could use blocks developed for bid management for example, for another process such as financial planning. These also have the advantage that you can change and amend processes quickly and with minimal disruption as your business needs change. For bid management, where no two bids will be identical, the tool-kit approach probably represents the best solution.

EXAMPLES FROM A TYPICAL WORKFLOW SYSTEM

Hydra, produced by SysGenics Limited, is an example of a workflow system that is suitable for bid management. Hydra adopts the tool-kit philosophy and provides the basic building blocks common to most workflow systems. Its flexibility allows you to construct a bid system that fits the way your business operates instead of having to change your work to fit the system.

The primary building blocks that Hydra provides are cases, procedures, states and work groups and these form the foundation of the bid management workflow application. Each new bid within the overall workflow system is called a case and consists of sets of procedures each of which form discrete parts of the bid process. So for each bid there will be many procedures such as action on receipt of the bid invitation, proposal preparation, review and authorisation. Each procedure goes through a number of stages which Hydra calls states, and movement between states is effected via transitions. There is no limit on the numbers of states and transitions or on how they interconnect. These blocks combine to form the workflow map for each stage of the bid. The illustration in Fig. 13.1 shows a simplified procedure for the action upon receipt of a client's invitation to bid.

This procedure is only a part of the complete bid workflow and illustrates typical states that you would expect to go through: invitation review, risk, bid decision, bid strategy and so on. These hold information about the tasks needed to be performed whilst in that state, and associate tasks

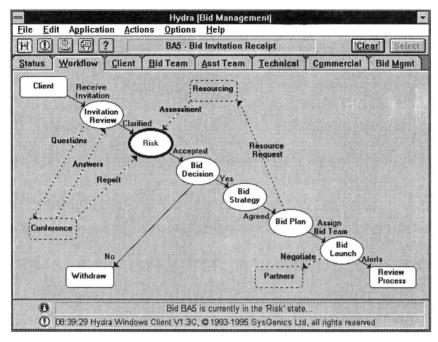

Fig. 13.1 Hydra workflow map

with specific procedures. Each task will be undertaken by one or more members of the bid team. Some tasks will be dependent upon others, while some can run concurrently. Where there is a dependency, the task in question must be completed in order to move on to the next. Hydra defines transitions as the means by which you move from one state to the next and in this example these include receiving the invitation, clarifying the invitation and accepting the risk. Making a transition usually requires a transaction of some kind. A transaction is a set of actions dynamically defined in the procedure. This could be a form or dialogue field that is presented to the team member for completion, or it could be one of several other actions including assigning a value to a variable (like bid costs) or invoking an external application (such as a resource database).

Every case has a history which is a permanent record of a bid's life and corresponds to the paperwork that would normally be associated with it. It contains an entry for every transition the bid has made so that you can browse through it to find out what has happened to each task, where it is in the bid procedure and how it got there. In addition the case maintains a list of bid team members with an interest in or responsibilities for completing each task. The bid manager can add or change any of these team members and define access at various levels depending on their privileges. Whenever something happens to the case, everyone concerned can be alerted to the change, in real time, wherever they may be in the network. Sometimes, of course, people work away from their desk, but they can still be kept informed by dialling up a simple terminal interface.

Fig. 13.2 shows some specific data relating to the *risk* state. This displays the deadline for completion of all the tasks, the persons responsible for doing them and their express responsibilities. It also shows the status of each task and what action has been taken to escalate it.

Every task requires some transaction to complete the transition to another state. In this example, the deadline for the transaction has passed, resulting in Hydra automatically generating an alert and sending this to the bid manager and the responsible team members. Alerts can be broadcast to screens, or sent as electronic mail messages when a specific event occurs. It will be sent to all relevant team members wherever they are and will consist of sufficient information to allow some action to be taken. Hydra maintains a record of every alert for the bid and when it was sent and so maintains an audit trail. Fig. 13.3 shows the alert resulting from the deadline for the risk state expiring.

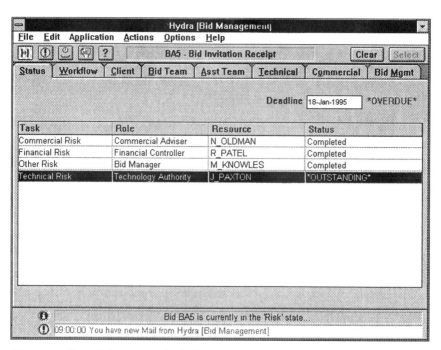

Fig. 13.2 State information for bid risk assessment

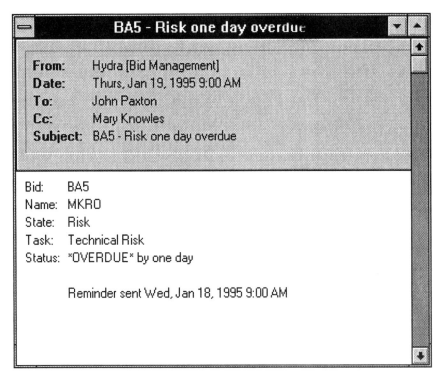

Fig. 13.3 Alert resulting from delayed transaction

When an alert is received, the recipient must take some action. In this case the bid manager will check the status of the bid team database to see why the member responsible for the transaction has not completed it. The bid team and resource database is an example of Hydra's work groups. Work groups define who is responsible for a task at any point in its life. The work group will be the bid team for any particular bid and people can be freely added to and removed from the group as necessary.

In the example in Fig. 13.4 the bid manager can see that the person needed to perform the transaction in the technical risk assessment task is not available. This explains why the transaction was not completed and why the alert was raised. The bid manager can select another resource from the list who can do the work and assign responsibility to them. All people concerned with the task then receive an alert telling them of the changes that have taken place.

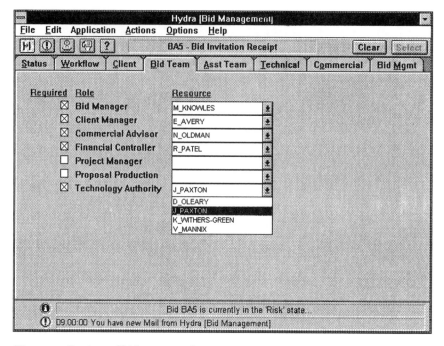

Fig. 13.4 Review of bid team work group

CHANGING THE BID PROCESS

Workflow management systems such as Hydra will allow you to transform your bid and business processes into working applications very quickly. They should allow you to prototype processes, explain them to the people who will use them and incorporate their feedback rapidly. Once you have set up your bid process you will begin to see the benefits of rapid, secure, traceable delivery of work to those who should do it, reduced paper flow, and unavoidable adherence to procedures.

Although these will provide you with significant benefits you still have to be able to cope with change. Some changes are clearly necessary when driven by external events, such as amendments to legislation or the acquisition of a new subsidiary. However, making changes to existing practices are sometimes harder to justify. Intuitive feelings that greater savings can be made here or efficiency improved there, are rarely good enough reasons. And pinpointing the aspects that require change is harder still.

The analysis features of an active workflow management system will help you to identify bottlenecks and areas of wasted effort. Once you have identified and quantified these, you can make changes to the people involved and the process that backs them up. Systems like Hydra allow you to change existing business processes simply and easily, even to the extent of modifying a system while it is running, resulting in minimum disruption to users.

SUMMARY

- *A good bid workflow system optimises the way work flows to and from the individuals within the bid and assignment teams. This leads to improvements in bid planning and management.*

- *By defining the workflow you can track and enforce progress so that nothing is missed during the bid process. Your system should initiate reminders automatically when deadlines are approaching.*

- *A key aspect of workflow systems is that they should ensure that some-one always has responsibility for the work to be done during the bid cycle. It should help you by allowing you not only to switch tasks to other people when resource problems arise but also to provide those people with all the information they will need to carry the tasks out.*

- *A key benefit of the workflow system is that the bid team will remain motivated and focused because those people responsible for each piece of work will be kept informed and reminded of what they have to do and can also see what other people are doing. The bid manager should be alerted to any delays caused by people not performing their individual tasks efficiently.*

- *In a well-defined and utilised workflow system bid costs will be reduced as less time is spent by people in tracking down documents and progress chasing. Productivity will improve because the bid manager can quickly identify resource problems or bottlenecks.*

CONCLUSION

Winning business in competitive tenders calls upon many management skills bundled under the umbrella of bid management. This book has shown that the successful bid manager has to exercise these skills in abundance: they need excellent commercial judgment to deal with the complex business issues that major bids often generate, they need a solid understanding of management and financial accounting coupled with creativity to turn bid financing into a benefit to the client, they need the ability to control a team of diverse people with varying skills across intricate matrix and hierarchical management boundaries, and above all they need to create new ideas and construct innovative solutions to difficult business problems.

People with these skills and abilities will prove to be valuable resources as bidding becomes increasingly important in the modern competitive business environment. As business processes become more efficient and purchasers more sophisticated, they will be seeking the advantages that competitive tendering can bring. Furthermore, enforced legislation and commercial sensitivity are major motivators for driving businesses towards buying through competitive selection. It is fair to say that most client organisations of any size will at some stage make significant purchases by this method. Suppliers will have to take cognisance of the fact that they will have to compete to win.

It is the bidder who stays one step ahead and influences the client early on in the bid process who will have the initial competitive advantage. But it is the bidder who shows supreme professionalism in responding to the client's needs and works quickly and effectively within tight time scales, that will convert that advantage into a winning bid.

The organisation, structure and constraints of the bid process are also fundamental to bidding. How you plan and prepare your response, arrange and control the people involved, and deal with problems when they arise are critical. There are few short cuts, but setting up an optimised bidding system will ultimately bring benefits and will make winning bids easier within your organisation.

This book has taken the core propositions of bid management and explored them to see what can be done to make them more effective. The importance of ensuring that the opportunity sits firmly within your own business objectives has been emphasised, with the corollary that you reject or withdraw from those bids which do not. The critical strategic issues on price, competition, products and dealing with the client, have been dissected to find their relevance to your bid, and reassembled to form the basis of your bid plan. Similarly, the execution of that plan through effective team work, and application of sound bid tactics has been investigated so that ways can be found to translate the strategy into action. Finally, all the organisational and process aspects of bidding and workflow management have been analysed, so that you can see where benefits of cost reduction and improved efficiency can be achieved.

You will not win every time you bid, but by putting into place the precepts and values of bid management that are contained in this book, you will win more often than you lose.

GLOSSARY

There are few standard terms used in bid management so it may help to clarify some of the terminology that is used within the context of this book.

Aid Funds, people and resources provided by an international lending agency to help developing countries.

Aid-funding When some or all the funds needed by the client to pay for the project is provided as aid.

Assignment The task to be carried out by the supplier when they are awarded the contract for which they have bid.

Best and final offer An offer in which the lowest price bid wins; no amendments or alterations are permitted once bids are tendered.

Bid bond A returnable sum of money submitted to the client by a bidder which is forfeited if the bid is withdrawn before its validity period expires.

Bidder The company or person who is preparing and submitting an offer to the client.

Bidding The process of inviting tenders by the client and submitting offers by potential suppliers.

Bid manager The person responsible for controlling the way a bid is prepared, produced and delivered to a client from the beginning to the end of the bid process.

Budgetary estimate Not a formal offer but a quote for consideration.

Business manager The owner of the potential profit and loss associated with a bid with responsibility for ensuring the offer fits with the supplier's business objectives.

Client A potential or actual buyer.

Client manager The main liaison with the client on all issues relating to the bid.

Commercial advisor The person in the bid team who deals with commercial and legal issues.

Consequential loss Financial losses to the client caused by a failure of the products or services that the supplier provides.

Financial controller The person in the bid team with financial knowledge responsible for all bid finance issues.

Fixed price contract A contract in which the price to be tendered is immutable and will apply irrespective of the time or resources required.

Heads of agreement A non-contractual outline of the commercial terms under which two parties will work together

Invitation for bids The same as an invitation to tender.

Invitation to tender A formal request by the client for offers from suppliers.

Liquidated damages A specified sum of money paid to the client by the supplier as compensation for a material breach of contract.

Lock-in A situation where it would be difficult for a client to change to another supplier.

Market testing Evaluating the way government departments are run by inviting bids for the services they provide from the private sector.

Memorandum of agreement Summary of the terms and conditions under which an agreement will be reached.

Memorandum of understanding Details the basis upon which two parties will work together and used in a simpler form to imply actions and resources required from internal divisions

Negotiated tender A tender where the client negotiates directly with one or more suppliers without formally advertising the bid opportunity

Open tender One in which any person or company can make an offer in response to a widely published invitation.

Operational requirement The operational needs of the client stated within the invitation to tender documents.

Opportunity A potential contract for which a supplier may bid.

Pre-qualification The client's process of evaluating potential suppliers prior to inviting bids.

Procedure A related set of tasks that follow a predetermined course of action.

Process Any business activity that takes information and performs an action upon it to produce a result.

Project The contracted work or supply of goods resulting from a bid.

Project manager Controls and manages the project or assignment if the bid is successful.

Proposal production manager Co-ordinates activity related to the supplier's bid proposal and controls the production of the proposal document.

Prospect The bid opportunity or sometimes the client who owns it.

Request for bids Another term sometimes used for an invitation to tender.

Request for proposals Similar to an invitation to tender although not always requesting firm prices.

Selective tender A tender where the client invites only certain suppliers to bid from those who respond to a general invitation.

Statement of requirement Normally the operational and commercial requirements needed to be met by the bidders.

Subcontractor The actual or potential supplier of products or services to the bidding company when a contract is awarded.

Supplier The company or person who can provide the products or services needed by the client.

Task A piece of work to be carried out comprising one or more specific and related activities.

Technology manager The person with responsibility for ensuring that the design and functional characteristics of the technology you are planning to bid meets the client requirements.

Tender A formal proposal document submitted as a bid.

Tendering The process in which a supplier submits a priced offer to a client.

Time and materials contract A contract where an estimate is provided of the time required to complete the total project which is then charged at a daily or weekly rate.

Transfer of Undertakings (Protection of Employment) Legislation aimed at preserving the rights, pay and conditions of employees where their contracts of employment are transferred to another company.

Transaction A single activity as part of a task.

Transition The movement of the bid process from one state to another.

Workflow The way in which tasks pass from person to person within an organisation and the modelling of this by computer software.

INDEX